INTERIOR PLANTING
IN LARGE BUILDINGS

INTERIOR PLANTING IN LARGE BUILDINGS

A handbook for architects, interior designers, and horticulturists

Stephen Scrivens

with contributions from
Leo Pemberton
John Baker
John Weir
Philip Cooper

THE ARCHITECTURAL PRESS, LONDON
HALSTED PRESS DIVISION
JOHN WILEY & SONS, NEW YORK

First published in 1980 by The Architectural Press Ltd, London.

First published in the USA by Halsted Press

Library of Congress Cataloging in Publication Data

Library Data

Scrivens, Stephen.
Interior planting in large buildings.

"A Halsted Press book."
Includes index.
1. House plants in interior decoration. 2. Indoor gardening. 3. Indoor gardens.
I. Pemberton, Leo. II. Title.
SB 419.S375 747'.98 80–23565
ISBN 0–85139–320–9 (British edition)
ISBN 0–470–27067–5 (United States edition)

Printed in Great Britain
by W & J Mackay Limited, Chatham

Contents

Acknowledgements

It will never be possible to thank in full all those who have contributed to this publication. To compile technical information over such a broad subject is a laborious and time consuming process which requires the goodwill and cooperation of many people. Those who had a commercial interest in the information which they supplied have been mentioned at the point where their contribution appears, to assist any interested party who wishes to pursue the matter further. For their assistance with specific sections of the text I wish to thank Mr M. Cracknell of Pershore College of Horticulture for his observations on the chapter on Plant Physiology; Dr R. Hurd of the Glasshouse Crops Research Institute for his comments on relating plants to the interior environment; Mr C. Major of the British Agrochemical Association for his advice on pesticides; Dr P. Callaghan of St Thomas's Hospital Medical School for his guidance on the functioning of ion exchange resins; Mr D. Richardson of Rochford Landscape Ltd for his advice on plant selection; Mr C. Bailes of the Royal Botanic Gardens, Kew for his assistance with the plant illustrations.

Once the basic information had been assembled it was necessary to bring a range of opinions to bear so as to ensure that the correct balance was achieved in a concise and accurate manner. For this time consuming activity a particular note of thanks is due to Peter Thoday of the University of Bath. His efforts were ably supported by those of Patricia White, Ellie Scrivens and John Parkinson who were able to provide a critical and non-horticultural input.

The effort which was required to produce and label the large number of diagrams which appear in this book was considerable. For her work in this area a particular mention must be made of Stephanie Crockett who devoted much time to this task.

I would also like to note that the progress of this book was greatly assisted by the effort and enthusiasm of Myrtle Sanchez who had the unenviable task of typing and retyping this tome several times over.

Such acknowledgements as these can only be a superficial indication of the actual energy which was supplied by these individuals mentioned above. However it is to be hoped that this book stands as a tribute to a team with whom it was a pleasure to work.

Stephen Scrivens

Decorative illustrations between chapters are from the following sources:
Oxford Development Group Ltd: frontispiece
The Architects' Journal: pp 5, 53 (photos Philip Sayer), 89
Harry Seidler & Associates: p 6, 20, 36, 54 (photos Max Dupain)
GGS Photography, Norwich: p 14
Redditch Development Corporation: pp 19, 35
Arndale Centre, Manchester: p 27 (Studio Photography)
Gardenair (Rentals): pp 28, 100
Gillinson, Barnett & Partners: p 44 (Fietscher Photos)
Willis, Faber & Dumas: p 60 (photo Jocelyne van den Bossche)
Associated Landscape Contractors of America: p 67
Tropica, Inc, Maryland: p 68
Stephen Scrivens: pp 76, 106 both
A C Rentaplant: p 105 (photo Pilkington Bros Ltd)

1 Introduction

In recent years plants have increasingly become an integral part of the interior design of buildings. This is due in part to fashion but also is an attempt to produce a working environment to which people can relate. Research studies have even suggested that productivity may be increased by 10–15% through the introduction of plants to an office (though this claim should be treated with caution).

This manual has been prepared to assist architects, landscape architects, and interior designers who wish to use plants in buildings, as well as the growing number of horticulturalists and maintenance operatives who are responsible for their upkeep. As with many developments in design, practical techniques and knowledge have tended to lag behind the aspirations of designers. It is often possible to transfer technology from other fields to produce efficient designs, and therefore an attempt has been made to collate such information as is relevant to those proposing to install or maintain plants in buildings. Every effort has been made to present this information in such a way as to aid practitioners with everyday design projects. Consequently certain topics are treated in a technical manner, although the amount of jargon has been kept to a minimum.

Whenever it is hoped to employ plants efficiently within a building every attempt should be made to account for their inclusion from the initial design stage. It is unfortunate that due to the complexities of modern building design, the requirements of plants are often overlooked until late in the design process. If, however, it is possible to make some allowance for an organic element from the outset, the chance of long term success is greatly increased.

The use of plants in buildings as a positive element in design is comparatively new. As a result, designers are often unsure of themselves in this field and fail to realise the full potential of an organic element. (This book does not enter into a full discussion of the role of plants as an element in architectural design, but instead concentrates on the non-subjective, practical considerations that are of relevance in a technical manual.)

The following diagrams indicate the space requirements of plants and people indoors, whilst the subsequent series of photographs (figs 1.2 to 1.5 inclusive) indicate some ways in which plants have been used in buildings. Some simple line drawings (figs 1.6 to 1.10 inclusive) have also been included to assist with project graphics.

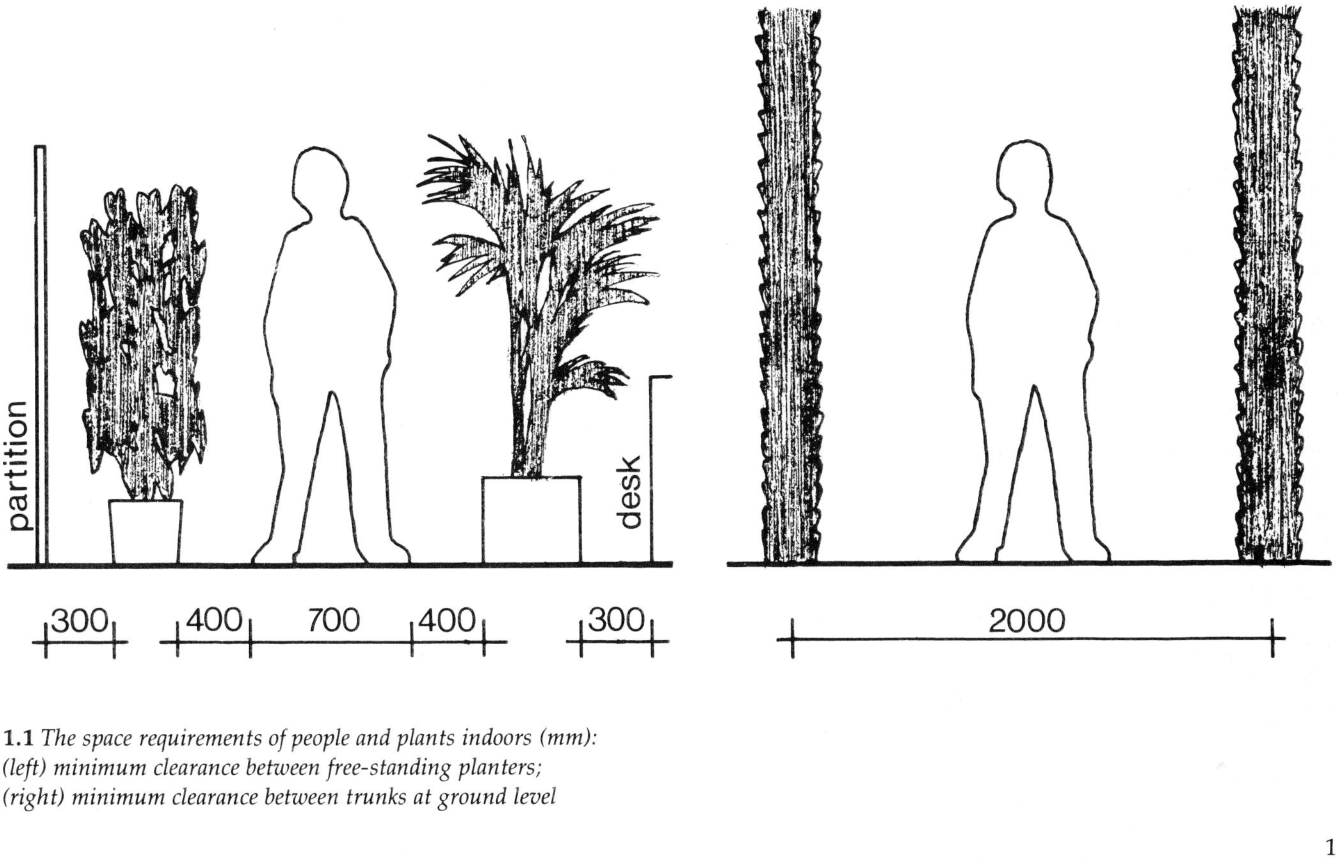

1.1 *The space requirements of people and plants indoors (mm): (left) minimum clearance between free-standing planters; (right) minimum clearance between trunks at ground level*

1.2 *To provide a feature for personal identity – Centraal Beheer Insurance Company Offices, Apeldoorn, Holland*
1.3 *To complete a prestigious effect – AMRO Bank, Nijmegen*

1.4 *To add interest – Swindon Leisure Centre, Swindon*

1.5 *To produce a foliar backdrop – John Deere Co, Illinois*

1.6 *Line drawing of*
× Fatshedera lizei

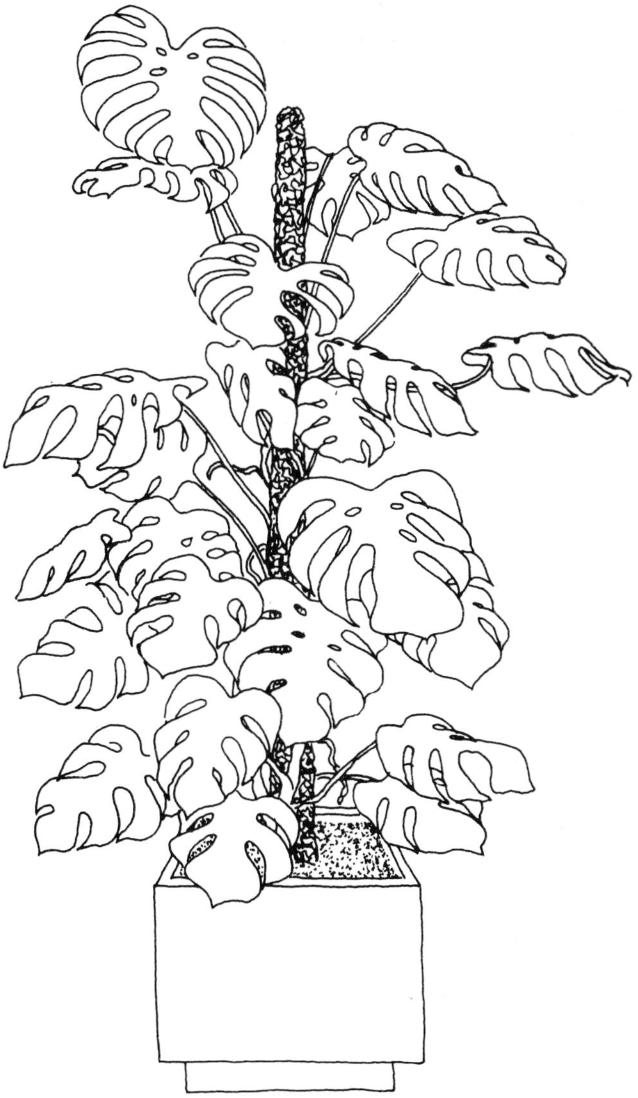

1.7 *Line drawing of* Monstera deliciosa (Philodendron pertusum), *scale 1:10*

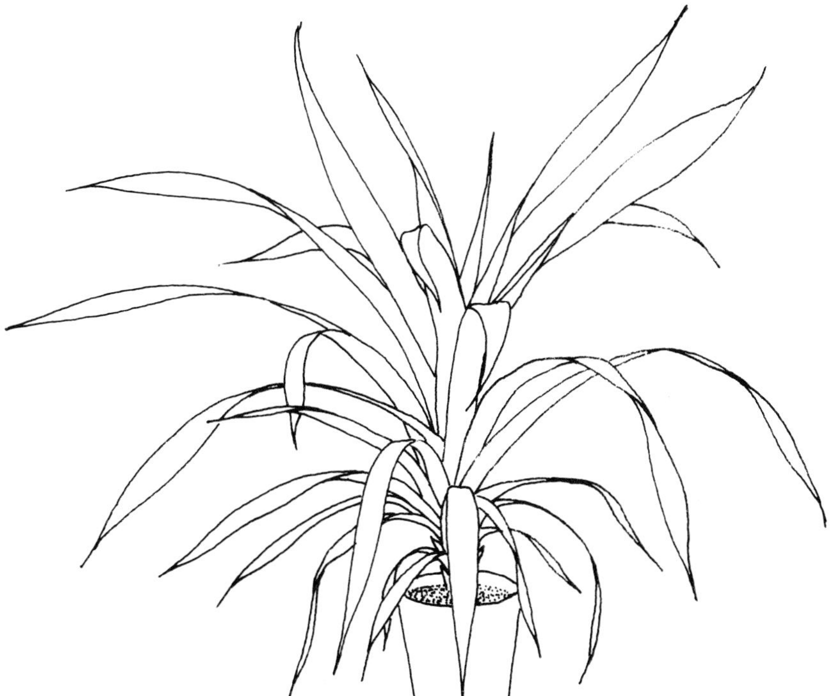

1.8 *Line drawing of* Pandanus veitchii *and* Philodendron erubescens (Philodendron 'Burgundy'), *scale 1:10*

1.9 *Line drawing of* Schefflera actinophylla *scale 1:10*

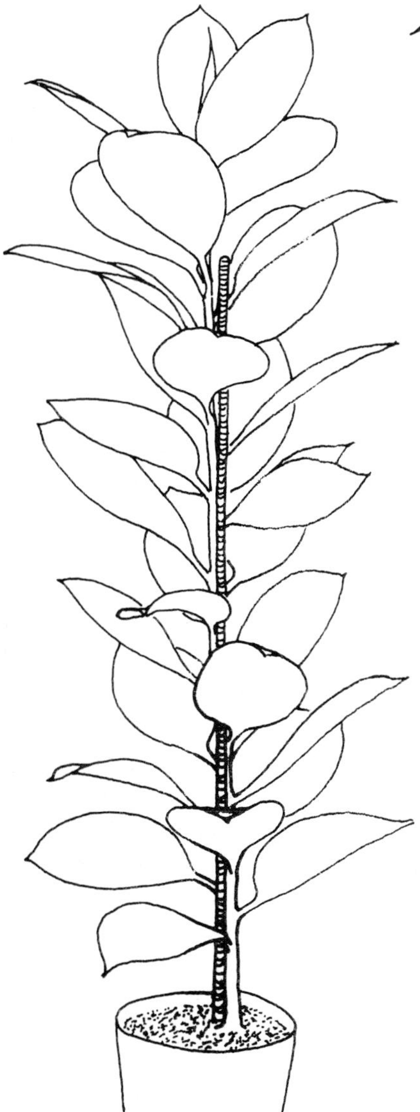

1.10 *Line drawing of* Ficus elastica *and* Dracaena fragrans 'Massangeana', *scale 1:10*

2 The history and origins of interior plants

*by Leo Pemberton**

The cultivation of plants in buildings has a long but poorly documented history. Certainly the Egyptians grew plants in containers and transported them long distances, but it is doubtful if these methods were particularly widespread. Some European plants such as the European fan palm (*Chamaerops humilis*) and bay laurel (*Laurus nobilis*) have been grown as "house plants" for centuries and are still very popular. They both come from the Mediterranean region and possess most of the features essential for an interior plant, ie they are evergreen, tolerant of a wide range of temperatures, will live in containers and tolerate a degree of neglect.

Early house plants tended to be flowering and annual because they could be grown in almost natural conditions and then brought indoors for a short display period. Many plants introduced from the New World did not survive because their minimum requirements could not be met by the technology which was then available. Also, most of the plants that were introduced were those from which it was easy to find fruits and seeds and/or dormant stages such as bulbs, corms and tubers. By the seventeenth century widespread exploration, the introduction of faster ships, and the construction of heated orangeries helped to awaken scientific interest in plants. Orangeries were used to overwinter container-grown plants which could then be moved to a warm terrace in summer (fig 2.1). The early structures were heated by hot flues and fired by coal. Later the flues were replaced by hot water pipes and the building structures were lightened to produce the greenhouse.

The eighteenth century saw the development of an orderly classification for plants (and animals) by Linnaeus and a rapid increase in the number of introductions. When travellers saw the richness of the tropical vegetation they often wished to reproduce the effect back in their European homes. It should not be thought, however, that the interest in ornamental plants was extremely widespread and strongly supported. The founders of the Royal Horticultural Society at the start of the nineteenth century were mainly interested in obtaining new varieties of fruits and vegetables, with ornamental plants as a secondary consideration. As the Industrial Revolution progressed wealth increased and so did interest in ornamental plants, reflected in the larger greenhouses which were then being built. The large conservatory at Syon House built between 1820–32, predated the Palm House at Kew (1848) (fig 2.2 & 2.3), and probably influenced Sir Joseph Paxton with his designs at Chatsworth and the Great Exhibition in Hyde Park. The Great Exhibition of 1851 not only stimulated interest in the arts but also the use of plants indoors. As the techniques of glasshouse construction became more reliable and widespread so the conservatory became a standard feature of suburban villas. There was now the money, time and opportunity for people to develop special interests in specific groups of plants such as ferns, orchids, and palms. As the world was combed for new territories and new resources, the list of decorative plants was

2.1 *The Orangery at the Royal Botanic Gardens, Kew (Crown copyright)*

2.2 *The Palm House at the Royal Botanic Gardens, Kew (Crown copyright)*

2.3 *The planting of the Palm House at the Royal Botanic Gardens, Kew (circa 1855)*

* Mr L. Pemberton is with the Royal Botanic Gardens, Kew, London

2.4 *A reconstruction of a Wardian Case being filled with specimens (Crown copyright)*

extended, encouraged by the Victorian era's obsession with collections.

One of the greatest difficulties for plant collectors was to transport living plants safely over long distances. In 1819 Dr John Livingstone, the chief surgeon of the East India Company in China and a Corresponding Member of the Royal Horticultural Society, wrote a long letter to the Secretary about the difficulties of transporting plants from China to England: "The plants should be collected in proper time, so as to enable them to be firmly rooted in wnich they are to be transported to England; a proper soil should be obtained, wherein they might be planted; they be arranged in their chests or boxes, accordingly as they require abundant, frequent, moderate, or slight waterings; when on board the covers of the chests should be well closed when the spray is flying over the ship, and opened at all times in temperate and fine weather; the plants should be duly watered with good water. . . ." If the collector was not travelling with his shipment such instructions were unlikely to be carried out. In 1856 the *Gardeners' Chronicle* noted in an obituary to John Reeves that, "Doubling the Cape was so difficult an operation that the freight of living plants was continually damaged or thrown overboard in order to clear the decks" – it is a wonder that any plants ever survived the rigours of such journeys but many did.

The difficulties of transporting living plants were greatly eased in the early eighteen forties by the introduction of the newly invented Wardian Case (fig 2.4). It was invented by Dr Nathanial Bagshaw Ward and was described by him in the *Gardener's Magazine* in 1839 and in his book on "the growth of plants in closely glazed cases" (1842). It removed the need for attention by the crew and as it was compact and robust the plants were less liable to be damaged or discarded. The famous collector John Fortune in 1843 was one of the first to use the Wardian cases, taking living plants out to China. Among his introductions from that trip were *Phalaenopsis amabilis*, *Anemone* × *elegans*, *Jasminum nudiflorum* and *Spiraea prunifolia* – all of which were originally grown in heated greenhouses, although today the latter three are well known as excellent hardy garden plants!

Probably the heyday for plant introductions was in the latter half of the nineteenth century. This was especially true for Great Britain where there was tremendous interest in all kinds of new plants, with private individuals vying with each other to be the first to introduce or flower plants for exhibition. The *Gardener's Chronicle* ran a regular feature "new and noteworthy plants," which included many interesting house plants that are still widely grown. The longest running horticultural periodical, *Curtis's Botanical Magazine*, started in 1787 and still published today, has featured about 11 000 different introductions.

2.5 *An early portrait of Sir Joseph Banks (Crown copyright)*

Whilst many of the plants introduced during this period have survived in cultivation many have not, and it is quite possible that re-introduction would prove to be successful due to developments in cultural techniques.

The competition in acquiring new plants is best exemplified by the orchid collectors. Although not strictly considered as interior plants, orchids had a big influence on the introduction of other families. The epiphytic orchids found on the upper branches of tropical rain forest trees share a similar habitat with many bromeliads and tropical climbing aroids. These associated plants are some of the most popular and striking of house plants but their exact origins are rather obscure. Orchid collectors were usually reluctant to disclose their sources and even destroyed plants so that others would not reduce the economic advantage of the first find. The sordid commercial reason seems more realistic as the explanation for lack of information about house plants than modesty – one cannot look at the catalogues of the late nineteenth century and feel there was much modesty in any of them! As a result the nineteenth century plant collectors are not renowned for their literary prowess, unlike their more modern counterparts such as George Forrest, Frank Kingdon-Ward and Henry Wilson who have written full and interesting accounts of their travels and discoveries. The reticence of the nineteenth century collectors is somewhat strange when one considers that there had been a tradition of recording plant introduction by such notable figures as Sir Joseph Banks (1743–1820) (fig 2.5). During the long period that he was Honorary Director of His Majesty's Garden at Kew (now the Royal Botanic Gardens) Sir Joseph Banks not only sent collectors to all parts of the world to find new plants but also arranged training courses, so that the young men from Kew could be relied upon to take care of the plants on board ship during their long journeys from Australia and the Orient. He not only encouraged and provided support for others to collect plants but also did some exploring himself and collected plants in Newfoundland in 1766. With Dr Solander he accompanied Captain Cook on his great voyage of exploration from 1768 to 1771, through the Pacific to Tahiti to observe the passage of Venus over the sun in 1769. They discovered such a great variety of plants in Australia that, in consequence, their principal stopping place was called Botany Bay. One of the major interior introductions from this voyage was the Australian Kangaroo Vine *Cissus antarctica*.

Possibly one of the most successful collectors to be dispatched by Sir Joseph was Francis Masson, who went with Captain Cook on his second voyage of discovery to the Southern Pacific. Masson collected over four hundred species that were new to botany and his contribution probably did much to establish Kew's early pre-eminence in botanical affairs (fig 2.6). It is interesting to note that at Kew there is one of the original plants introduced by Masson over 200 years ago, a cyad called *Encephalartos longifolius* which is still growing and therefore probably the oldest "pot plant" in cultivation. Among other plants that he introduced were several of the beautiful and delicate cape heaths and the well known succulent *Stapelia grandiflora* and *Aloe dichotoma*. As early as 1770 Benjamin Tarrin, an East Indian clerk at Canton, safely sent to Kew different plants – *Cordyline terminalis*, *Daphne odora*, *Osmanthus fragrans* and *Saxifraga stolonifera* (*S. sarmentosa*).

Johann Reinhold Forster and his son Johann George Forster were the naturalists attached to Captain Cook's second voyage of discovery in the South Seas from 1772 to 5. They were originally intended to be the official recorders for the voyage but the Admiralty, under the advice of Captain Cook, decided to withdraw their support. Despite this they rushed through their private report some months before the official version, a

2.6 *A recent view inside the Palm House at Kew*

typical action. They had been unpopular with the crew, who disliked the Forsters' dictatorial attitude and constant interference. The family name is commemorated by one of the Kentia palms *Howea forsteriana* – a paradox really, for it is very popular and millions of seeds have been exported from the tiny Lord Howe Islands for growing as house plants. In fact for many years up to the second world war the seeds were the islands' main source of revenue. In 1946 Thomas Rochford and Sons noted that they imported 250 000 seeds to help restore the firm's pot plant production. Recently the supply of seeds on the open market seems to have been reduced, due to monopolies in the supply chain, so that the Kentia palm has almost taken on a scarcity value.

Another famous name in connection with plants is that of Veitch; this English firm covered all aspects of the nursery trade from hardy to hothouse plants. In *Hortus Veitchii* they listed 1274 of the plants that the firm had introduced; orchids were the main section, although it is interesting to see how these influenced other introductions. Not only did they have correspondents sending them plants, but they also sent collectors to given areas for specific plants. One of their collectors was a Christopher Mudd, and to quote from *Hortus Veitchii*, "This collector, son of a former Curator of the Cambridge Botanic Gardens, went on an expedition to South Africa in 1877 and great things were expected to result from the undertaking. These expectations, however, were not realised for Mudd, who seemed to have no special aptitude for collecting and entirely lacked the explorer's instinct, sent home little of horticultural value and the mission, which was practically a failure, had to be recalled." Actually Mudd is said to have introduced one good

2.7 *An engraving of* Asparagus plumosus nanus *taken from* Hortus Veitchii *(1882)*

plant, the Asparagus fern, *Asparagus setaceus*. It is perhaps better known by its synonym *A. plumosus nanus* (fig 2.7). This rather delicate looking plant is surprisingly tough and drought resistant, and is particularly interesting as it is raised from seed produced in Europe rather than being imported from the country of origin as is usually the case. Asparagus fern was a very important foliage plant for cutting and there were specialist nurseries that concentrated solely on the production of *Asparagus setaceus* and its coarser, more vigorous and slightly easier to grow relation *Asparagus "Sprengeri"*.

Messrs Veitch did introduce many new plants, and one of the family, John Gould Veitch, was a collector who made two expeditions to the East, the first to Japan and the Philippines, and the second to Australasia and Polynesia, whence came the attractive screw pine *Pandanus veitchii*. It is of interest to note that although Mr Veitch wrote extensively about his travels in the *Gardeners' Chronicle* over many issues he did not mention – where his new introductions came from. This was still the age of commercialism, with the source of supply often a secret so that the first specimens of *Pandanus veitchii* sold for £10 a plant in 1868. Another very interesting plant introduced by Veitch from the same expedition was *Dizygotheca elegantissima* (syn. *Aralia elegantissima*).

Some plants have histories which serve as poignant illustrations of the hardship of the early collectors. For example, *Dracaena godseffiana* was introduced from the coast of Guinea by Mr H. Millen, the curator of the Botanical Station, Lagos, and described in the *Botanical Magazine* in 1893. He had been a student at the Royal Botanical Gardens, Kew for only one year and at the age of 19 was made Curator of the Botanical Station. In 1895 Mr Millen wrote: "There is no doubt that horticultural and agricultural work is most trying and dangerous to Europeans engaged on the Coast, as they are compelled to be out in the sun and about the grounds. The frequent and lengthy vacations which are necessary for all Europeans on account of the unhealthy nature of the climate are a drawback to the development of the Colony; still, considerable progress has been made already in the direction of planting and improved methods of cultivation, and we hope to do a great deal more before we retire into that nice little place in the country of which all Colonists dream." Unfortunately Mr Millen, like many others, did not reach his "nice little place in the country" because he died in Trinidad following an accident in 1908.

Some plants have interesting stories behind them and their names, eg *Dieffenbachia sequine*, the dumb cane, got its name from a rather cruel trick often played on young gardeners. The stems of *Dieffenbachia spp.* are ribbed and bare and look rather like sugar cane, but if bitten the stems are found not to be full of sweet juice but an extremely poisonous sap. When sucked the sap can cause agonising throat swellings, so that the victim cannot speak for several days.

2.8 *Many interior plants come from the tropical zone*

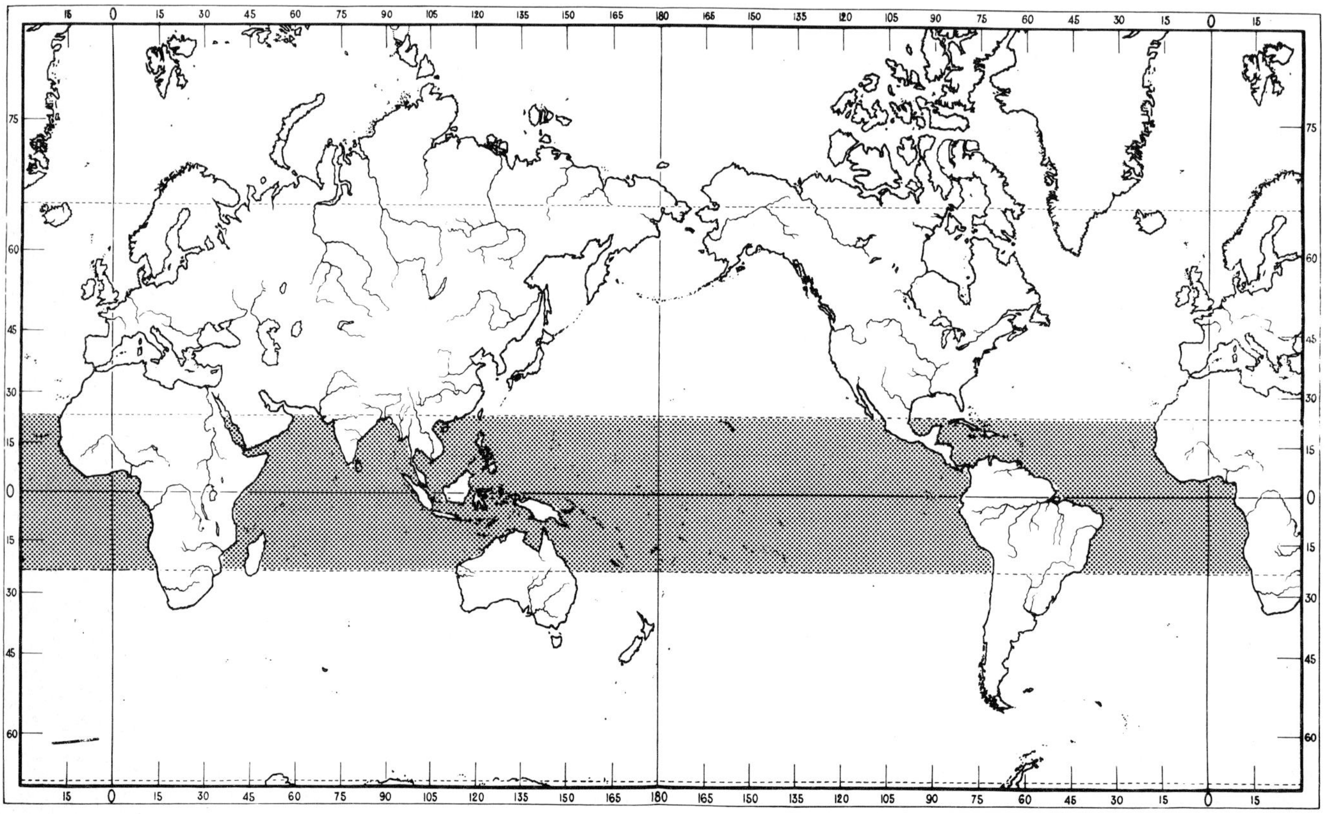

2.9 *A specimen of* Monstera deliciosa

2.10 *A group of* Yucca elephantipes

2.11 *A specimen of* Dieffenbachia amoena

Probably the most surprising aspect of interior plants is that specimens from disparate sources are frequently grown together. Today's house plants have come from all over the world, from every continent and even more surprisingly from almost every type of climatic zone. In the main they are perennial species including herbs, shrubs, vines and small trees from the wet and arid tropics and sub tropics ie the region between latitudes 40°N and 40°S (fig 2.8).

In the moist tropical zones of South America there is a wide range of showy flowering plants as well as dramatic foliage plants. Not all these plants require high temperatures, for example *Monstera deliciosa* is found in the state of Chiapas in Mexico, where the temperature can fall to 10°C (50°F) and there is a dry season of two months (fig. 2.9). Fascinating cacti are also found on the dry plateaux, along with other plants such as *Yucca elephantipes* (fig 2.10). In Central America both Costa Rica and Guatemala possess extremely rich and diverse floras, eg for its size Costa Rica has the greatest concentration of orchid species in the world. As a consequence the orchid collectors combed the rich forests and brought out a great variety of other plants. The islands of the Caribbean also yielded many plants similar to those of the mainland.

Equally rich, with a very diverse flora, is the northern part of South America, where there are still many plants waiting to be introduced. In this area there are many epiphytic species of *Araliaceae*, *Araceae* and especially *Bromeliaceae* such as *Vriesia splendens*. Further south in the great Amazon basin there are also epiphytic species and on the forest floor many useful house plants such as *Dieffenbachia spp* (fig 2.11), *Maranta spp*, *Cryptanthus spp*, and *Peperomia spp*. Still further south there are more epiphytes such as *Aechmea fasciata*. To the west in Ecuador, Colombia and Peru are other areas potentially rich in plant material which have yet to be fully studied.

The African continent is a direct contrast, for although there are a similar number of genera to those found in America there is a lack of diversity within them and few plants which are suitable for use indoors. Yet there are some interesting plants such as the showy *Dracaena godseffiana* which is found in the West African jungle. From the south come more drought tolerant plants whose appearance almost belie their drought tolerance, eg *Asparagus setaceus* (*A. plumosa*). Perhaps it is surprising that off the East African coast on the island of Madagascar there is a very interesting flora in the tropical rain forest such as the well known *Dracaena marginata* (fig 2.12) and many epiphytic orchids. In North Africa probably the best known plant is *Phoenix dactylifera*, which is widely cultivated and is increasingly being used as an indoor tree in Europe because large plants can be successfully transplanted with a small root ball (fig 2.13).

In the main, Asia Minor has not yielded many house plants, although it is the home of many interesting bulbous and herbaceous plants. In the far south eastern part of the continent, however, there is an example of the rich tropical plant diversity found in South and Central America. Particularly noteworthy are the many different foliage shapes of *Ficus spp* (fig 2.14). The multi-coloured *Codiaeum variegatum* is found throughout South East Asia, along with *Pilea spp* and *Platycerium spp*, and leads on to the richness of the Indies. In Indonesia are found some of the richly coloured foliage forms of aroids, such as *Aglaonema spp* and *Scindapsus spp*, and a wealth of orchids.

From China and Japan comes a wide range of hardy plants including *Aspidistra elatior* and *Fatsia japonica* (syn *Aralia sieboldii*) which are widely grown. From the South of China comes the creeping fig *Ficus pumila* which occurs as far south as Queensland. This fig is well known, due to its extensive use on pillars in the Great Conservatory at Longwood Gardens (fig 2.14).

The vast continent of Australia has a great diversity of

2.12 *A group of* Dracaena marginata

2.13 Phoenix dactylifera *(Date Palm) is widely used in Europe as it can be transplanted successfully with a small root ball (Skyline Hotel, London)*

2.14 *The pillars in the Great Conservatory at Longwood Gardens, Pa. are covered with* Ficus pumila

2.15 *A clump of* Howea forsteriana

2.16 *A group of* × Fatshedera lizei

mainly sun loving plants. Few are suitable for growing in poor light conditions, and they usually grow too quickly if given adequate moisture. However there are some very effective plants, such as the Kangaroo Vine *Cissus antarctica*, from New South Wales and Queensland. Also from Queensland comes the umbrella plant *Schefflera actinophylla* (syn *Brassaia actinophylla*).

Further east in the Pacific Ocean and from Polynesia in particular have come many decorative plants, such as *Asplenium nidus*, *Dizygotheca elegantissima* and *Pandanus veitchii*. Even relatively tiny islands have made their contribution. From the Lord Howe Islands come the two Kentia palms, *Howea belmoreana* and *Howea forsteriana* (fig 2.15), and the Norfolk Islands are the home of *Araucaria excelsa*.

The variety of house plants is still being added to. Not all the plants are from introductions of long ago and some, such as *Peperomia caperata* from South America, are of very recent date and proving to be very popular. Cultivation has its good points too – *Pilea cadierei*, the aluminium plant, has only been found once in the wild in Indo-China: surprising when it is so easy to grow!

Although the temperate regions have produced very few house plants it should be remembered that one of the best indoor plants with a wide range of cultivars is the common ivy, *Hedera helix*. Of course the common ivy has had a long history of cultivation, with little drama. It is very tough and hardy yet it possesses the ability to retain its inherent neatness and character even when grown under more favourable conditions, ie warmth with freely available nutrients and water although excessive temperatures can however cause etiolation. A few house plants have actually been created rather than found in the wild. An interesting example which has remained very popular for over 60 years is the bi-generic hybrid × *Fatshedera lizei* which originated from the French nursery of Messrs Lize Freres of Nantes in 1910 (fig 2.16). The parentage, although a little uncertain, was said to have been *Fatsia japonica var moseri*, the female parent, and *Hedera helix var hibernica*, the pollinator. There has not been any further successful hybridisation and so all plants in cultivation have been derived as cuttings from the original, including the cream margined variegated form.

From a study of the origins of interior plants it can be seen that they have not evolved in any particular ecological environment, but that a rather crude "prosper or die" process of selection has ensured that there is a reasonably large range of tough and resilient plants available to the designer. With improved interior environments it will almost certainly be possible to grow an even wider selection of plants than are now available.

3 Plant physiology

INTRODUCTION

Whenever it is proposed to instal plants in buildings it should be remembered that they are living organisms which have evolved in situations far removed from our urban environments. For this reason it is necessary to have an understanding of their structure and mode of functioning. It is also important to understand that plants must successfully exploit two distinct situations, ie that which exists above ground level and that which exists below. The dissimilarity in these situations necessitates fundamental structural differences between the various plant organs. For this reason a plant should be regarded as a structure composed of several components, each with its own specific function and requirements (fig 3.1). The most relevant of these for an understanding of interior plant cultivation are described in this chapter.

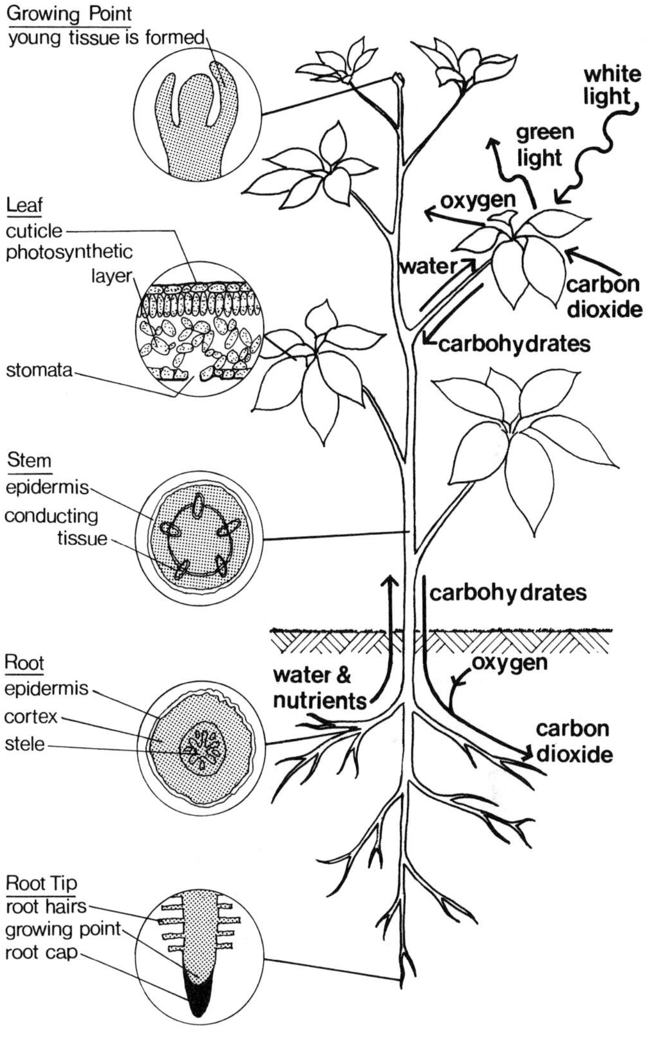

3.1 *Diagram of the anatomy of a typical plant*

THE AERIAL COMPONENT

The growing points

These are the main areas of cell division, active areas in which many small young cells develop rapidly to form stems, leaves, and flowers. This zone also produces many of the hormones which control the growth of the plant, eg when supplied with nutrients, shoot tips produce hormones which accelerate the rate of growth. Another function of all major growing points is to produce hormones which suppress the activities of other buds so that the main growing points occupy a dominant position on the plant and so preserve the overall shape, ie effect apical dominance. In many plants these zones, in conjunction with young leaves, detect changes in day length to effect the seasonal control of flowering.

The stems

The stems give a plant form, support the leaves and flowers, and transport materials. These functions are achieved by a large number of fine "tubes" that are interspersed with reinforcing tissue. They are arranged in bundles or rings towards the outside of the stem to give maximum rigidity. The tubes are filled with a solution of nutrients and/or carbohydrates which is being moved around the plant (see "Translocation"). In most cases the stem is a rigid structure which is easily damaged by bending, particularly in monocotyledonous plants like palms and grasses which have non-renewable conductive tissue. Overall stem length is usually reduced by high light levels, which affect the hormone balance in the growing point, but is compensated for by an increase in the stem diameter and the total plant dry weight. Conversely, plants which are grown in the shade tend to be taller, have weaker stems, and less carbohydrate reserves.

The leaves

The leaves are typically the area for carbohydrate manufacture. They are usually covered by a waxy cuticle which reduces water loss and resists the activities of pests and diseases. The cuticle is carried on a barrier wall of cells called the epidermis which covers a mass of regular soft thin-walled cells or parenchyma which have a high chlorophyll content. These in turn rest on a much more open mass of cells which enclose numerous air spaces called the spongy mesophyll. Some plants like ferns have a poorly developed cuticle through which as much as 30% of the total water loss can occur. In contrast xerophytic species (drought tolerant) have evolved to reduce this loss to a minimum by having such features as a system of hairs and scales on the leaf surface to produce a static layer of air, as well as to increase their reflective value. An amount of water is also lost from the stems by means of pores or lenticels but as a plant ages these pathways are closed by the formation of bark.

The internal air spaces of leaves are continuous with the

surrounding atmosphere via small pores called stomata. These facilitate the exchange of air between the voids in the leaf and the external environment. By this means carbon dioxide can enter the leaf, and oxygen and water vapour can leave. This latter function is most important, as the evaporation of moisture from the leaf during periods of bright light prevents overheating. Despite their ability to absorb light, leaves usually collect less than 3.5% of that which falls upon them; the remainder being reflected or serving to raise their temperature. Each stomata consists of a variable aperture between two special guard cells whose dimensions vary, according to their turgidity, in response to the osmotic effect of their soluble carbohydrate content (fig 3.2). In dicotyledonous plants, eg *Ficus benjamina*, the majority of the stomatal apertures are on the lower surface, whilst in monocotyledonous plants such as grasses they tend to be evenly spaced on both surfaces. The stomata usually have the ability to open and close, but as their behaviour is so variable throughout the plant kingdom it is most practical to regard them as partially open pores. During periods of actute drought all stomata will close because the guard cells become flaccid due to dehydration. Similarly at low light levels the guard cells will also close because their carbohydrate content is insufficient to maintain turgidity.

The leaves of plants grown in full sunlight tend to be thicker and have a smaller area than those which are grown in the shade (fig 3.2). High light levels tend to encourage more layers of palisade cells, whereas shading produces more of the spongy mesophyll type. High light levels also lead to the formation of more stomata, thicker cells walls and cuticles, few large chloroplasts and a deeper structure, eg *Ficus benjamina* when grown in high light conditions can develop thicker epidermal and palisade layers (fig 3.2). In the case of larger plants it follows that as the leaf area increases so the average light intensity throughout the plant decreases, ie photosynthesis per unit area falls, and so there will always be a situation where growth is optimal for a given leaf area. This is one of the main reasons why leaves are frequently shed from the inside of the canopy ie to maintain the maximum surface area.

The most important characteristic of leaves is that they absorb carbon dioxide and combine it with water in the presence of light and chlorophyll to produce carbohydrates. The chlorophyll is located in highly organised units called chloroplasts which are found primarily in the palisade layer and are specifically designed for the absorption of solar energy. The chloroplast contains discs ("grana") bedded in a colourless matrix or stroma, contained by a membrane. Chlorophyll has a characteristic absorption curve as indicated in fig 4.3 with a double peak of activity in both the "red" and "blue" regions of the spectrum. Chlorophyll consists of a complex molecule of carbon, hydrogen and nitrogen with an atom of magnesium at the centre. The reason why a nutrient deficiency causes a plant to appear low in chlorophyll, ie pale in colour, is because its formation depends on certain oxidation systems. These systems consist of nitrogenous organic compounds containing sulphur, phosphorus and iron. A deficiency in any of these elements will result in a decline in all physiological processes due to a loss of oxidation activity (eg. iron) as well as the lack of component elements (eg. magnesium for the chlorophyll molecule).

The chlorophyll is contained in chloroplasts which are independent organelles surrounded by a membrane. They contain the range of complex organic compounds necessary for the production of carbohydrates, such as chlorophylls a and b, in association with other pigments like carotenes and xanthophylls. These other pigments serve to increase efficiency and protect the chlorophyll from the denaturing which would otherwise occur at light intensity in excess of 20 000 lux. The grana in the chloroplasts contain the photosynthetic pigments which absorb light and release electrons to the reactions in the stroma which reduce carbon dioxide to carbohydrates. Shade-plant chloroplasts contain particularly large grana stacks which are slightly mobile, and can respond to bright light by forming tight vertical units. In low intensity light they spread out to increase the area of interception. This is a very gradual process which occurs only in certain species over a four or five weeks period.

Most of the plants grown for interior use are unable to utilise excessive quantities of light due to the way in which their

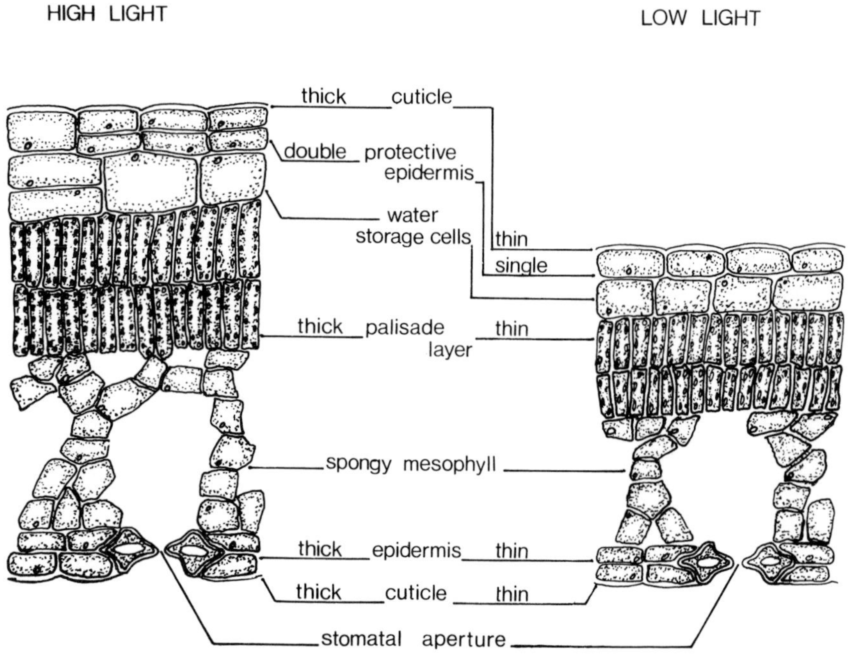

3.2 *Sections through leaves of* Ficus benjamina *grown in high and low light conditions to indicate some of the variations in leaf morphology associated with extremes of light intensity*

biochemical systems operate, and have to achieve a high level of efficiency at relatively low light levels. In a shade leaf there tend to be fewer chloroplasts across the leaf section but they are usually larger and contain more chlorophyll than those in plants grown at higher light intensities. Therefore the increase in the size of chloroplasts and the amount of chlorophyll per chloroplast in shade leaves is more than offset by the decrease in the number of chloroplasts per unit area of leaf surface. Shade plant chloroplasts are, however, saturated at much lower light intensities than those formed under high light intensities probably due to the increased size of the photosynthetic unit.

Photosynthesis consists of two distinct phases – a dark reaction and a light one. The light reaction is reasonably robust as it operates whenever light falls on the chlorophyll producing a reduction capability for the dark reaction. The dark reaction is different, as it is sensitive to the availability of water and the prevailing temperature, with most of the activity taking place between 10 and 30°C (50–85°F). In the dark reaction hydrogen is split from the oxygen in water and combined with carbon dioxide to form carbohydrates. The leaves retain some carbohydrates to enable them to function in the dark, and the surplus is dispersed to the points of growth, eg the root and shoot tips, and to storage areas, eg stems and roots. However, when a plant is stimulated into other activities such as producing flowers and fruit, all the surplus carbohydrates from the leaves and stores may well be diverted to these functions, thereby restricting growth.

The release of energy from the products of photosynthesis is called respiration, and occurs in all the parts of the plant to maintain basic functions and to permit growth. The rate of respiration is directly related to temperature and although necessary to maintain the activities of the plant its rate is often independent of the plant's needs. For this reason a plant which experiences high temperatures will consume energy faster than one which experiences lower ones. In broad terms the rate of respiration doubles with every 10 deg C rise in temperature.

Every plant has a compensation point, where its ability to produce carbohydrates equals its minimum respiratory requirements but cannot support further growth. This represents a balance between photosynthesis and respiration but as a plant becomes acclimatised to adverse conditions such as low light, so its compensation point can be lowered. Probably the best index of viability in shade conditions is the reserve of respirable materials, as these are largely dependent upon the rate of conversion of photosynthates into plant structure. In some high light species, however, the consumption of photosynthates by growth may be so great that reserves do not accumulate. This is not a simple matter as recent work has shown that the controls of a plant's photosynthetic and respiratory processes are closely linked to metabolic and environmental factors. These complex relationships exist not only in photosynthetic tissue exposed to light but are also found with respiratory processes in the rest of the plant.

When a leaf is no longer required by the plant it is isolated and then detached. The area where this separation occurs is called the absiccion layer. During the life of the leaf the permeability of this zone is maintained by the hormones which it produces to counteract others from the growing points which would promote its isolation. When the leaf becomes weak its hormone level falls so that those from the growing points dominate and cause the leaf to be shed. This hormone pattern is influenced by ethylene which is a gas produced naturally by plants when they are stressed, eg by low temperatures, and explains why plants suffer in the presence of partially burnt hydrocarbons, for example from open gas fires.

The flowers

The flowers are the sexual reproductive component of the plant. There are few examples of interior plants being selected primarily for their flowers, because the growth potential which exists at the low light levels to be found in buildings is generally poor. In nature the flowers serve to attract insects to encourage cross-pollination, and can represent a considerable strain by consuming much of the available carbohydrates. If carbohydrate levels are low the flowers may not be initiated or may even abort. The petals consist of thin-walled cells and can be a major source of water loss for a plant which experiences drying conditions. Further information on the behaviour of flowering plants is included in chapter 4.

THE SUBTERRANEAN COMPONENT

The root system is totally dependent upon the leaves for carbohydrates so that if photosynthetically active radiation levels are low, root development will be retarded. Conversely, if a plant experiences high light conditions the amount of top growth will be low relative to the amount of subterranean growth. If light is not limiting each plant will develop a root system which is in proportion to its aerial component. This is called the root/shoot ratio and the exact balance for any given plant is dependent upon its genetic composition and the prevailing environmental conditions. Unlike the aerial portion of the plant the root system serves many functions within one structure and is best considered in terms of a few easily identifiable components:

The growing points

The growing points are the major area of cell division. Root extension occurs in a similar manner to that of the aerial parts as a result of rapid cell division in this zone. To avoid damage when penetrating the soil it carries a protective cap. Roots will not usually develop in a dry soil but extend readily into wet soils to the ideal root/shoot ratio even if the system is already large enough to supply the plant's current water requirement. There is evidence that the failure of roots to penetrate dry soils is usually due to physical impedance rather than the lack of water. If the nutrient level in the substrate falls the ability of this zone to produce new tissue becomes limited. A similar situation develops in low oxygen conditions when the ability of the root to absorb nutrients is reduced.

The root hairs

The root hairs have the closest possible association with the substrate. They consist of thin-walled cells which project from immediately behind the growing point and ramify between the soil particles. Normally they live for only a few days and frequently they are completely absent although in most species they absorb some water and mineral salts.

The main roots

The main roots are the basis of the system. These roots consist of concentric rings of specialised cells, the middle portion providing tensile strength with flexibility by virtue of their central location. This inner zone or stele also serves other functions, such as the transportation of materials and the thickening of the root. Surrounding this core is a mass of cells called the cortex, which provide protection and carry out a number of functions such as carbohydrate storage and water absorption. The functions of the main root system are described below.

Anchorage

Typically the quantity and distribution of the roots is sufficient to anchor the plant, but with high nutrient levels (by feeding) it is possible to reduce this ability by producing a plant with a small root system.

Water uptake

Without an adequate water supply the plant may become stressed and even die. Although some water is absorbed by the root hairs the majority enters the conductive tissue of the plant by passing between the cells of the cortex.

Nutrient uptake

Roots are able to take up a range of salts from the soil water by selectively absorbing those which are required. The rate of absorption is usually proportional to the supply when nutrient concentrations are low, but at higher concentrations an increase in actual levels leads to a smaller rate of intake. The movement of nutrients through the root to the vascular tissue requires the expenditure of metabolic energy. Although most salts are actively transported to the vascular system it would appear that their movement up the plant is dependent upon the rate of transpiration. Overall the rate of absorption is largely dependent upon the requirements of the plant unless the nutrients are in short supply, and means that plants will tolerate a wide range of nutrient levels.

Food storage

The roots are usually supplied with only sufficient carbohydrates for their immediate use, although it is common for many plants to store excess carbohydrates in an insoluble form in the cells of the cortex to resupply the aerial components at a later date.

TRANSLOCATION

Translocation, the movement of materials around the plant, occurs in the conductive tissue which is found in both stems and roots. In general terms water and minerals move up the plant and a "sugar solution" moves downwards. The translocation of photosynthates is directional and gives evidence of being highly organised, ie translocation from each leaf is directional to specific parts of the plant. The rate of translocation also tends to be proportional to the growth of the plant in the same way that photosynthesis tends to be proportional to the needs of the parts of the plant for carbohydrates. It is still not known exactly what controls the rate of photosynthesis and the translocation of its products but the existence of specific areas of demand, such as flowers, may cause translocation away from the leaves which in turn, may result in increased photosynthesis. It would appear that these operations are signalled by certain groups of plant hormones, although the details are still unclear.

There appear to be two main methods by which water passes up a plant. The most significant of the two is described as the "cohesion tension theory", which assumes that as water is lost from the leaves so more is drawn into them from the conductive tissue. As the conductive tissue consists of minute water-filled tubes running the height of the plant, any extraction of water from the top of the column will serve to draw water in at the base. A much less significant contribution is made by the osmotic pressure in the root produced by the high salt concentration in the cells when compared to the surrounding soil water.

4 Relating plants to the interior environment

INTRODUCTION

Most building interiors are designed to provide standards of environmental comfort suited to the activity and normal clothing of the occupants. The exact nature of interior environments is so variable that it is outside the terms of reference of this book to consider them further than the information contained in table 4.1.

For a plant to survive there must be a successful interaction between its "aerial" and "subterranean" components and the interior environment. A failure with any of these interactions will result in a reduction in the rate of growth and may even cause death.

FOLIAR ENVIRONMENT

The more important environmental factors which affect the aerial parts of the plant include temperature, humidity, air changes, gases and light.

Temperature

A low minimum temperature will reduce the rate of growth whilst a wide diurnal range, or very cold periods, such as might occur when the heating system is turned off over weekends or bank holidays, can kill plants. Optimum plant growth normally occurs when the night temperature is 5 to 8 deg C lower than the day temperature, although plants appear to develop a preference for lower night temperatures when they mature. Most interior plants prefer a day temperature of 21–24°C (70–75°F) and a night temperature of 15–18°C (60–65°F). Many will tolerate a minimum temperature of 13°C (56°F) and frequently 10°C (50°F) or even a little lower will suffice. Where temperatures are expected to fall as low as 2°C (36°F) the use of hardy plants may be considered. Temperatures below this level are seldom experienced, due to the danger of ice formation in the general plumbing and the need to safeguard fire sprinkler systems.

Leaf temperatures have a particularly marked effect on growth rates, since leaves are the site of photosynthesis and transpiration, as well as most of the respiration and protein synthesis. The effect of draughts is therefore particularly pronounced on thin leaves. At higher temperatures plants have an accelerated respiration rate and so it may be necessary to provide more illumination than normal in areas of high temperature.

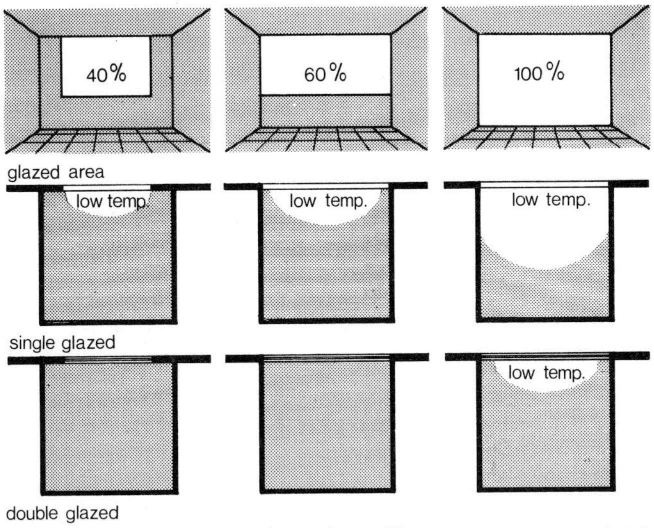

4.1 *Three examples of interior regions of low temperature associated with single and double glazed windows of different areas*

Planting should be kept away from localised low air temperatures, and from cold draughts which occur at the entrances of buildings and against single glazed windows. The area of low temperature associated with a window is related to the outside temperature and the area of glazing as illustrated in fig 4.1. Proximity to ducted air outlets should also be avoided as a "blast" of hot dry air can cause foliar damage.

Humidity

For much of the year, building interiors are maintained at higher temperatures than the external air, so that when air is

TABLE 4.1 THE CHARACTERISTICS OF SOME BUILDING ENVIRONMENTS IN RELATION TO PLANTING

Site	Examples	Suitable temperature (°C) Mean	Min	Light level (Lux)	Comments	Degree of abuse
Enclosed public thoroughfare	Shopping precincts, leisure centres, exhibition centres	18	10*	200 to 500	Generally poor—requires supplementing	Very high, unless the plants are at high level or are large
Enclosed private thoroughfare	Reception areas, landings, lift lobbies, corridors	20	13	200 to 500	Generally poor – requires supplementing	Little damage except for petty theft
Dining areas	Restaurants, cafetearias, coffee lounges	22	13	100 to 700	Often variable – may need supplementing	Moderate – planters can become filled with rubbish and coffee
Offices and showrooms		24	13	300 to 750	Normally adequate	Seldom any problems
Humid recreation	Swimming pools	25	10	750 to 2000	Adequate	Occasional petty vandalism

* In certain cases temperatures may fall to just above freezing for a considerable period of time

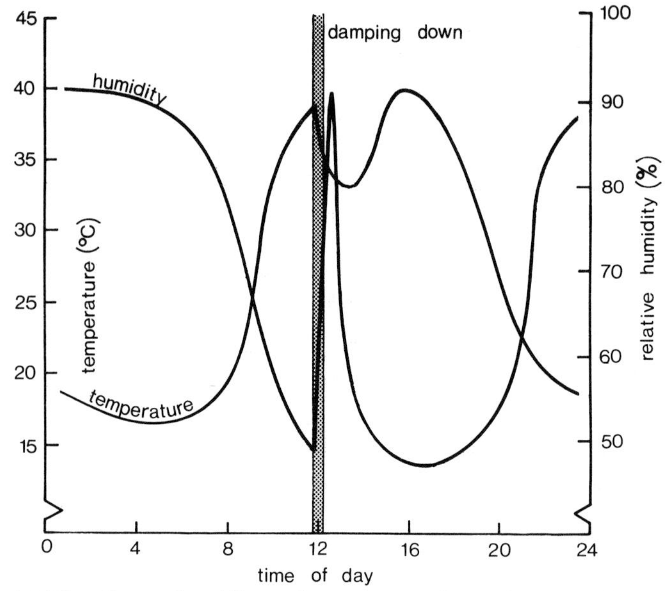

4.2 *The effect on humidity and temperature of spraying a glasshouse floor with water*

drawn into a building its temperature is raised and its relative humidity falls. As an approximate guide it may be assumed that a 1 deg C rise in temperature will lead to the humidity falling by 4%. In most buildings it is usual for the humidity to be between 50 and 55%, although it can fall to 20% in some parts of the world particularly if the external temperatures are very low.

Due to their structure most interior plants will tolerate humidities as low as 40% unless they are suffering from water stress. Plants usually have a preference for much higher levels, although humidities over 85% can encourage certain disease pathogens. Many plants are apparently unaffected by humidities as low as 20% although humidities below 40% must lead to some stress. Fortunately people also tend to experience discomfort at these low humidities and so humidifiers are frequently installed.

There is little evidence to indicate that plants benefit from high humidity unless they are suffering from a shortage of water. The practice of spraying plants with water or damping down the surrounding floor area serves to raise the humidity for such a limited period that it must be of minimal benefit (fig 4.2). The value of the humid zone over a plant substrate is also questionable as its extent is limited and it is rapidly dissipated by air currents. The presence of plants in a building does slightly increase the overall humidity, which has the advantage of substantially reducing the level of static electricity in office fittings.

Air changes

Normal air changes should have little effect on plants, except those placed directly in the hot or cold draughts at the outlets of air conditioning systems. Plants should not be used where rapid air changes have been specified which produce linear air speeds in excess of 1.5 m/sec and localised temperature fluctuations of 15 deg C. Such a drying stream of air can desiccate foliage causing "die-back" from the leaf tips or margins.

Gases

There are few phytotoxic gases which are tolerated in inhabited buildings, although some difficulties may be experienced with high levels of partially burnt hydrocarbons from heating units. The single most serious pollutant is ethylene, which is produced by the incomplete combustion of organic compounds. It occurs naturally in plant cells where it controls such functions as leaf senescence and root formation. However, when supplied from the outside in even small quantities it induces a range of symptoms such as wilting, premature leaf senescence, and flower abortion. The old forms of town or manufactured gas contained 20% carbon monoxide and 4–8% unsaturated hydrocarbons such as ethylene and were therefore harmful.

Natural gas is almost pure methane and therefore safe at concentrations up to 20 000 ppm. Carbon monoxide is produced from the same sources as ethylene and has a similar effect, but only at 5000 times the concentration, at which level it becomes harmful to people.

Halogens such as chlorine do not appear to be detrimental to plants at the concentrations which are found in buildings. High concentrations due to accidental release usually affect old tissue first, whilst young tissue appears to be able to develop a degree of resistance. Spraying plants with water chlorinated to 100 ppm does not appear to have an effect, although irrigation with water containing chlorine at 500 ppm can cause damage. The normal concentration of chlorine in drinking water is 0.5 ppm and seldom exceeds 1.5 ppm, which means it is not phytotoxic. Similarly there is little chance of damage at the concentrations to be found in the atmosphere of swimming pools, although one air change per hour should avoid any difficulties. Fluorine is also added to municipal water supplies in some areas, and can cause leaf tips to "die back" or dead patches to form on the leaf blade in a limited number of sensitive species.

The vapours from strong cleaning materials often contain compounds such as ammonia and carbon tetrachloride, which can cause foliar damage. The usual symptom is that the leaves curl and turn black, by which stage the damage is irreparable.

Light

Light is used by plants in three ways:

1 Photosynthesis – the production of carbohydrates
2 Photoperiodism – the monitoring of the seasons
3 Photomorphogenesis – the modification of morphology

The most important aspect of light for plants in buildings is its role as the energy source of plants. Of all the factors which exert a regulating influence on the growth of plants, low light levels are the primary limiter. In most cases the more light a plant receives the faster it grows, and the better it appears. However, many of the plants used for interior work have evolved in the world which exists below a jungle canopy, where regeneration depends on the survival and growth of seedlings at low light levels. Plants which naturally occupy shade habitats usually have low photosynthetic rates and reach their maximum at low light intensities. It is also usual for shade-tolerant species to maintain a uniform pattern of growth over a wide range of light values. Frequently they can modify their physiology to utilise more fully that light which is available, eg by increasing the number of cells in the palisade layer – a characteristic which is not common in high light species.

It has been found that most shade tolerant plants survive because they conserve the energy which is available rather than being efficient at its capture. Shade species are not limited to low visible radiation levels and can usually exist in direct sun although in some cases they may become light saturated and overheat, with consequential foliar damage. Even plants like *Dracaena marginata*, *Ficus benjamina*, and *Schefflera actinophylla*, which grow in full sun in the tropics, can be scorched by sunlight when placed in windows after a period of acclimatisation to shade conditions. This phenomena is not fully understood, as light which has passed through glass is almost unchanged in composition, but minor variations in spectral composition and irregularities in the glass may be the cause.

High light levels can cause problems, but with interior

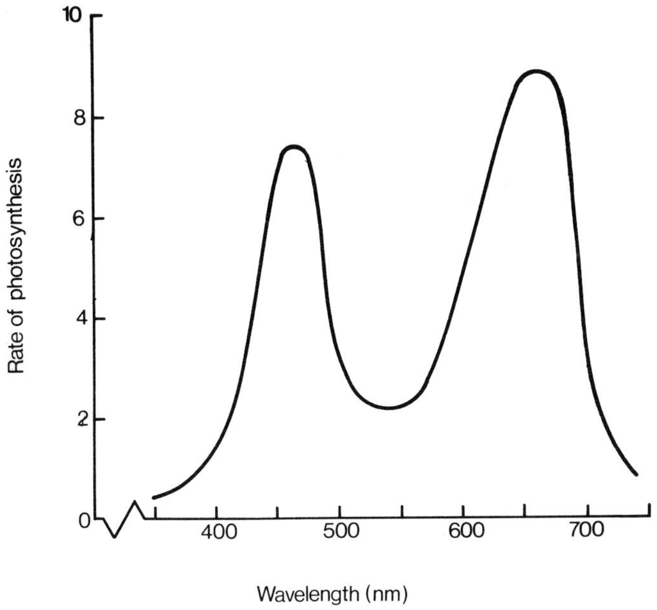

4.3 *Graph of the selective absorption spectra of chlorophyll, with its two peaks in the "blue" and "red" wavebands*

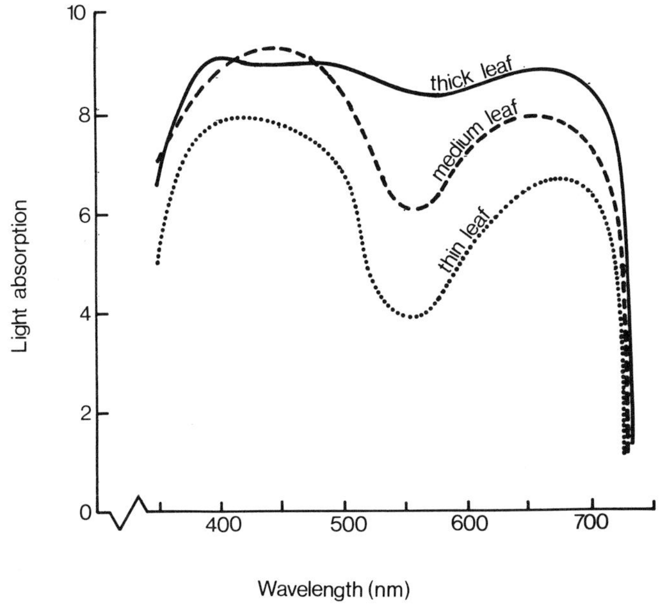

4.4 *The selective absorption spectra of leaves of various thickness*

work the concern is usually with low radiation levels. Most interior plants require only 0.07 to 0.08 MJ per day (600–700 lux for 12 hours) to grow satisfactorily and in some cases this can be reduced to 0.06 MJ per day (500 lux for 12 hours). At these lower illuminances plants with coloured or variegated foliage tend to appear less vivid due to the need to produce photosynthetic pigment in preference to colour pigment.

Light quality

Not only is the quantity of light important but also its spectral composition. The significance to the plant of light of different wavelengths is illustrated in table 4.1. That light which is not absorbed is reflected, giving the plant its characteristic colour. The most widely illustrated graph of plant behaviour is the double peak of chlorophyll absorption with maximums in the "red" and "blue" areas of the electromagnetic spectrum (fig 4.3). This is correct for chlorophyll when extracted from the leaf

TABLE 4.2 THE GENERAL RESPONSE OF PLANTS TO DIFFERENT PORTIONS OF THE ELECTROMAGNETIC SPECTRUM

Wavelength (nm)	Colour	Growth	Photosynthesis	Photoperiodism
315 or less	Far ultraviolet	Harmful	Destructive	Destructive
315 to 400	Near ultraviolet	Causes phototropic (movement) responses. Rate of internode extension reduced. Leaf thickness increased	Little effect	Little effect
400 to 510	Blue	Amount of extension growth restricted	High activity	Slight activity
510 to 560	Green	Little effect	Moderate activity	Little effect
560 to 610	Yellow	Little effect	High activity	Little effect
610 to 700	Red	Causes weak etiolated growth	Very high activity	Strong activity involving photoperiodic response, eg flowering
700 to 800	Far red	Stimulates weak and etiolated growth	Low activity	Counteracts effect of red light in photoperiodic response, eg flowering
800 and over	Infra red	Heats plants	Can cause damage	Can cause damage

but a complete plant has an absorption pattern which is much less distinct. This is due to other pigments which are present and the light scattering properties of the leaf cells. When the absorption spectra of leaves of varying thicknesses are expressed graphically a much flatter plot is found, with only a slight trough in the 550–600 nm range (fig 4.4). This ability to use any radiant energy within the 400–700 nm range is probably to be expected when the spectrum of natural daylight is considered, as it is unlikely that a utilisable source of energy would have been left untapped during the course of evolution. For this reason almost any light source which emits between 400 and 700 nm, eg most fluorescent lamps, is suitable for plant illumination provided it does not have a marked imbalance between the 'blue" and "red" areas, or a high level of infrared radiation which could cause distorted morphology (fig 5.4). Of course this broad utilisation of light does not apply to the other physiological responses, which are far more closely related to light quality.

Of the light which impinges on a leaf only a proportion is absorbed, whilst the remainder is either reflected or passes straight through. Far red light in particular passes through a foliar canopy and causes rapid extension growth in the plants underneath, ie it encourages plants to grow through any foliage which overshadows them. This tendency of plants to etiolate (develop thin weak stems) in the presence of a high "far red" light source, eg from incandescent lamps, can seriously reduce the value of a display. Conversely, plants which are grown in light with a high "blue" content tend to be hard and dark with a compressed appearance. Plants also tend to etiolate in total darkness, although this can be suppressed by small quantities of "red" light, but not "infrared". This would seem to indicate that certain of the mechanisms which control photoperiodism and photomorphogenesis are the same.

Illumination periods

It may safely be assumed that plants which have originated from the tropics have a preference for a day length of thirteen hours. Some plants require a period of dark each day to maintain their growth patterns, eg tomato seedlings become pale and stunted, and even die, particularly at higher temperatures, without a dark period. Continuous illumination may well cause undesirable growth responses in sensitive species although no clearly documented cases on interior plants are yet available although some preliminary work indicates that the results can be serious. To avoid any chance of growth irregularities a dark period of at least four hours should be arranged, though a period of six hours is probably desirable. This means that where possible security lighting should be absent from intensively planted areas. If continuous illumination is unavoidable then care should be taken to monitor the plants in case they show stress with no apparent reason.

Problems from low light

A leaf operates at its highest photosynthetic efficiency when it is new and expanding. With time its efficiency declines and immediately prior to shedding the leaf is stripped of re-usable materials. This is a perfectly normal process which usually takes from one to two years depending on the species, eg the leaves of *Philodendron scandens* and *Ficus benjamina* last about two years, whilst those of *Dieffenbachia spp* last only one. If the plant is functioning near to its compensation point it will not have sufficient reserves to make good this natural foliar loss. This is one reason why plants used in difficult situations can appear to be successful for a year or two before declining.

An important feature of shade plants is their continued resistance to disease, even at low light levels, which seems to depend on the ability of the plant to maintain a critical rate of physical development. It would therefore appear that disease resistance at low light levels is directly related to carbohydrate levels in the plant, ie production of secondary cell wall material and tissue differentiation would normally provide a physical barrier to penetration by fungi, and reduce the time for which juvenile tissue is available for colonisation.

ROOT ENVIRONMENT

A compost consists of a solid material in which there are voids filled with air and/or water.

Solid phase

One important function of a plant's root system is to provide anchorage for the aerial parts, and therefore it requires a suitably dense mass of material to get a grip on. Normally there is sufficient anchorage available in composts, although care should be taken in schemes where large specimens are to be grown in low density peat based composts.

Some major substrate constituents such as clay and peat have the ability to absorb nutrients when they are freely available and to release them slowly over a protracted period. The retention of nutrients is significantly affected by the intensity of watering, ie if large volumes of water are passed through the substrate the nutrients can be leached out. The possible exception to this general pattern are hydroculture systems which use an inert substrate for support and ion exchange fertilisers to achieve long term nutrient availability.

Mineral absorption by the root system is an active metabolic process and so is affected by the temperature of the substrate. Prolonged cold periods can reduce the rate of mineral absorption so that symptoms of iron induced chlorosis may develop ie the plants yellow; or similarly phosphate deficiency, ie they turn blue.

Gaseous phase

All plant substrates contain voids filled with air and/or water. The air changes slowly with that in the surrounding environment by diffusion and by displacement when the compost is heavily watered. The oxygen in the air is necessary for the roots to respire and if a substrate is saturated with water there will be a decline in oxygen availability and an increase in carbon dioxide levels. This leads to a decline in respiration efficiency with a reduction in the permeability of the root cells and a reduction in the rate of water uptake. The plants can then lose turgidity and even wilt in the presence of water. Some plants possess a mechanism which enables them to function in the absence of oxygen but these are reasonably few in number. However, the most damaging aspect of waterlogging is that the ethylene level in the compost can rise to 10 ppm, which inhibits the growth of roots and so renders them susceptible to attack by disease. Roots which receive sufficient oxygen tend to be long, light in colour and well supplied with root hairs, in contrast to roots that have developed with insufficient oxygen, which tend to be short, thick and dark, with few root hairs.

Liquid phase

All actively growing plants require continuous supplies of water if they are to develop to full potential. After light, water is probably the most important factor in controlling plant growth. Although many plants are able to absorb liquid through their leaves their main source of moisture is through the root system. Any major reduction in the compost moisture level below field capacity will prevent the plant from absorbing water at its maximum rate (see chapter 9, "Plant Substrates"). Probably the most important function of water is cell enlargement, ie the walls of young cells are stretched by their internal osmotic pressure and the increase is made permanent by the incorporation of new material. Any shortage of water reduces this ability to expand, so that the benefit of tissue production is not fully realised and further potential is lost. A slight moisture stress can, however, be desirable, as it prevents excessively soft growth from developing.

The quality of water used for interior planting is seldom of concern as the water is derived from municipal drinking supplies. Continuous applications of very hard water, however, can slowly raise the compost pH. Similarly, in areas where there is a high sodium chloride level in the water potentially toxic salt concentrations can develop.

TRANSPIRATION

Although 85% of a plant's total weight is usually water, less than 5% of that which enters is incorporated in the structure and of this less than 1% is converted into carbohydrates. The remainder is lost mainly by transpiration through the stomata in the leaves, although some is lost through the cuticle itself. Transpiration is a complex interaction between the aerial and subterranean components of the plant and is largely dependent upon the quantity of radiant energy which impinges on the foliage. Transpiration is intensified by radiation and so occurs during periods of illumination, when it has the effect of cooling the foliage. This loss of water can dissipate over 65% of the solar energy absorbed by a leaf. Some plants transpire over half their weight in water each day, although in the absence of high radiation levels most interior plants are characterised by having very low rates of transpiration. The cooling effect of transpiration can be used to reduce foliar damage in shade species by providing good ventilation in a bright location. Unfortunately many interior plants are unable to transpire rapidly and so are still susceptible to sudden exposure to direct sunlight.

Transpiration is most intense in conditions of high light,

high temperatures, low humidities, and fast air movements, and should it exceed the rate of water uptake the plant may wilt. As moisture stress increases the stomata tend to close, reducing the water loss but also reducing the carbon dioxide supply for photosynthesis. Further stress affects the rate of protein synthesis and cell division as well as causing carbohydrates to be diverted to thickening cell walls and/or storage rather than growth. Growing points and very young leaves are more able to adapt to water stress than older tissue, with the result that it is the older leaves which normally die first in drought conditions. When the drought ends the young growth extends rapidly to make good the foliar loss, which may produce unsightly interior plants. An additional effect of water stress on many plants is that the foliage becomes darker, because pigment production remains unaffected despite a reduction in the volume of new growth, ie there is an increase in pigment density.

ACCLIMATISATION

Most of the plants that are used for interior landscape schemes are produced in glasshouses or subtropical nurseries where they are encouraged to grow rapidly. When they are moved to the inhospitable environment inside a building they undergo acute shock induced mainly by low light levels. For a period after the move there is a rapid decline in the rate of water loss, an increase in photosynthetic pigment content and a drop in the rate of growth. Stress during this period may result in the loss of leaves, the aborting of flowers, a loss of leaf colour, or even death.

When plants are transferred abruptly from optimum to very low light conditions, normal growth is maintained for a short period as the carbohydrate reserves within the plant fall. The rate declines until growth ceases altogether at which time the plant's structure weakens and becomes increasingly susceptible to disease. Most interior plants are able to function at very low light levels although the products of photosynthesis may only be sufficient to maintain life, without a surplus for developing new tissue. As a result it is common for large plants to appear healthy for many years before weaknesses in their basic structure become apparent.

The shock of being moved into adverse conditions can be reduced by slowly subjecting the plants to less ideal conditions over a period of several weeks. Probably the most significant benefit to a plant from such acclimatisation is to allow the physiology of the leaf to adjust to the reduction in light. The time required for the less major of these modifications, such as the spreading of the grana, is very variable but is usually in excess of six weeks.

The light levels which are recommended for acclimatising plants grown in the sub tropics are seldom experienced in a temperate glasshouse. However, any acclimatisation process will increase the chances of the whole plant surviving and minimises the leaf fall which can occur when light levels are suddenly reduced. The acclimatisation of plants to a dark interior environment is difficult but the reverse process is almost impossible to achieve without damage. This problem is illustrated by plants which succumb to high light levels when withdrawn from an interior location to a well lit glasshouse.

A period of acclimatisation also provides an opportunity for the plants to receive special attention. The relatively high nutrient levels to which the plants have been accustomed in production can be leached from the compost by heavy flushing with clean water. The plants can also receive a heavy application of a powerful commercial insecticide to ensure that they are free from pest problems before use. A sudden reduction in humidity can also prove to be stressful to plants especially if they are produced in moist glasshouses. The adaptation of leaves to low humidities and the development of roots to supply additional water is rapid, but the intervening period of stress can lead to foliar loss. If plants are to be used in extremely unfavourable conditions arrangements should be made for a period of hardening off before moving to the final location. Large specimens of plants like *Ficus benjamina* and *Schefflera actinophylla* can lose much of their canopy if they are not acclimatised and may take over a year to recover. In North America it is common practice for plants produced in California, Florida and Texas to be conditioned for use in large cities by growing them at about half their normal light levels for six to ten weeks before use. Such an acclimatisation service is not normally available in Western Europe and will have to be made by special arrangement with the supplier.

FLOWERING PLANTS

Few plants used in buildings are chosen for their flowers, although some plants such as chrysanthemums, poinsettias and cyclamen are used as short term sources of colour.

Flowering can be triggered by many factors such as temperature, time, light, or any combination of these. A period of low temperature in the case of bulbs, or a rise in temperature in the case of corms, can cause flowering. Certain other responses are governed by day length, such as the amount of leaf growth in *Begonia rex* and stem elongation in rosettes, but they are fairly rare. However, of all these stimuli light is probably the most important as it is the main cause of flowering in house plants as well as being the source of the energy necessary to complete the process. The bulk of the information in this section relates to *Chrysanthemum morifolium*, although the basic concepts may be transposed to all house plants which exhibit a photoperiodic "short day" response.

Plants which are stimulated to flower by certain night lengths are said to exhibit photoperiodism. The night lengths are monitored by a pigment in the leaf called phytochrome; it can exist in one of two forms which are transmuted by light in a daily cycle. One form absorbs red light (Pr) with a peak at 660 nm (fig 4.5) and is converted into a far red absorbing form (Pfr). This slowly reverts to the red absorbing form in the dark, although the process can be accelerated by far red light.

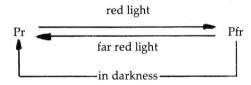

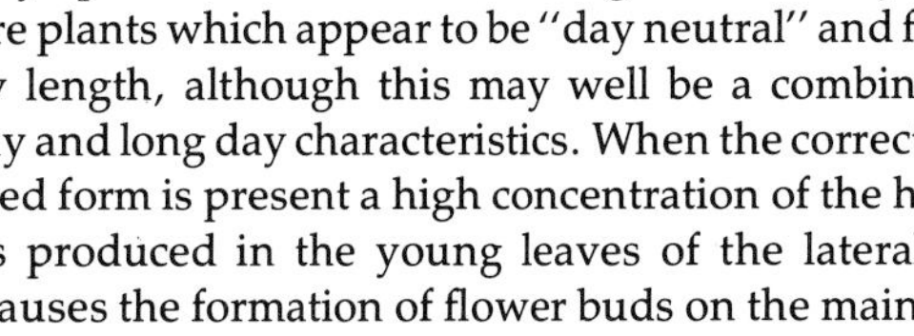

This means that after a long night there is proportionately more of the far red phytochrome which stimulates flowering in "long day" plants but inhibits flowering in "short day" plants. There are plants which appear to be "day neutral" and flower at any day length, although this may well be a combination of short day and long day characteristics. When the correct level of the far red form is present a high concentration of the hormone auxin is produced in the young leaves of the lateral shoots which causes the formation of flower buds on the main shoots. At this stage any inhibitory treatment such as changes in day length become ineffective as the juvenile florets produce their own auxin.

The development of flowers often requires most of the plant's carbohydrate production which is surplus to its basic respiratory needs. For this reason the main factor which determines the display life of flowering plants is their ability to produce sufficient carbohydrates when placed in areas with low radiation levels. Under such conditions the flowers continue to develop as they would in high light, thanks to the

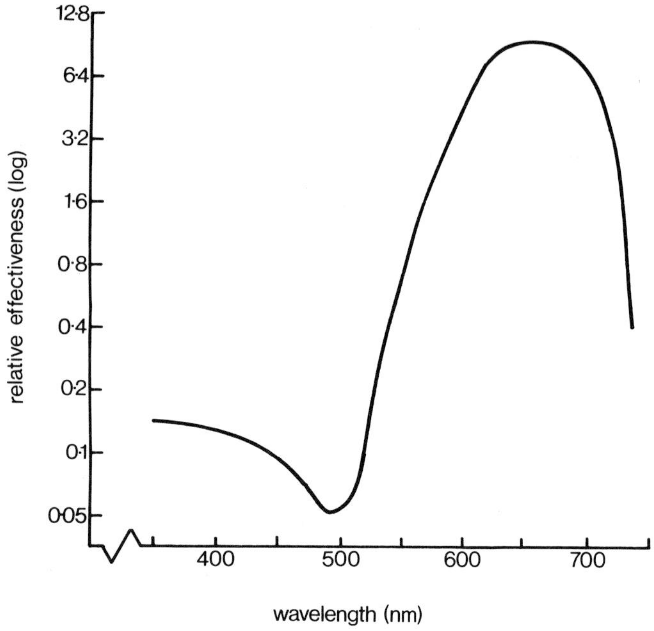

4.5 *The absorption of light of different wavelengths by phytochrome*

plant's carbohydrate reserves. With radiation levels of 900 mW/m^2 for 12 h/day (about 3600 lux h per day) flower development ceases after ten to fifteen days. At 300 mW/m^2 for 12 h/day (about 1200 lux h per day) development ceases after only five days. As the flowers act as the main sink for photosynthates it would indicate that the plant reserves are completely exhausted by the end of these periods. This would imply that if a plant is to receive therapeutic high light treatment it is necessary one week after introduction to difficult conditions. At radiation levels below 900 mW/m^2 there is a rapid decay of young buds which is accelerated by high temperatures and low humidities. At these low radiation levels an increase in temperature from 20°C to 28°C can effectively halve display life probably as a result of increased respiration rates. Obvious disease symptoms are apparent in the buds after 20 days of low light and become progressively worse. It would seem that although light intensity affects the time of initial infection it is temperature which controls its rate of development. This is to be expected for as the carbohydrate reserves are reduced so the cell walls become weaker, until the plant succumbs to disease whose spread is then dependent upon temperature.

High radiation levels increase the ability of the plants to grow and develop, until a point is reached where the light levels cause the display life to be reduced due to completion of the flowering cycle.

Flowering plants are often characterised by a high rate of water loss from the foliage when first introduced to a dry situation, although this is reduced as the plant becomes accustomed to its new environment. This acclimatisation process is usually countered by the increased rate of water loss from the thin cell walls of the flowers as they expand.

CONCLUSION

Interior plants can suffer from a range of stressful situations, and experience indicates that a low light level is probably the most harmful. If the light levels are adequate then water availability usually becomes the limiting factor, although many other environmental factors can have an adverse effect. Fortunately plants possess a great ability to come to terms with their environment if they have sufficient time. For this reason a period of acclimatisation can be beneficial before introduction to a stressful situation.

5 Lighting for plants

*by John Baker, John Weir and Stephen Scrivens**

INTRODUCTION

The ways in which light influences the growth and development of green plants, and the effect of the various photoreceptive mechanisms on these activities, have been described earlier. The highly simplified description in fig 5.1 emphasises the fundamental differences between the main light-stimulated activities of the plant. In the process of photosynthesis the green plant uses light as an energy source to promote the synthesis of basic food materials, and for this purpose almost any radiation within the visible spectrum has some effect. This response is quantitative in that, provided other factors are not limiting and the chlorophyll within the plant is not light saturated, the rate of carbon fixation is approximately proportional to the lighting level or illuminance. Photomorphogenetic and photoperiodic responses are in general qualitative in that light of certain wavebands will "trigger off" specific responses even at very low illuminances (fig 5.2). Daylight which has passed through clear glass or almost any of the special tinted/reflective glasses is adequate for all photomorphogenetic and photoperiodic requirements. Even mercury-discharge sources with their high "blue" content are satisfactory, although the "red" light from incandescent or sodium-discharge sources is undesirable unless mixed with daylight or "blue" light.

Of the total solar radiation which impinges on a plant less than 45% is capable of photosynthetic activity. All radiation within the 400 to 700nm band is of some value, with "red" light being the most effective. If plants are grown in "red" and "far red" light only, they can become etiolated, although this may be overcome by the addition of a small amount of "blue" light. In general plants grown in predominantly "red" light are pale in colour, with soft growth, and tend to show signs of etiolation. In contrast, plants which are grown in predominantly "blue" light have a darker colour and a more squat habit. A high emission of radiation in the "far red" ("infrared") portion of the spectrum increases the rate of foliar heating, whilst excessive amounts of radiation below 360 nm ("ultraviolet") can cause foliar damage and in extreme cases death.

The majority of species which have proved to be suitable for use indoors come from the tropical or sub-tropical regions and thus tend to have a "day-neutral" response (see chapter 4). They have often evolved to permit growth in shade conditions and therefore have a low light demand. Such shade adapted plants often have the additional advantage that they can grow without undue etiolation in light with a high "red" content. However in practice it is photosynthetic rather than photomorphogenetic requirements which limit growth, and so it is the plant's photosynthetic requirements which should be determining the minimum light requirement. The radiant-flux density within the visible spectrum is the main parameter in establishing such a requirement but this must be related to a time scale to give a daily energy integral. It should be remembered that the total daily energy requirements which are necessary for net growth are substantially higher than those required for basic activities, ie above the "compensation point".

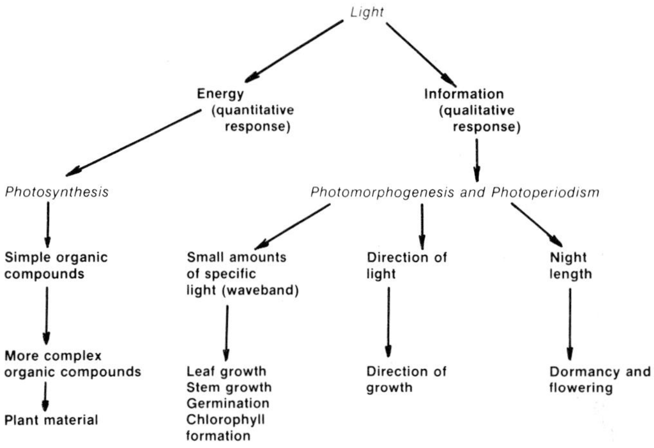

5.1 *The responses of plants to light*

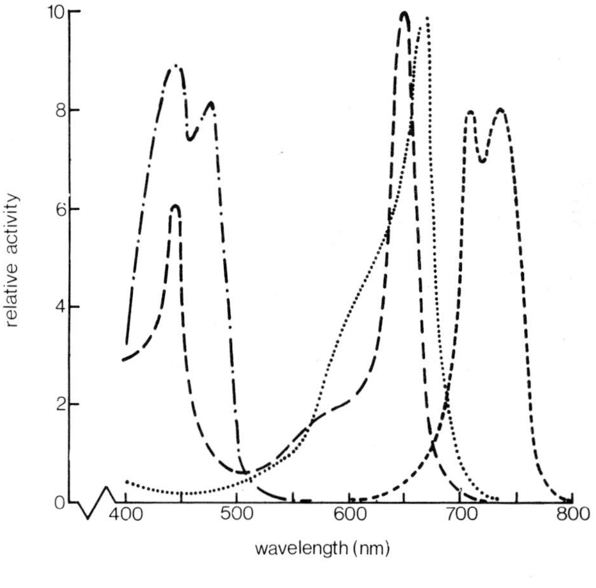

5.2 *The areas of absorption associated with different plant pigments over a range of wavelengths (– – – – chlorophyll; –·–·– phototropism; ······· red phytochrome conversion (Pr → Pfr); ––––––– far red phytochrome conversion (Prf → Pr)*

LIGHT REQUIREMENTS

When siting plants in buildings a high priority should be given to using whatever daylight is available. This is not only because the source is guaranteed but because experience has shown that a proportion of daylight is always conducive to good growth

* Messrs J. Baker and J. Weir are with The Electricity Council, Millbank, London

TABLE 5.1 SOME TYPICAL ILLUMINANCES FOUND IN COMMON SITUATIONS IN LUMENS/M² (LUX)

Bright sunlight	80 000 lux
Overcast day, outdoors	5000
"Bad light stops play"	1000
Modern office or factory	500
Side road lighting	5
Moonlight	0.2
Clear starlit night	0.02

(table 5.1). In situations such as conservatories, areas adjacent to large windows, or below partially glazed roofing, daylight will often be sufficient to support growth. As plants are sited further away from the source of daylight so the resulting illuminance is progressively reduced, until a point is reached where the daylight penetration becomes insufficient to support satisfactory growth and must be supplemented by artificial sources. In the extreme case where daylight is completely absent, light from artificial sources must be capable of supporting all the plant's growth requirements. Providing for normal growth in the latter circumstances might seem to be complex, but fortunately plants have a good measure of tolerance so that most commercially available lamps can provide the desired energy level within acceptable photomorphogenetic limits.

A generalised indication of the minimum illuminances that are required to maintain healthy growth are given in the plant selection tables. When the minimum has been determined it is necessary to decide if such values are already available from daylight, and if not then how they are to be obtained artificially. This need to determine prevailing daylight values is equally true with existing or proposed structures, although in the latter case it is to be hoped that such information will be available from the lighting engineer or architect. In most cases it is neither possible nor practical to provide the full light requirement by daylight, so electric lighting must be used.

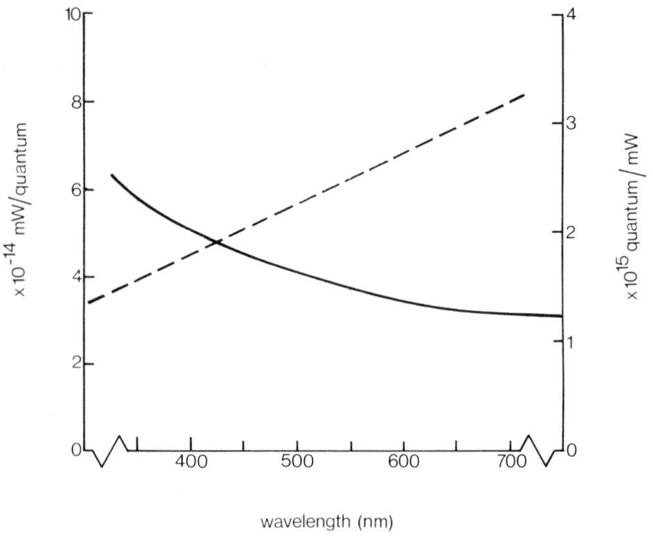

5.3 *The interaction between wavelength, energy, and quantum number: energy in mW per light quantum at different wavelengths (————), and the number of quanta per mW at different wavelengths, (– – – –)*

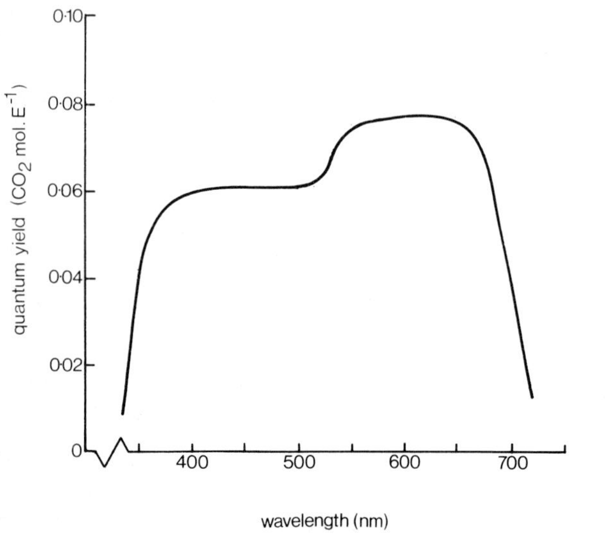

5.4 *The effect of light of different wavelengths on quantum yield measured as CO_2 uptake*

THE QUANTIFICATION OF PHOTOSYNTHETIC REQUIREMENTS

The relative effectiveness of light of different wavelengths for photosynthesis is best described by an "action spectrum" based on quantum input. A quantum is a definite unit of radiation whose energy content is inversely proportional to its wavelength, ie the amount of energy per quantum varies with wavelength.

$$\text{energy} = \frac{\text{quanta}}{\text{wavelength}}$$

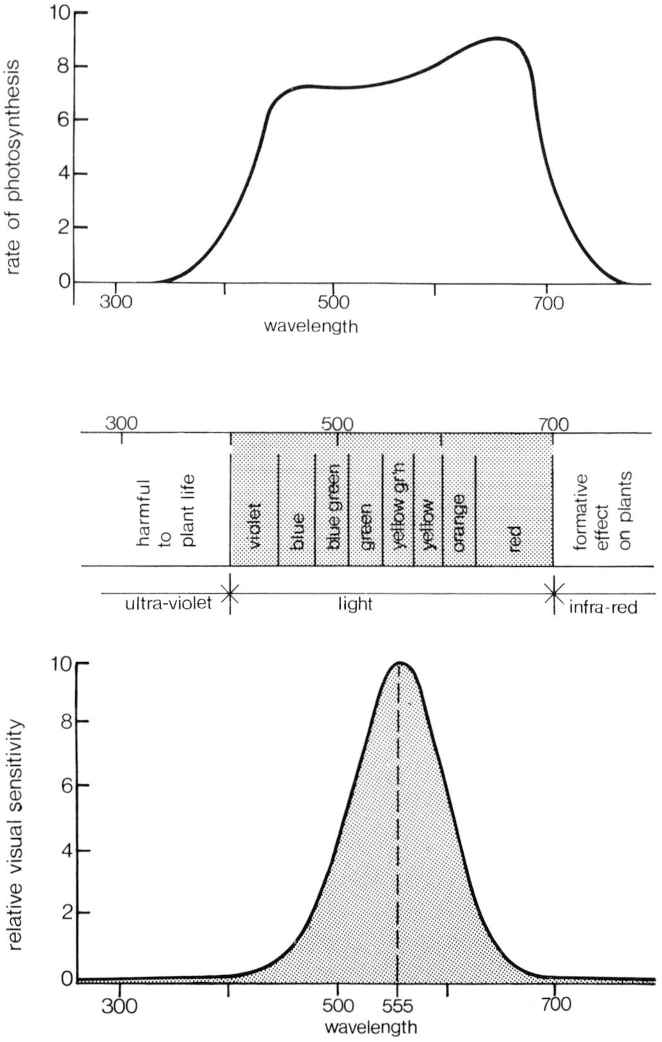

5.5 *The rate of photosynthesis relative to the sensitivity of the human eye to light of different wavelengths*

This system of measurement is the most accurate as it allows the relative energy content of light from different sources to be compared in terms of their potential photosynthetic value, eg red light contains more quanta than blue light for a given amount of energy (fig 5.3). The actual number of quanta in a given emission can be determined empirically by the application of Planck's Constant, which expresses energy as a simple ratio of wavelength. Recently it has become practical to quantify an existing illuminance by the use of a portable "quantum" meter. Only a limited number of the quanta which pass through the leaf are intercepted by the plant's pigments for use in the process of photosynthesis. Of those which are fixed some ten to twenty are then required to fix a molecule of carbon dioxide in the form of a carbohydrate.

Despite the development of quantum meters it has been found in practice easier to use the existing photometric techniques for measuring luminous flux in lumens per unit area, ie lux (lm/m^2) or lm/ft^2 (ft cd), as a rough standard. This system is based on the response of the human eye with its maximum sensitivity in the region of 555 nm and very different from the broad utilisation pattern (action spectrum) of plants (fig 5.5). However it is possible to convert these values to more serviceable units of radiant energy such as joule (J), or alternatively ergs or calories. These are less closely linked to a photosynthetic response than a quantal input but have the advantage of being easily interpreted. The total amount of useful light energy to which a plant is being exposed can therefore be determined by measuring the average illuminance received over a given period of time. The resulting values are approximate but are satisfactory for practical purposes.

The minimum radiation levels which are tolerated by species used for interior planting are given in the tables of plant characteristics. These are minimum figures and should be exceeded by a significant margin wherever possible. The minimum energy values which are necessary for achieving satisfactory growth have been determined on an arbitrary basis, as relatively little empirical data is available. It has been shown that the minimum daily energy requirement for satisfactory growth in *Chrysanthemum morifolium*, which is a "high energy" species, is 1.2 MJ/m^2. On a comparative basis it would seem desirable for most species suitable for indoor planting to receive a daily energy input of say 0.3 MJ/m^2, although many will tolerate daily inputs as low as 0.05 MJ/m^2. A more generally acceptable target which is suggested as a universal norm for indoor planting is 0.1 $MJ/m^2/day$. The only remaining problem lies in translating total energy input into terms of an average illuminance from one or more light sources for a given number of hours per day, and this is covered in the next chapter on electric lighting.

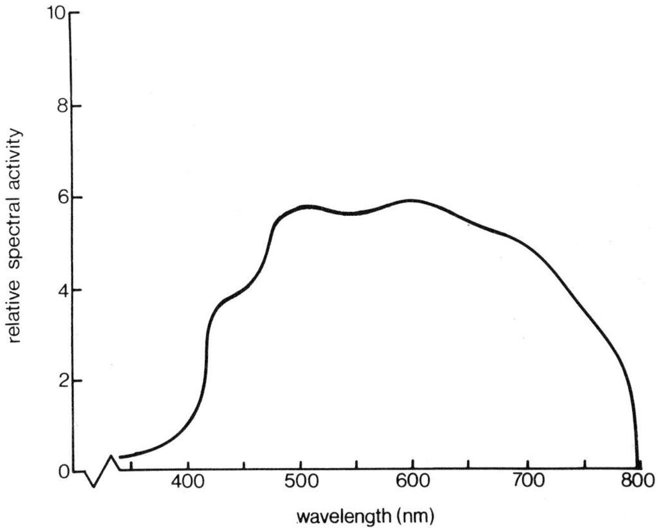

5.6 *The spectral distribution of sunlight at noon*

The duration of illuminance

With most plants at very low illuminances the benefit of light for photosynthesis can be regarded as being cumulative, eg a luminous flux density of 3000 mW/m^2 (about 1000 lx) for 10 hours is the same as 1500 mW/m^2 for 20 hours (see chapter 4). This effect can also be enhanced at low visible radiation levels by the use of a source with a high red content. However, due to the complexity of the subject it is always advisable to ensure that a radiant flux density (400 to 700 nm) of at least 2000 mW/m^2 (about 700 lx) will impinge on the plant for at least twelve hours and preferably sixteen hours a day. The visible radiation levels in the plant selection tables are minima which should be exceeded by a factor of 50% if good growth is desired.

DAYLIGHT

Daylight is a mixture of radiation across the 400 to 700 nm band which varies slightly during both the course of the day and the seasons due to the changing angle of the sun. This means that daylight has a higher red content when the sun is low than when the sun is overhead (fig 5.6). The main difference between daylight and electric lights is that the latter have definite peaks of radiation which are substantially different from daylight and which give them their characteristic "colour". Any deficiencies in the spectral composition of artificial sources can be overcome by relatively small amounts of natural light and therefore it is best to employ both types of light together.

Due to continuous fluctuations in daylight illuminance both on a daily and seasonal basis the light values which impinge on a point in a room cannot be expressed as a simple numerical value. However, the resulting illuminance can be described as a proportion of that which would be received if the point were exposed to an unobstructed hemisphere of overcast sky. This ratio is known as the Daylight Factor and is expressed as a percentage with typical values ranging from less than 1% to over 20%. This technique assumes that direct sunlight is not involved but even so the luminance (brightness) of the sky varies from nadir to zenith with a value at angle θ which is proportional to

$$\frac{(1 + \sin\theta)}{3}$$

In most buildings daylight can enter via side windows or rooflights, and these two routes are very different in their effectiveness. The sky which is observed through a side window has the potential to yield only about half to one third of the illuminance of that from the sky which is directly overhead through, say, a skylight. Higher daylight factors are therefore possible from roof lights where a brighter portion of the sky is observed. Also the potential of side windows is often reduced by adjacent buildings or rising ground and by structural features such as overhangs intended to reduce solar gain. Overhead rooflights have the added advantage that plants tend to grow towards the light in what is considered a "normal" direction. With side windows, plants will grow towards the light and give problems of support or uneven growth (fig 5.7). This may be corrected by rotating the plants, if convenient, or by providing sufficient electric lighting on the side away from the windows to correct for potential irregularities in growth (fig 5.8).

5.7 *Illumination from side windows may cause uneven plant growth*

5.8a *Tree grows in drum beneath floor, which revolves very slowly to ensure vertical growth.* **b** *Cross section (right). Coutts Bank; courtesy Frederick Gibberd & Partners, architects*

Calculating daylight factors

To arrive at the total amount of daylight received at a point within the space it is necessary to add together the contributions from:

1 The unobstructed sky, ie direct sky view.

2 The externally reflected components, ie light reflected from adjacent buildings or the ground.

3 The internally reflected component ie from the floor, ceiling and walls, (fig 5.9).

It is possible to correlate this information and so calculate daylight factors but a more simple and sufficiently accurate method is to use the BRE daylight protractors (developed by the Building Research Establishment) in conjunction with a scale plan and sectional elevation of the space. Overall this method provides an assessment of the direct light with the internal and external reflected light components being derived from tabulated data. Once the daylight factor has been established for the position of the planting within the space, reference to average daylight illuminance curves for the relevant latitude permit light quantity values (eg lux-hours) and energy values (eg MJ/m^2) to be calculated.

It would be tedious to calculate all the daylight values throughout the year, but fortunately it is only a minimum that must be provided and so a start can be made on the winter months. If the minimum light energy values can be provided naturally throughout the winter then electric lighting is unnecessary, although it may still be used for aesthetic reasons. If the minimum energy level cannot be provided by daylight during the winter months, then it is necessary to determine if it can be provided for at least part of the year. Similarly if supplementary sources are necessary then the magnitude of the shortfall must be determined both in terms of illuminance and duration.

Estimating daylight factors

In the case of an unbuilt space the only way to determine the daylight factor will be that outlined above. In an existing building an approximation can be made with the aid of a light meter or of a photographic exposure meter fitted with an incident light attachment. As the daylight factor is a ratio, actual light

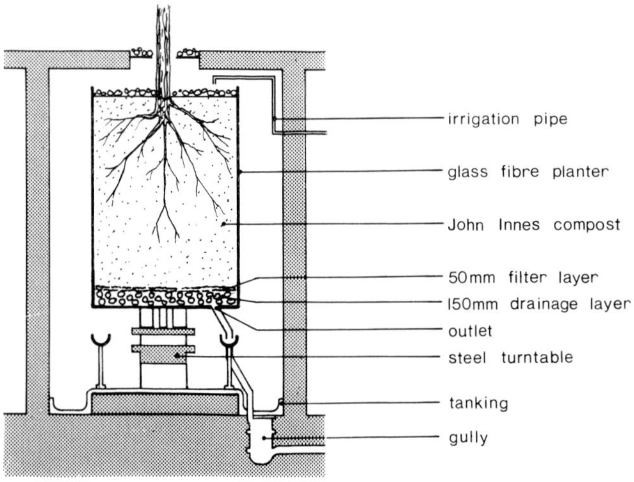

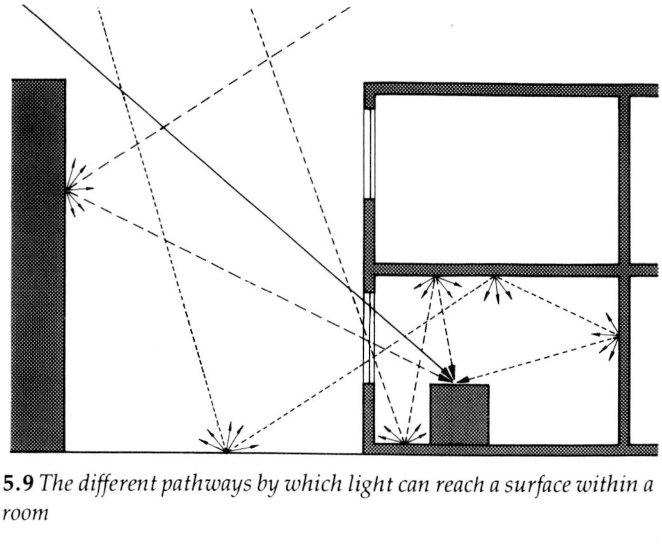

5.9 *The different pathways by which light can reach a surface within a room*

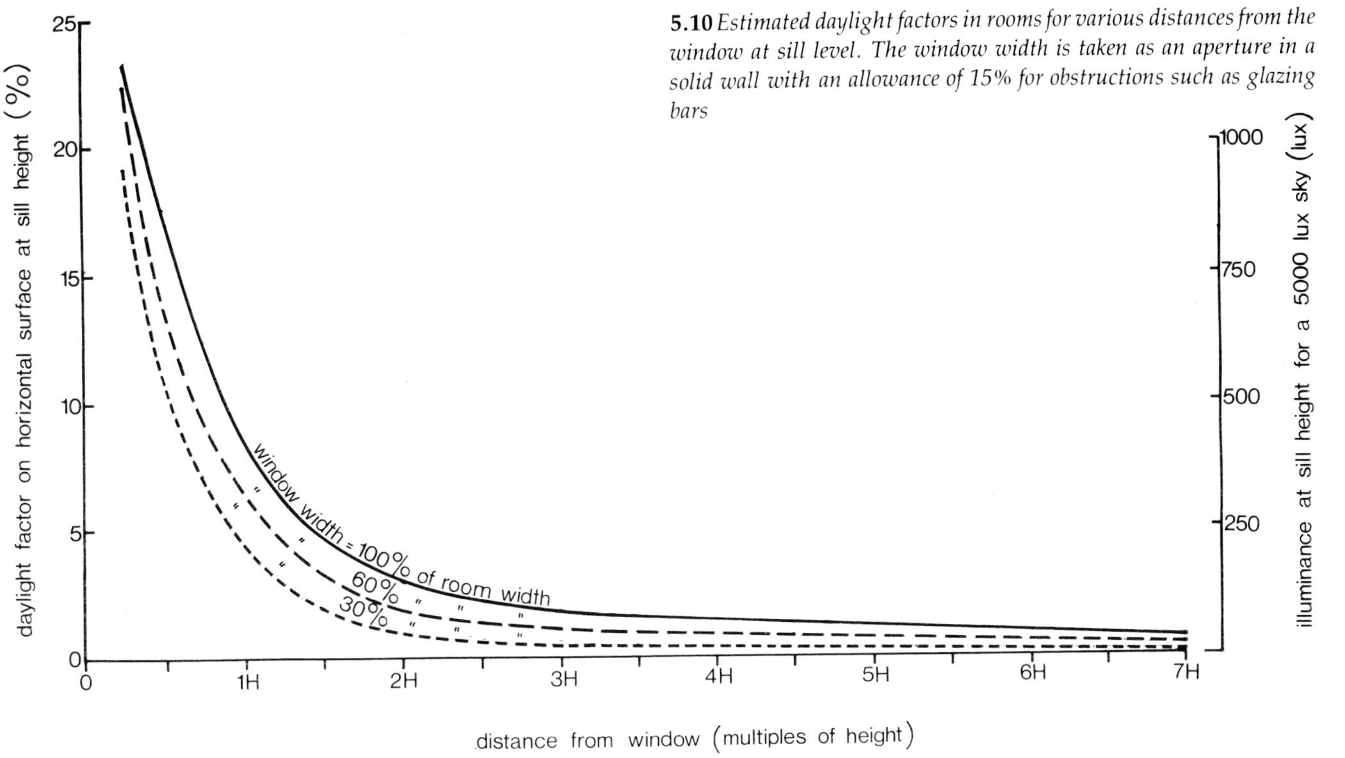

5.10 *Estimated daylight factors in rooms for various distances from the window at sill level. The window width is taken as an aperture in a solid wall with an allowance of 15% for obstructions such as glazing bars*

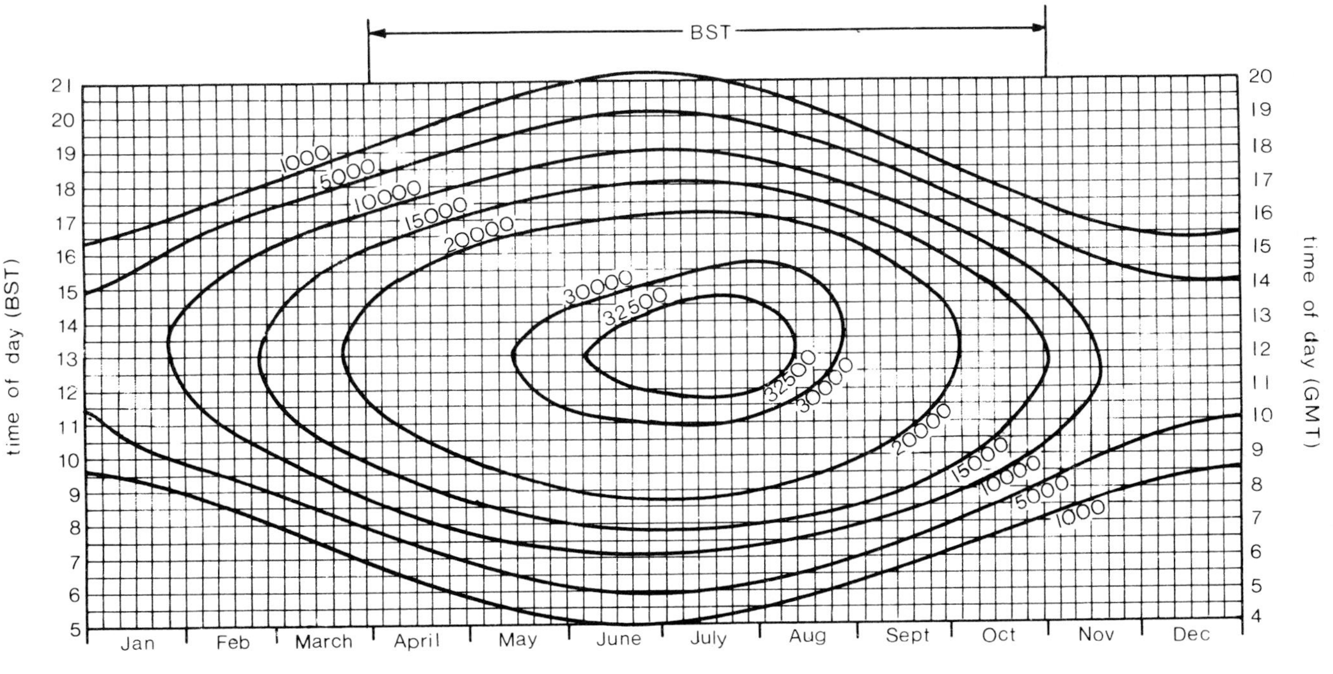

5.11 *Average daylight illuminance curves for Britain and the northern US*

5.12 *The passage of radiation through "Antisun Insulight Bronze" glazing*

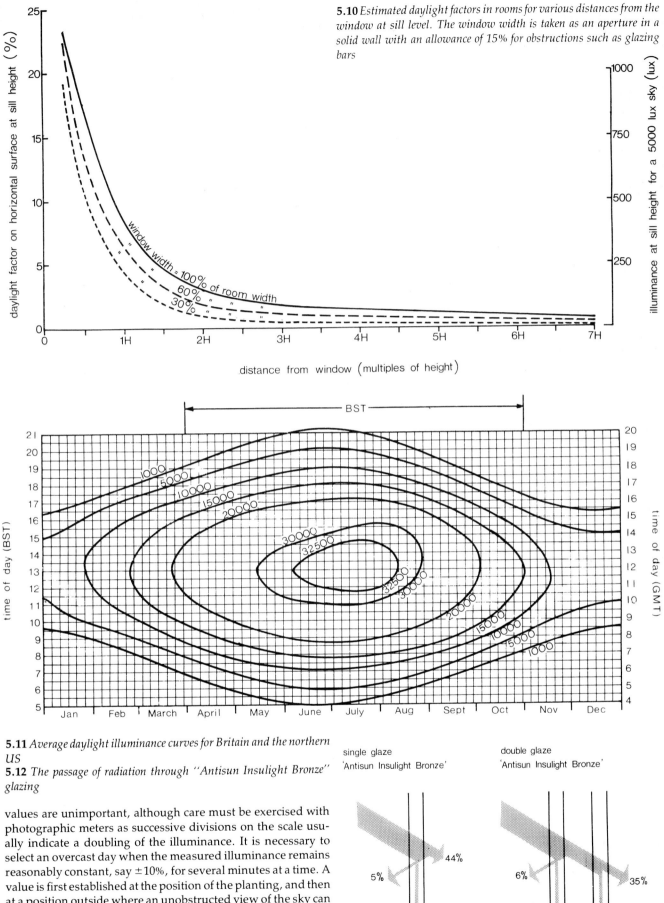

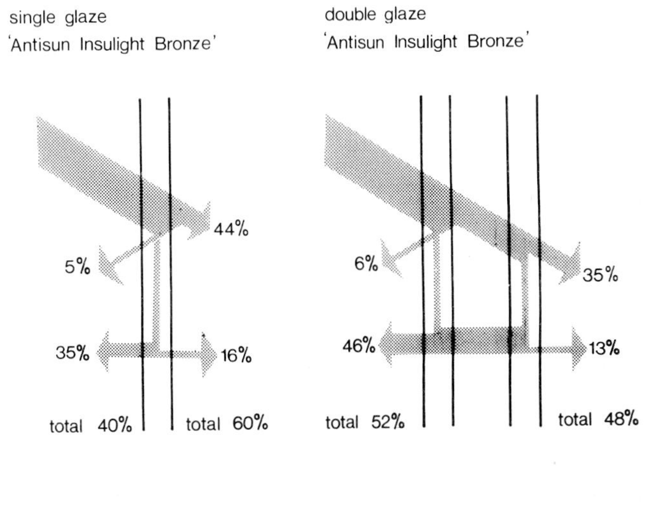

values are unimportant, although care must be exercised with photographic meters as successive divisions on the scale usually indicate a doubling of the illuminance. It is necessary to select an overcast day when the measured illuminance remains reasonably constant, say ±10%, for several minutes at a time. A value is first established at the position of the planting, and then at a position outside where an unobstructed view of the sky can be obtained. Returning to the first position a check can be made on the original value to confirm that it has not varied significantly. The ratio of the two values can be expressed as a percentage to give the daylight factor.

Finding an unobstructed view of the sky may be difficult but a measurement on the roof of the building will usually suffice. Alternatively, if a window gives an unobstructed view of a half hemisphere of sky then a measured value on the window ledge can be doubled as a reasonable approximation, although poor orientation can cause inaccuracies. The use of two observers with two identical meters will permit the simultaneous determination of both values and so improve accuracy.

If this system is inappropriate then an approximate daylight factor can be obtained from fig 5.10 which indicates the factors achieved at sill height for various distances from the window. The daylight factors are then related to mean annual daylight charts which are available for most parts of the world, although fig 5.11 will suffice for most cities in Northern Europe and the northern USA. The orientation of windows has an effect upon the direct light which enters a room, and so a window orientation compensation factor may be utilised: 0.0 for East and West; 1.25 for South; and 0.75 for North.

Tinted glazing

It has been stated earlier that various types of tinted glass, particularly the infrared absorbing or reflecting types, will modify the spectral composition of daylight but this appears to have little effect upon the quality of plant growth (fig 5.12). But a tinted glass may well reduce the transmitted daylight by as much as 80%, and the exact value should be established with the manufacturer (table 5.2).

It is possible to estimate the percentage light reduction caused by a specific glazing system by the use of a light meter. Readings are taken through an opening window or a glazed door with and without the glass in place to enable a comparison to be made. The light which passes through the glass can then be expressed as a percentage of the unobstructed daylight and correlated with other factors such as orientation and standard illuminance conditions.

TABLE 5.2 TYPICAL PERFORMANCES OF A REPRESENTATIVE RANGE OF SOLAR CONTROL GLASSES AVAILABLE IN BRITAIN

Single glazing	Visible light Trans	Visible light Refl	Total transmittance
Clear glass	0.87	–	0.84
Heat absorbing Monolithic			
Green	0.75	–	0.60
Bronze	0.50	–	0.60
	0.20	–	0.42
	0.14	–	0.38
	0.08	–	0.31
Grey	0.40	–	0.60
	0.20	–	0.44
	0.14	–	0.39
	0.08	–	0.33
SM (surface modified) bronze	0.50	–	0.66
Laminated			
Green	0.73	–	0.75
Light brown	0.55	–	0.67
Medium brown	0.28	–	0.52
Dark brown	0.09	–	0.40
Heat reflecting Monolithic			
Clear	0.61	0.35	0.64
	0.46	0.39	0.58
	0.39	0.35	0.53
Light topaze	0.48	0.38	0.62
Green	0.50	0.35	0.43
	0.38	0.39	0.39
Bronze	0.33	0.34	0.45
	0.21	0.35	0.40
Grey	0.30	0.34	0.46
	0.18	0.35	0.38
Silver	0.20	0.27	0.37
	0.14	0.33	0.35
	0.08	0.44	0.23
Gold	0.20	0.24	0.38
	0.14	0.26	0.31
	0.08	0.28	0.26
Laminated			
Bronze	0.17	0.22	0.28
Gold	0.30	0.26	0.34
Gold	0.16	0.37	0.22
Heat strengthened			
Clear	0.50	0.34	0.60
Bronze	0.30	0.34	0.46
Grey	0.24	0.34	0.44

Double glazing	Visible light Trans	Visible light Refl	Total transmittance
Clear glass	0.76	–	0.73
Heat absorbing Monolithic			
Green	0.66	–	0.48
Bronze	0.44	–	0.48
	0.30	–	0.38
	0.18	–	0.30
	0.07	–	0.20
Grey	0.37	–	0.48
	0.30	–	0.42
	0.18	–	0.32
	0.07	–	0.22
SM (surface modified) bronze	0.43	–	0.56
Laminated			
Green	0.64	–	0.64
Light brown	0.48	–	0.55
Medium brown	0.24	–	0.40
Dark brown	0.08	–	0.27
Heat reflecting Monolithic			
Clear	0.54	0.37	0.57
	0.42	0.41	0.51
	0.35	0.35	0.44
	0.20	0.38	0.17
Light topaze	0.42	–	0.54
Green	0.46	0.37	0.35
	0.35	0.40	0.31
Bronze	0.33	0.29	0.25
	0.30	0.35	0.36
	0.20	0.35	0.30
Grey	0.27	0.35	0.39
	0.19	0.35	0.28
Silver	0.40	0.35	0.36
	0.30	0.42	0.26
	0.18	0.27	0.27
	0.07	0.44	0.16
Gold	0.40	0.33	0.31
	0.36	0.40	0.28
	0.34	0.22	0.30
	0.30	0.42	0.23
	0.26	0.19	0.22
	0.18	0.24	0.28
	0.07	0.28	0.17
Azure	0.47	0.18	0.33
Grey/blue	0.45	0.20	0.34
Purple	0.39	0.15	0.31
Laminated			
Bronze	0.15	0.22	0.18
Gold	0.34	0.26	0.27
	0.14	0.37	0.15
Heat strengthened			
Bronze	0.25	0.33	0.38
Grey	0.21	0.34	0.34

* Published by courtesy of Pilkington Brothers Ltd

Kingfisher Walk
Buses Trains
Evesham Walk
Worcester Square
Evesham Street
Telephones

6 Electric lighting

*by John Baker and John Weir**

INTRODUCTION

Probably the most important characteristic of electric lighting is its controllability both in terms of quantity and duration. Unfortunately the excessive use of electrical energy can prove to be expensive, so every effort should be made to reduce consumption to a minimum consistent with maintaining plant growth. It is not proposed to discuss the lighting of buildings for human activities but to consider those lighting installations which can satisfy the requirements of plants.

INSTALLATIONS

In general any lighting installation used in a commercial building for general illumination will be suitable for plants, providing that the quantity and duration are adequate. There are exceptions to this general statement: for example incandescent filament lamps require additional sources of illumination to produce a more balanced spectrum. Seldom is it economic to provide the illuminances required by plants in all work locations, and should certain locations require less than say 750 lux, it may be advantageous to arrange for additional lighting for specific planted areas rather than to extend the overall illumination period. The choice of luminaires must be in keeping with the design of the interior, but in general directional units will concentrate the light where it is wanted and so increase the efficiency of the installations. Where fittings are local to the plants, sufficient clearance must be maintained to allow for plant growth and to avoid the risk of scorching. An indication of such clearances is given in the table of light source characteristics (table 6.1).

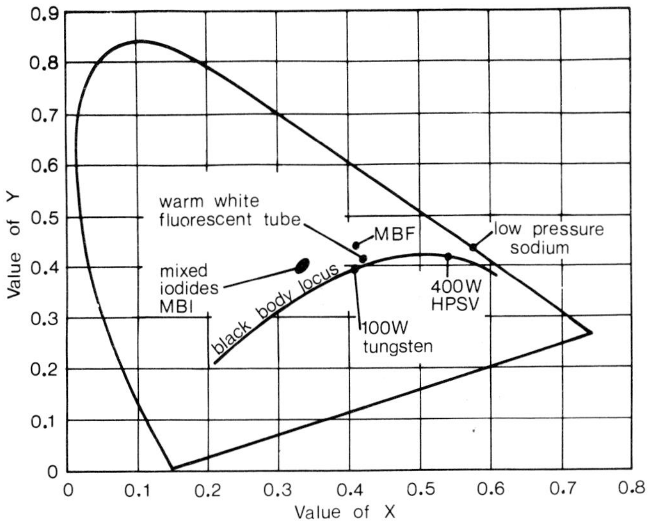

6.1 *Within the CIE chromaticity diagram all colours fall within the triangular figure. Pure colours lie near the perimeter while "white light" sources lie near the centre. The black body locus is the path that the full radiation of a filament lamp follows as its temperature is gradually increased from red to blue-white. If the X and Y co-ordinates of the light source are know its position can be established relative to other light sources*

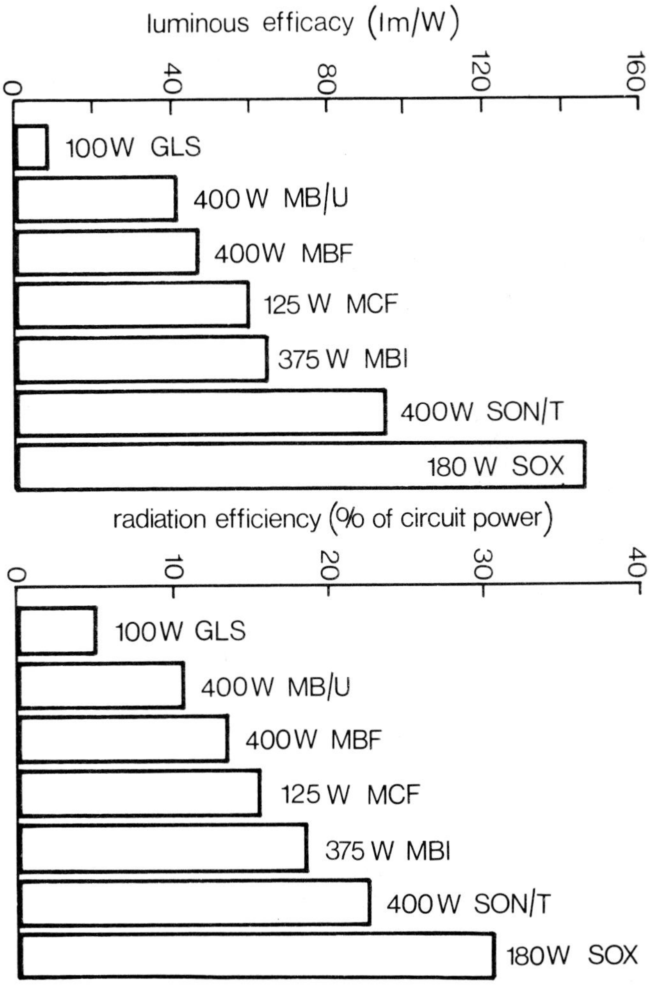

6.2 *The efficiency of various common light sources in terms of: (left) luminous efficacy in lumens per watt; (right) radiation efficiency as a percentage of circuit power*

LIGHT SOURCES

The following section does not cover all those light sources which are available but concentrates on those which are compatible with commercial buildings and homes. Other lamp types are suitable for lighting plants but not for interiors where people live or work. With the exception of fluorescent (MCF) lamps, once the type of lighting system has been chosen little variation in colour appearance or colour rendering is possible, although this of course does not prevent the use of colour filters to obtain particular effects. Colour rendering is a term which

* Messrs J. Baker and J. Weir are with the Electricity Council, London

TABLE 6.1 LIGHT SOURCE CHARACTERISTICS (CONSULT MANUFACTURERS FOR CURRENT DATA)

Lighting source	Efficacy lm/W	Recom-mended lamp types	Nature of source	Average life in hours	Nominal power in watts	Control gear	Integral reflector	Practical clearance above plant	Comments
Incandescent filament type – GLS and others	Low		Compact	1000 or 2000	15 to 1500	No	Sometimes	500 mm to 1.5 m de-pending on wattage	Not recommended as sole source
Tubular fluorescent lamp type – MCF	High	Daylight White Warm White Colour 84	Linear	7500 h over 1.2 m long	8 to 125 in practice	Yes		Sometimes 500 mm	Maximum light for minimum power Good colour rendering available from some lamps at higher cost
	Medium	Natural Kolor-rite	Linear	5000 h under 1.2 m long	15 to 125 in practice	Yes	No	500 mm	Improved colour rendering if lower efficacy can be tolerated
	Low	Homelight Warmtone Deluxe Natural Philips Softone 32	Linear	do	15 to 125 in practice	Yes	No	500 mm	Has extra emission in 700–750 nm range Can help develop good plant form Should be mixed with fluorescent tubes of a higher efficacy.
	Horticultural specials	Grolux Agrolite	Linear	do	8 to 80 in practice	Yes	No	500 mm	For relative growth response there is no evidence that these lamps are superior to those of higher efficacy. Colour rendering may be preferred in certain circumstances
Blended lamps type – MBTF	Low		Compact	6000	100 to 500	No	Sometimes	1 m	Good for highlighting individual focal points. Usually needs reflector housing. Relatively high far red light content but insufficient to cause problems
High pressure mercury fluorescent type – MBF (no reflector) type – MBFR (integral reflector)	Medium		Compact	7500	50 to 1000	Yes	Sometimes	1 m	Some plants may exhibit damage due to ultra violet light below 350 nm – unlikely at normal lighting intensities
High pressure mercury fluorescent horticultural special type – HLRG	Medium		Compact	7500	400	Yes	Yes	1m	Claimed to be free from ultraviolet radiation (below 350 nm)
Metal halide type – MBI (clear envelope) type MBIF (fluorescent envelope)	High		Compact	6000	250 to 1000	Yes	No	1 m	Very natural colour rendering.
High pressure sodium type – SON/E (no reflector) type – SON/T (no reflector) type – SON/R (integral reflector)			Short linear	6000	50 to 400	Yes	Sometimes	1.5 m	Spectrum relatively unbalanced so may cause growth problem with some species. Some lamp forms can cause foliage to appear dark. Manufacturers vary

* "Low efficacy" tubular-fluorescent lamps should be mixed with lamps of a higher efficacy. The exact ratio must be determined empirically but a good starting point is two "low efficacy" tubes in five

relates the perceived colour of an object under a given electric lamp to its appearance under a standard light source, ie daylight.

Colour appearance is a term which describes the colour of a truly white surface when illuminated by a given source in terms of its apparent "warmth". In general most mercury discharge lamps (MBF, MBTF and MBI) are said to be "cool" to "intermediate" in appearance, while GLS and SON lamps are "warm" (fig 6.1). Discharge lamps are to be preferred for their higher efficacy and long life but while the operating costs are relatively low, the initial purchase price must include the control gear and its installation (fig 6.2).

Incandescent filament lamps

The most inefficient of the commonly used light sources: it consists of a tungsten filament housed in an evacuated glass envelope (fig 6.3 & 6.4). To improve efficacy (light output for energy input) the vacuum is usually filled with an inert gas. Efficacy of the general lighting service (GLS) lamp, which is pear shaped, ranges from about 8 lumens per watt (lm/W) for the low wattages up to 13.6 lm/W for the 200 W rating which is the highest commonly employed. Many other shapes are available, particularly the internally silvered reflector lamps (ISL) which can direct the light into a spot or flood distribution. The main advantage of this system is small physical size which leads to a good optical control and low initial cost. The main disadvantages are low efficacy, ie high energy consumption for a given illuminance, short life (1000 to 2000 h) and high radiant heat output. Tungsten halogen lamps are similar in principle but the envelope is tubular, single or double ended, and made of quartz or fused silica. Additives in the gas filling prevent the envelope blackening and permits the filament to be operated at an elevated temperature which improves efficacy to 25 lm/W for a 1 kW rating. Their life is usually in the order of 1000 h for ratings up to 100 W and 2000 h for ratings of 300 W to 2 kW.

Tubular fluorescent lamps

These are low pressure discharge lamps of the MCF type (fig 6.5 & 6.6). Other suffix letters may be used to denote particular types, eg MCFRE are tubular fluorescent, reflectorised and silicon coated. In an MCF lamp an electric current is passed through a mercury vapour within a glass tube to produce far ultraviolet (235.7 nm) radiation with a small quantity of visible blue light. The ultraviolet light is converted into visible light by a phosphor coating on the inside of the tube. By varying the mixture of the phosphor it is possible to produce light with a particular spectral composition. Probably the most widely used lamps are those with a high output in the yellow region of the spectrum, where the human eye is most responsive, and which therefore have a high visible light output efficacy but poor colour rendering. Lamps with a more even output throughout the spectrum have better colour rendering but a lower light output (fig 6.7). In both types there is a choice of colour appearance ranging from cool to warm. In recent years developments in phosphor technology have led to the adoption of new materials capable of producing a light of good colour without a drop in light output. These have made it possible to produce more

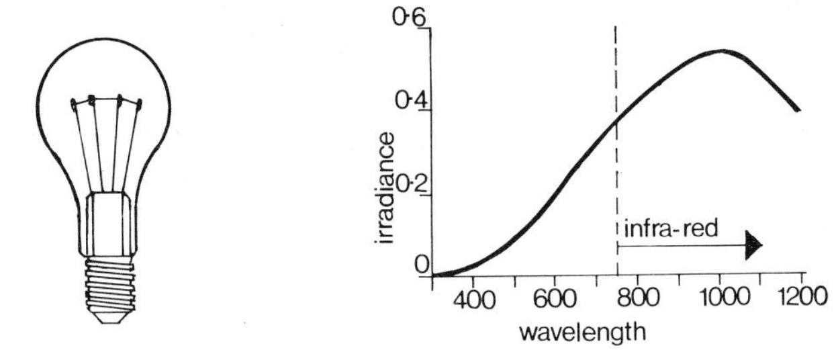

6.3 *A 100 W incandescent filament lamp (GLS)*

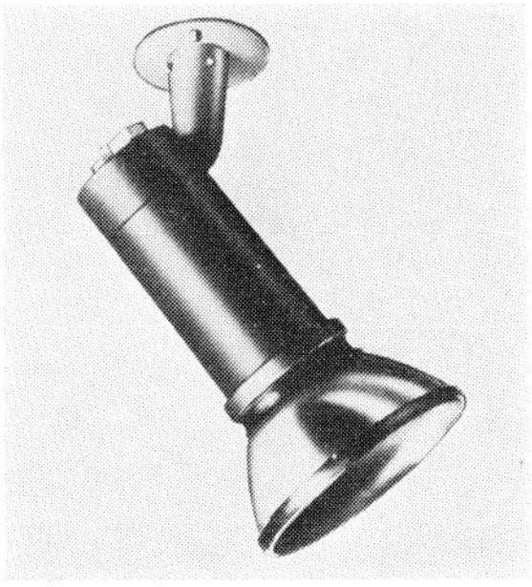

6.4 *An incandescent lamp in a directional luminaire (courtesy of Philips Electrical Ltd)*

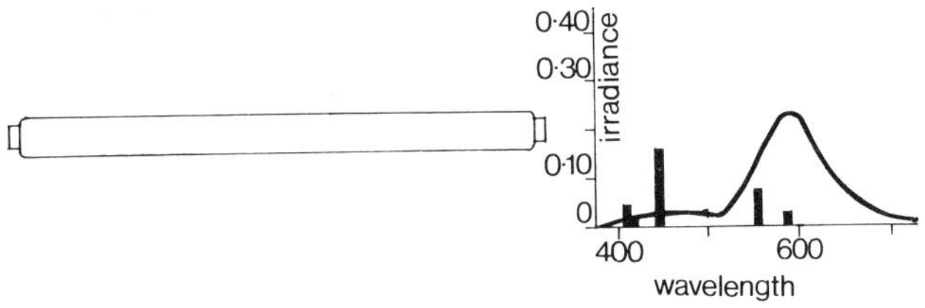

6.5 *A 40 W tubular fluorescent lamp (MCF)*

6.6 *Luminaires containing tubular fluorescent lamps (courtesy of Tropical Plants Display Ltd)*

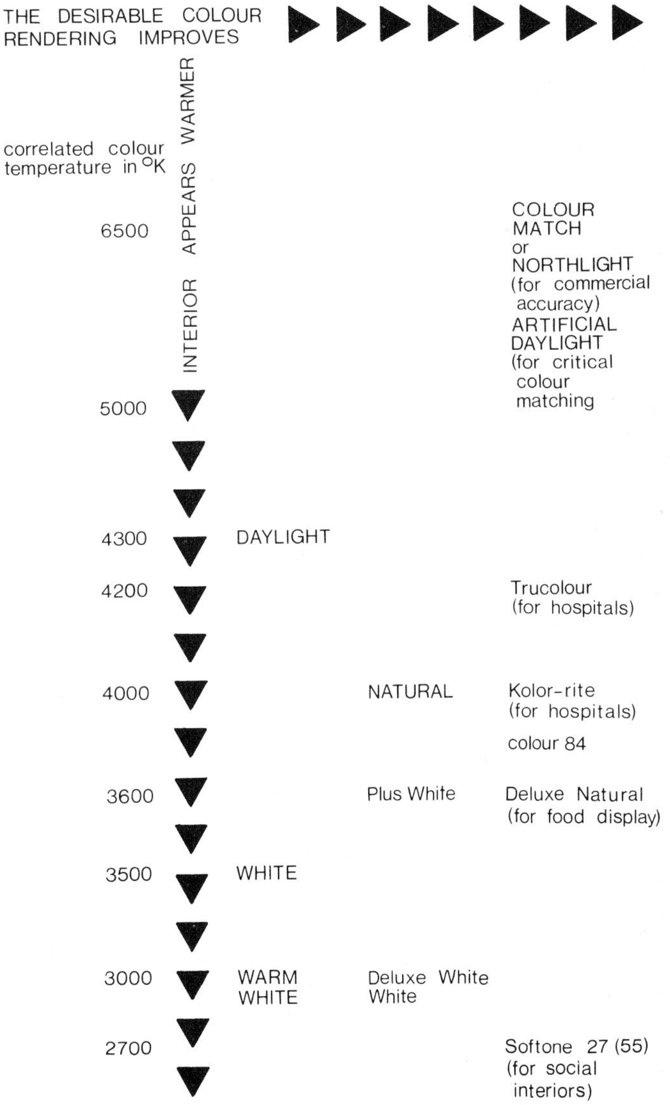

6.7 *The colour rendering properties of white fluorescent lamps can be chosen independently from their colour appearance. From top to bottom are shown lamps of an increasingly warm appearance. From left to right are shown lamps of improving colour rendering.*

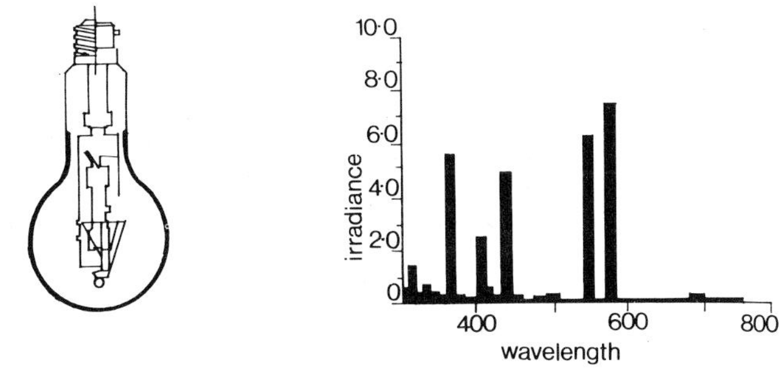

6.8 *A 250 W mercury blended lamp (MBTF)*

efficiently a light with a good colour although the cost of such polyphosphor lamps is substantially more than that of the more traditional lamp. Fluorescent lamps have been produced which are claimed to have a spectral emission tailored to requirements of plants. In practical trials these have proved to have little, if any, advantage over conventional lamps, although they may be preferred on aesthetic grounds.

Nominal wattages and sizes are from 4 W for a 150 mm (6 in) lamp to 125 W for a 2.4 m (8 ft) lamp, although those less than 40 W (for 1.2 m) are not widely used for general lighting purposes. To these lamp wattages must be added the control gear losses which are in the order of 25% of the lamp rating, ie the total consumption of a 40 W lamp is about 50 W. Lamp efficacy will depend on the size and the "colour" but over 60 lumens/circuit-watt is common.

Mercury blended lamp (MBTF)
These are high pressure discharge lamps which have an internal filament to act as a ballast (fig 6.8 & 6.9). The light output is therefore a mixture of light from the filament and light from the discharge with a phosphor coated envelope to improve the colour rendering. One useful version (160 W MBTFR) of this lamp uses a PAR38 reflector envelope to provide directional control of the light output. The efficacy ranges from 12.5 to 23.0 lm/W and wattages from 100 W to 500 W. Various claims are made for lamp life; some manufacturers suggest 6000 h although some quote much longer periods. The main advantage of these lamps is their compact size combined with good life, but as their efficacy is little more than that of a filament lamp they are more likely to be used as an addition to a lighted interior or for a small area of planting than as the prime source for a substantial area. If desired they may be used to replace filament lamps, since the sockets are compatible.

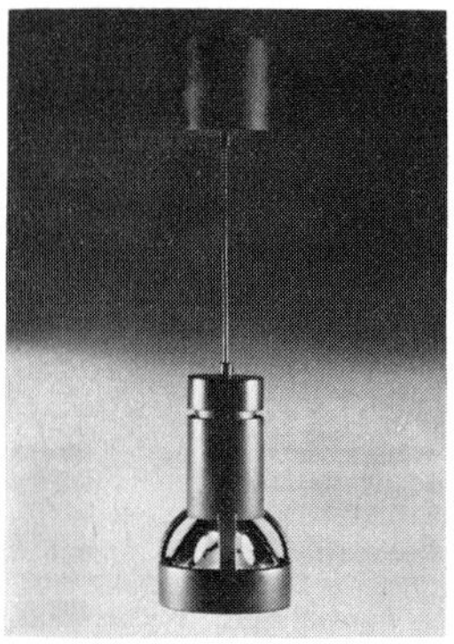

6.9 *A Wotan Flora Set with an 80 W mercury reflector lamp (courtesy of Wotan Lamps Ltd)*

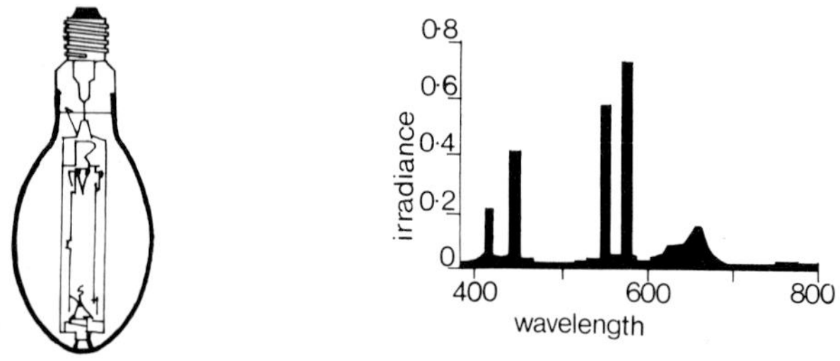

6.10 *A 400 W colour corrected mercury lamp (MBF)*

6.11 *A 600 mm square modular luminaire for a colour corrected mercury lamp*

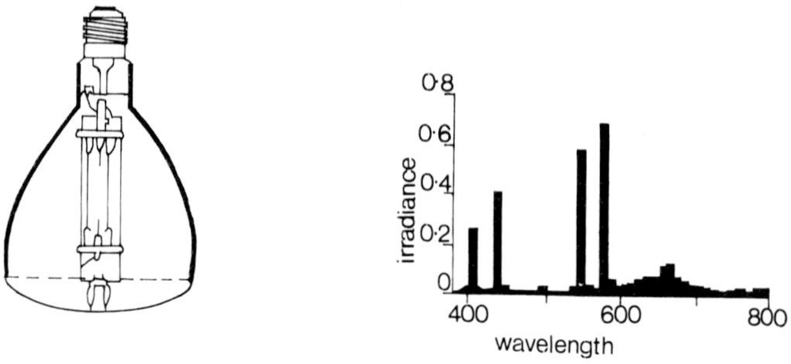

6.12 *A 400 W high-pressure mercury fluorescent lamp with internal reflector (MBFR)*

6.13 *A high-pressure mercury lamp (MBFR/U) with control gear and reflector (courtesy of Thorn Lighting Ltd)*

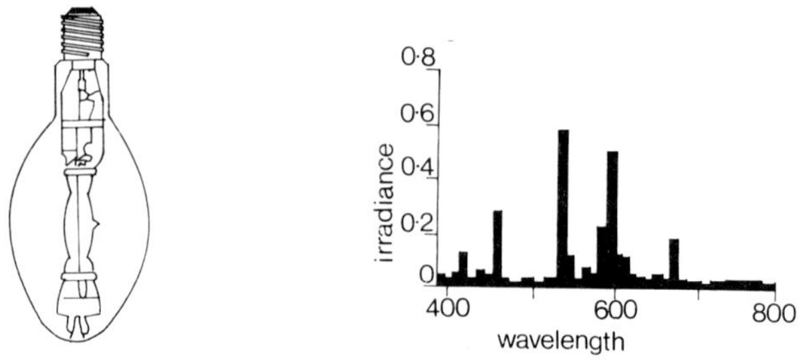

6.14 *A 400 W metal halide lamp with eliptical envelope (MBI)*

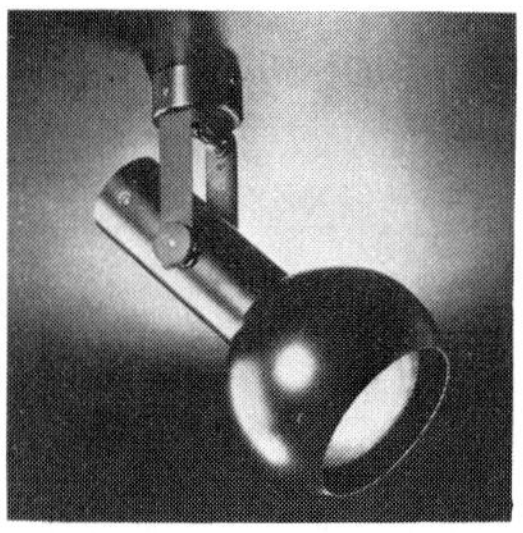

6.15 *A Wotan power star set with 250 W metal halide reflector lamp (courtesy of Wotan Lamps Ltd)*

Colour corrected mercury lamp (MBF) (fig 6.10 & 6.11)
These are the most common mercury lamps, consisting of a high pressure discharge tube with a phosphor coated outer envelope. An external choke is necessary to control the lamp current, and gear losses increase the system rating by 10 to 15%. Several ratings are available with an internal reflector (MBFR) which have the advantage of providing some directional control without the need for a large external reflector (fig 6.12 & 6.13). Wattages range from 50 W to 2000 W for MBFs and 125 W to 1000 W for MBFRs, with efficacies from 35 to 50 lm/W. A de luxe phosphor is available from some manufacturers for the standard MBF type: it improves the "colour rendering" and warms the "colour appearance". But the claims for light output do vary, so a check should be made to see if a reduction in the lamp efficacy adversely affects the economics of the system.

Metal halide lamp

This is a mercury discharge lamp with additives in the discharge tube to improve the colour rendering and light output (fig 6.14 & 6.15). It is available in a linear form (MBIL) for use in a trough floodlight or in an elliptical or tubular envelope (MBI). A phosphor coating (MBIF) may be added to the elliptical envelope further to improve the colour rendering. The most common ratings are 250 W, 400 W and 1000 W with efficacies from 55 to 75 lm/W. Lamp life is variously quoted between 6000 and 8000 h. A compact source lamp (CSI) is available for use in long range spotlights but their life is only some 1000 h.

High pressure sodium lamp (SON) (fig 6.16 & 6.17)

This is a lamp with very poor "colour rendering" and a very warm "colour appearance" which has the advantage of producing an efficacy of around 100 lm/W. Ratings from 50 W to 1000 W are commonly available. A reflectorised version is also available in some ratings.

Special versions of this lamp are available as a direct substitute for 250 W and 400 W MBF lamps and require no modifications to the existing circuitry. However, it is advisable to get the lamp manufacturer to agree the substitution as some problem may be found with older installations. The advantage of the substitution is a significant increase in light output with a decrease in energy consumption. The SON lamp has a considerable potential for energy saving due to its efficiency in converting electricity to light. This type of lamp is the subject of intensive development and an even higher efficacy and cooler "colour appearance" can be expected in the next few years. However care must be exercised with the use of this source as it can make some human skin types look strange.

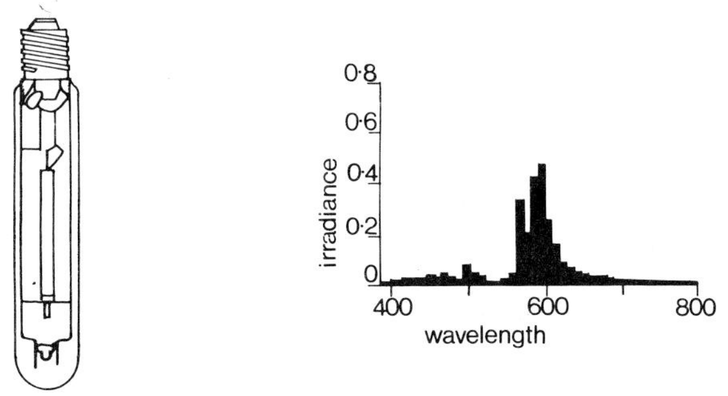

6.16 *A 400 W high pressure sodium lamp*

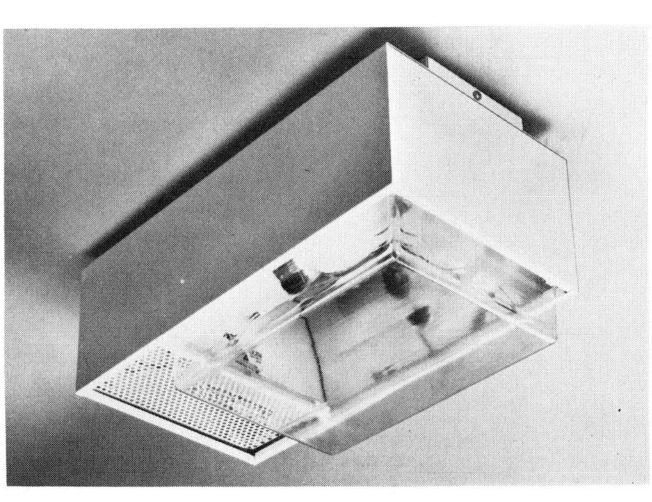

6.17 *High-pressure sodium lamp in luminaire (alternative to luminaire shown in fig 6.11); (courtesy of Thorn Lighting Ltd)*

CONTROL SYSTEMS

In many situations it may be that electric light is only necessary to "top-up" the available daylight energy, perhaps at certain times of the day or at certain times of the year. In such cases it is necessary to make a decision as to the method of control, ie either manual or automatic. Manual control has the disadvantage of being both inconvenient and unreliable, particularly if the duration needs to be varied seasonally. An automatic control has the additional advantage that it will function even when the building is unoccupied. The simplest automatic system is a time switch with a solar dial to allow for seasonal variation in day length. Such time switches are commonly used for the control of street lighting, with a sequence of operations that switch on at sunset and off several hours later. For example the lights can be on from sunset to 22.00 h and on again at say 06.00 h until sunrise. If the set time operation conflicts with variable operations no switching is necessary, eg when the 06.00 h switch-on occurs after sunrise no switching would be performed. Such a time switch enables seasonally shorter days to be extended for the required minimum duration.

Another simple automatic control is a photo-electric switch used in conjunction with a time switch. If the daylight fails to provide the minimum illuminance required within a given period determined by the time switch, the photo-electric controller switches on the lamps. A more complex version of this would be to use a photo-electric controlled dimmer which would not only turn the electric light on and off but would vary the illuminance to complement daylight and so maintain a chosen minimum value. The disadvantage of the latter approach is that it is restricted to dimmable lamps such as incandescent and tubular fluorescent.

All these control systems are readily available but usually have the limitation of fixing "day length" regardless of the energy received by the plant. It must be within the ingenuity of the microprocessor industry to devise an integrating unit which can measure the energy received by a plant, in order to calculate the deficiency to be made up from electrical installations.

SOURCE ENERGY DETERMINATION

It is common practice to measure photosynthetically active radiation in visual (photometric) terms using the unit of illuminance lux (lx), ie, lumens per m^2, or lumens per ft^2 (lm/ft^2); the conversion factor being $lm/ft^2 \times 10.76 = lx$ and $lux \times 0.0929 = lm/ft^2$. As has been discussed earlier, illuminance can only be loosely related to a photosynthetic rate although a simple derived unit can be corrected according to its source and then related to an area/time base to give total effective power. The most easily applied unit for this purpose is the watt (W), or more particularly the milliwatt (mW). A unit of illuminance can then be converted directly to photosynthetically-active radiant power by the use of the correction factors given in table 6.2 eg an illuminance of 1000 lx of fluorescent (MCFE) light is equal to 2900 mW/m^2.

When interior plants are grown at lower illuminances the rate of growth is proportional to a given illuminance eg a 2 hour period of exposure to an average illuminance of 1000 lx will give a growth response which is double that of one resulting from a similar exposure for 1 hour. For all practical purposes it may be assumed that the growth response is directly related to the total energy received by a given area of leaf in a given period of time. For example a 2 hour period of exposure to 1000 lx of fluorescent (MCFE) lighting will give a total energy input of 5800 mWh/m^2 (2×2900 mWh/m^2). This may be expressed in units of energy by using the conversion factor, 1 mWh = 3.6 Joules (J) so that the total energy received in this example is 20880 J/m^2 or 0.0209 MJ/m^2.

Example

To determine the average illuminance from daylight required to provide an energy input of 0.1 MJ/m^2

From table 6.2 the energy constant for daylight is 4.3. Thus

$$\frac{100\,000}{3.6 \times 4.3} = 6460 \text{ lmh/m}^2.$$

The average illuminance required for a twelve hour day would therefore be:

$$\frac{6460}{12} = 538 \text{ lux}$$

and for an eight hour day would be:

$$\frac{6460}{8} = 808 \text{ lux}.$$

Example

To determine the average illuminance from fluorescent lamps to provide an energy input of 0.1 MJ/m^2

If Warm White fluorescent lamps are used instead of daylight an increased illuminance is required to compensate for the lower effectiveness of the light source.

From table 6.2 the energy constant for fluorescent lamps is 2.7. Thus

$$\frac{100\,000}{3.6 \times 2.7} = 10\,288 \text{ lmh/m}^2.$$

The average illuminance required for a twelve hour day would therefore be:

$$\frac{10\,288}{12} = 857 \text{ lux}.$$

and for an eight hour day would therefore be:

$$\frac{10\,288}{8} = 1286 \text{ lux}.$$

From the above it can be seen that 60% more illuminance would be necessary to provide the same energy level from fluorescent lamps than from daylight.

Example

To determine the additional electric lighting required to provide an energy input of 0.1 MJ/m^2, assuming the daylight contribution to be an average of 400 lux for eight hours per day.

Daylight contribution $= 400 \times 8 \times 4.3 = 13\,760$ mWh/m^2
or $13\,760 \times 3.6 = 49\,536$ J/m^2

The electric light required is therefore:

$$100\,000 - 49\,536 = 50\,464 \text{ J/m}^2$$

Assuming a working day of eight hours with fluorescent lamps:

$$\frac{50\,464}{3.6 \times 2.7 \times 8} = 649 \text{ lux}.$$

If the working day were extended to ten hours this value would be reduced to

$$\frac{50\,464}{3.6 \times 2.7 \times 10} = 519 \text{ lux}.$$

TABLE 6.2 CONSTANTS FOR CONVERTING THE ENERGY CONTENT OF THE EMISSION OF SOME COMMON LIGHT SOURCES FROM LUMENS TO MILLIWATTS

Light source	Conversion factor (mW/lm)
Daylight	4.3
GLS (100–200W)	4.3
MCFE ("Warm-white" fluorescent, 40–125 W)	2.7
MCFR ("Warm-white" fluorescent, 40–125 W)	2.7
MB/U (400–1000 W)	2.5
MBF (400–1000 W)	2.9
MBFR/U (40–1000 W)	2.9
HLRG (400 W)	3.0
MBI (400–2000 W)	2.9
SON/T (400 W)	2.4

CALCULATING ILLUMINATION FROM LINEAR SOURCES

Example

To provide 0.1 $MJ/m^2/day$ over an area measuring 5 m wide by 3 m deep for a planted feature.

Assume:

1 that the light source is to be tubular fluorescent lamps which correspond with the rest of the interior lighting system
2 that the natural daylight levels are negligible
3 that the illumination period is that of the normal working day ie 09.00 h to 18.00 h or 9 hours a day.

The total energy required to provide 0.1 MJ for 9 hours will be

$$\frac{100\,000}{3.6 \times 9} \text{ or } 3086 \text{ mW/hours}.$$

To express this as illuminance measured in lux refer to table 6.2 to find the conversion factor for tubular fluorescent lamps, ie 2.7.

Therefore

$$\frac{3086}{2.7} = 1143 \text{ lux}.$$

The area to be illuminated measures some 15 m^2 so that the total illuminance required will be:

$$1143 \times 15 \text{ or } 17\,145 \text{ lux}.$$

Due to the inefficiency inherent in all luminaires it is necessary to increase the installed flux by a utilisation factor obtained from the manufacturer (assume in this example 0.55). Therefore the installed flux will be

$$\frac{17\,145}{0.55} \text{ or } 31\,172 \text{ lux}.$$

Similarly a correction factor should be used to allow for the soiling of the luminaires which occurs in most situations (assume in this example 10%).

Therefore the total flux requirement will be

$$\frac{31\,172}{0.9} \text{ or } 34\,635 \text{ lux}.$$

From the manufacturer it is found that a 1.5 m long 65 W warm white lamp yields 4650 lumens. Therefore the number of lamps required is

$$\frac{34\,635}{4650} \text{ or } 7.44.$$

For a practical solution this may be taken as 8 tubes or four twin lamp luminaires.

Resumé: The procedure described above can be expressed more simply in the equations

$$\text{illuminance (lux)} = \frac{\text{J/m}^2\text{/day}}{3.6 \times h \times LCF}$$

where $J/m^2/day$ = the required energy level
h = the number of hours of illumination per day.
LCF = the lamp conversion factor to be found in table 6.2.

and

$$\text{Number of luminaires} = \frac{\text{lux} \times \text{area}}{UF \times MF \times N \times lm}$$

where UF = the utilisation factor (data from the luminaire manufacturer).
MF = the maintenance and soiling factor.
N = the number of lamps per luminaire.
lm = the lumen output of the lamp (data from the lamp manufacturer).

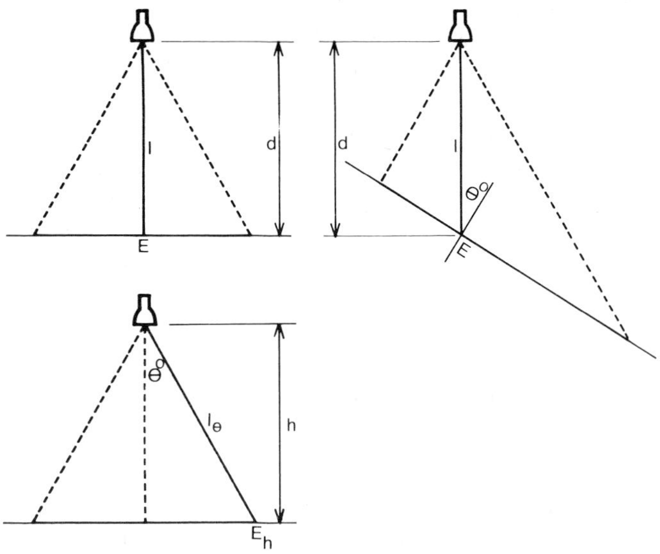

6.18 *Example – calculating illumination from point sources*

CALCULATING ILLUMINATION FROM POINT SOURCES

In many interior situations the general lighting installations will be suitable for planted areas. But special treatment may be required if an existing layout is inappropriate or if it is intended to highlight a feature. For these functions spot-lighting may be necessary.

At the mounting height given below, an MBFR/U lamp is considered as a point source, so the inverse square law applies (fig 6.18):

$$E\ (\text{lux}) = \frac{I\ (\text{candelas})}{d^2\ (\text{metres})}.$$

(the intensity of the source in candelas is obtained from manufacturer's data).

If the plane of illumination is not normal to the direction of lighting it is necessary to take the appropriate intensity and multiply it by the cosine of the angle of incidence (fig 6.18):

$$E = \frac{I \cos\theta}{d^2}.$$

This procedure will involve calculating a new distance d, as the illuminance must be determined at different points. For this reason a modified formula is used which has only two variables: the intensity and angle of the incident light.

$$E_h = \frac{I \cos^3\theta}{h^2}.$$

In practice a cosine correction is unnecessary with angles of less than 20°, since the foliage is normally orientated in a random manner.

Example

To illuminate the area to the level described in the previous example from a 7 m high ceiling using reflectorised high pressure colour corrected mercury lamps (MBFR/U).

$$\text{illuminance (lux)} = \frac{\text{J/m}^2\text{/day}}{3.6 \times h \times \text{LCF}} = \frac{100\,000}{3.6 \times 9 \times 2.9} = 1064\ \text{lux}$$

With the centre of the MBFR/U lamp 7 m above the foliage the required intensity is:

$$1064 \times 7^2 \text{ or } 52136\ \text{cd}$$

From the lamp manufacturers intensity distribution data for a 400 W MBFR/U lamp the peak intensity is found to be 7670 candelas. This level is maintained within 20° of the vertical and as the planting falls within this area it can be assumed that the illuminance will be reasonably uniform. It is therefore necessary to provide

$$\frac{52136}{7670} \text{ or } 6.8 \text{ lamps.}$$

In practice this may be interpreted as 7 lamps which will provide 1100 lux if clustered in a ceiling area of 1 m × 3 m directly above the centre line of planting.

7 Planters and their planting

INTRODUCTION

Traditionally a limited range of container materials were used whilst the plants were grown in loam based composts. Recently a range of new materials have been used; plastics and aluminium for containers, and bark and vermiculite for composts. More recently hydroculture techniques have become widespread, but for many reasons the more traditional systems continue to represent the bulk of the plants used for interior planting. This chapter deals mainly with those techniques which are necessary to produce a complete planting scheme in traditional plant substrates. Hydroculture is considered later in chapter 10.

PREFABRICATED PLANTERS

Containers for plant display are either prefabricated "off the shelf" models or built insitu. Small individual units have the advantage of being relatively light so that they do not represent an excessive point loading and can be easily manhandled into position. They are unlikely to leak and require little attention to maintain their appearance. They normally range in volume from 0.005 m^3 to 0.2 m^3, and are available on plan as squares, rectangles, hexagons and circles in various heights (table 7.1). There are several models of prefabricated planters designed for use with compost grown plants that have a limited water storage capability, where the water is slowly released into the compost. Most companies specialising in interior planting market a complete range of prefabricated plant containers, and most of those which offer a planting service have their own range of economically priced containers.

Planters are available in a number of materials, the more common of which are described below:

Plastic

The smaller prefabricated planters are usually composed of smooth high gloss polystyrene whilst the larger ones are usually made of glass reinforced polyester (grp) in a range of basic colours (fig 7.1 & 7.2). Most of these planters have a smooth finish but some are available with embossed decorative finishes. There is a selection of more ornate finishes such as copper, silver and even mirrored, but these are expensive.

7.1 *Prefabricated planters in grp*

7.2 *Grp planter on top of filing cabinet avoids a potential obstruction at floor level*

TABLE 7.1 THE MORE COMMON PLANTER DIMENSIONS (MM)

Circular planters: polyester and grp

Diameter	Weights			Major material	
	low	medium	high	polyester	grp
150		200		0	
200		250		0	
300		**300**		0	
350	250		350	0	
400	**300**		360	0	0
450	**300**	**450**	600	0	0
500	**300**	400	630	0	0
550	**300**	**450**	**500**		0
600		**300**			0
700	**300**	**450**	**600**		0
900		**450**			0

Circular planters: aluminium

Diameter	Heights
250	150
300	**200**
350	250
400	**275**
450	300
500	**330**

Rectangular planters: polyester and grp

Length	Width	Height	Material	
			Polyester	grp
450	**200**	**220**	0	
570	200	200	0	
675	200	200	0	
750	400	300		0
800	300	270		0
900	**300**	**300**		0
	400	**300**		0
	350	350		0
970	**300**	**400**		0
1000	**250**	**250**		0
	300	300		0
1200	**400**	**350**		0
1500	750	300		0
1600	400	300		0

Square planters in polyester or grp

Sides	Height	Material	
		polyester	grp
400	250 or **350**	0	0
450	300 or 400	0	0
500	**300** or 350 or 400	0	0
600	or 350 or 400	0	0
750	300		0
900	400 and 500		0

Hexagonal planters: usually in grp only

Width	Height
500	**300**
550	300
600	400
700	300
750	**250**
	300
	400
	450

Goblet planters; usually in spun aluminium only

Diameter	Height
200	**180**
500	**450**
700	**500**

Note Figures used in this table have been adjusted by up to plus or minus 10 mm. Figures in bold type indicate styles of planters most commonly used.

Aluminium

There is a range of spun aluminium planters available. They offer a very striking base, with their slightly reflective finish, but are very expensive. They are normally of a simple cylindrical pattern, although there is a range of planters with a goblet shape (fig 7.3).

7.3 *A planter in spun aluminium (courtesy of Lune Metal Spinning Co Ltd)*

Terra cotta pots

These are the traditional unglazed clay plant containers and in the last few years there has been a marked return to such planters. Terra cotta pots are usually characterised by a perforated base and plain unglazed sides (fig 7.4). The unglazed sides mean that the planters require irrigation more frequently than those made of other materials. If such containers are used in a dry building the evaporation of irrigation water through the container walls soon results in efflorescence on the surface. Not only is this unsightly but it is virtually impossible to remove. It is possible to overcome these problems by purchasing containers with a glazed inner surface or by the application of a proprietary waterproofing compound. The presence of perforations in the base of most terra cotta planters can cause difficulty in many office situations due to the need for a "saucer" and the associated danger of flooding. For this reason it is advisable to purchase containers without drainage holes, or to seal existing holes and then use half hydroculture, full hydroculture, or a proprietary reservoir system.

Glazed ceramic containers

Recently a range of simple glazed ceramic containers have been produced for interior planting. These are usually of a simple cylindrical form without drainage holes and finished with a subdued colour wash before glazing. It is unfortunate that such planters appear to be relatively hard to locate and are rather expensive. Even though these containers are glazed it is advisable to apply a sealing compound to the inside to ensure that the walls are not permeable. Such planters can be stood directly on any surface and are best employed with a half hydroculture, full hydroculture or proprietary self watering system (fig 7.5).

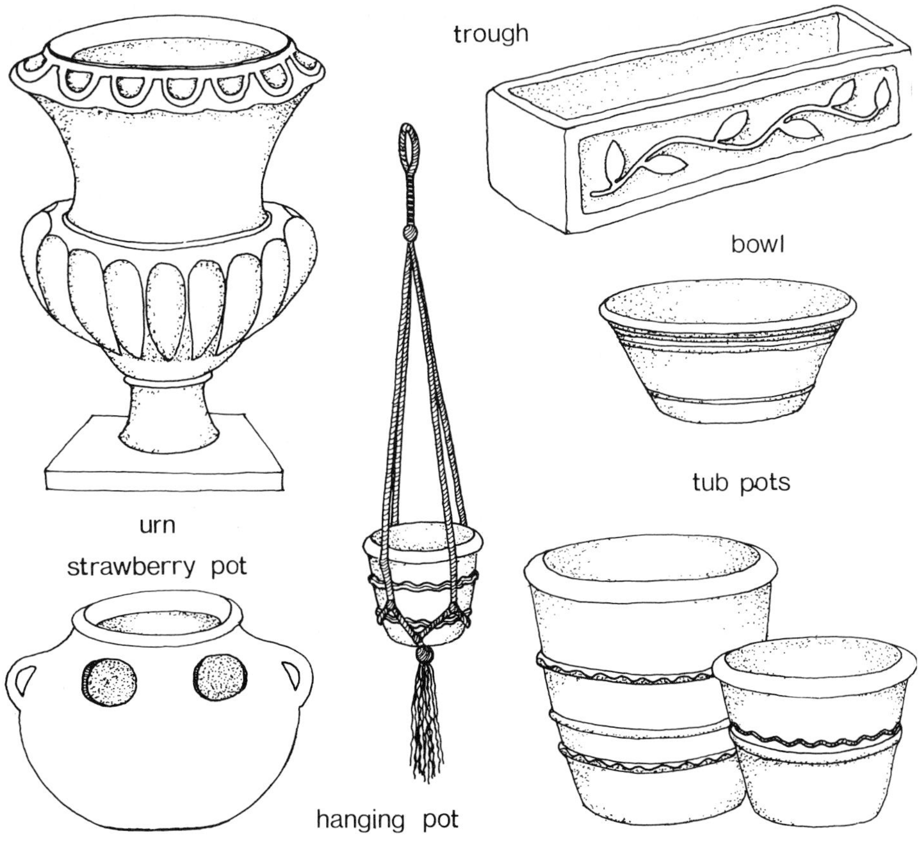

7.4 *A range of the planters available in terra cotta*

7.6 *A "smoked perspex" hanging planter which contains a considerable volume of compost*

7.5 *Simple glazed ceramic planters*

Wood
Timber offers a great deal of flexibility in the design of larger containers for use with interior planting, particularly in a conservatory situation. It is always advisable to use moisture resistant wood like cedar or keruing, although some interesting results have been produced with marine plywood sealed with elastic waterproofing compounds.

WATERING SYSTEMS
The function of a compost is to make oxygen, water, mineral salts and anchorage available to the plants. Air will diffuse freely into a compost providing it has pore spaces, and nutrients are easily absorbed on to the surface of the clay or organic matter components to become available to the plant when required. Water is therefore the only addition which is frequently required and represents a significant maintenance problem. An excess of water will completely fill the air spaces in a compost, leading to the asphyxiation of the root system, whilst too little will result in the plant experiencing water stress which results in a reduced rate of growth or even death. Techniques have been produced for reducing the chance of such irrigation problems due to a reliance on manual skills. The more important of these self watering systems are considered below whilst hydroculture is considered in a later chapter.

Manual watering
This is still widely used but it is the least reliable as the amount of water required must be assessed by an operator who is often untrained. Even if a compost is raised to field capacity (see glossary) it will normally require attention every two to four days (see plant substrates). The main problems associated with manual watering are therefore:

1 the lack of control and/or expertise may result in over or under watering
2 watering must be carried out every three to seven days
3 frequent watering, particularly of loam based composts, can compact the surface, restrict the passage of air to the roots, and leach nutrients
4 for water to move down through the compost the upper layers must be saturated.

With manual watering the only safe way to ensure that the complete compost mass is moistened is to apply sufficient water for an excess to escape. If such a policy is adopted drainage should be provided to avoid the danger of the lower layers becoming saturated. Some planters are designed to receive a nursery production container without the need for additional compost but they should be constructed in such a way that a drainage void is provided in the base.

Hanging planters usually contain compost grown plants which often suffer from water stress because of the relatively small volume of substrate which is available. Frequently they retain so little moisture that daily watering can be necessary. The main consideration when selecting hanging plant containers is to ensure that the compost volume is as large as is practical (fig 7.6).

Reservoir based systems

These are an attempt to reduce the labour requirement of manual watering by producing a display container with a reservoir (fig 7.7). The water is introduced to the reservoir by means of a pipe opening on the upper surface of the container, and is transferred from the reservoir to the compost by the "capillary action" of fired clay discs or fibre wicks. In most interior situations watering is reduced to refilling the reservoir every two to three weeks, at which time liquid feed can be added. The high level of evaporation which would normally occur from a moist compost is avoided because the "capillary lift" of the substrate is insufficient to raise moisture to the surface layers. This means that a deep substrate can appear to be totally devoid of moisture at the surface even though the lower levels are moist. As a result there have been cases where well intentioned people have irrigated plants in the traditional manner from the top and killed the plants by waterlogging. The low maintenance requirement of these systems results therefore from the low transpiration rates associated with interior plants and the isolating effect of a dry surface layer of compost. Some examples of such patented reservoir based watering systems are described in the following sections.

The gardenair system

The Gardenair watering system utilises fired clay discs fitted into the base of a hollow walled trough to transfer water from the reservoir to the compost (fig 7.8). The water level is monitored with a dipstick and the reservoir level is corrected by additions made via a filler tube. Large planters can be made self watering by placing several double-skinned liners into them before planting in the normal manner.

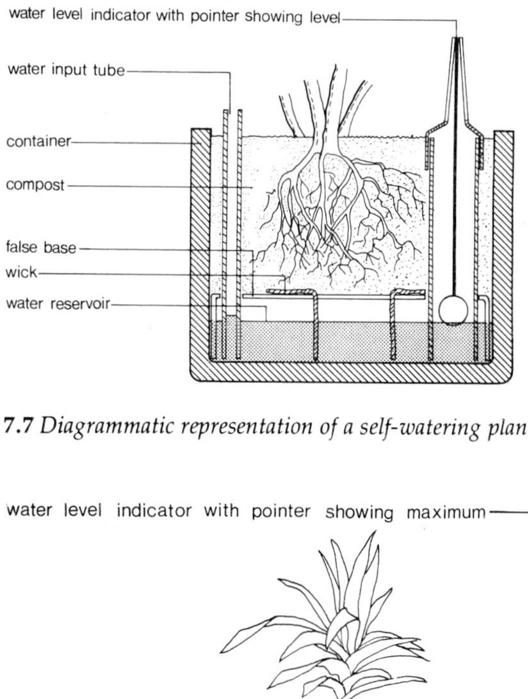

7.7 *Diagrammatic representation of a self-watering planter*

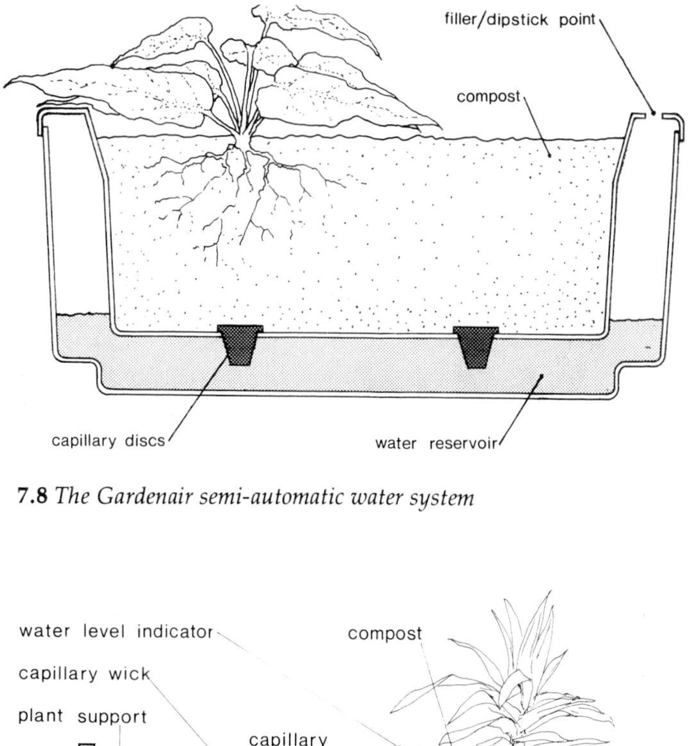

7.8 *The Gardenair semi-automatic water system*

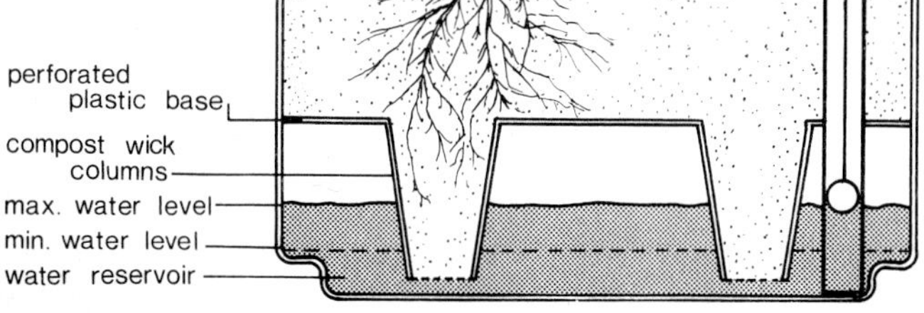

7.9 *The Mona semi-automatic watering system*

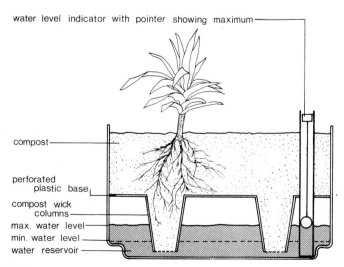

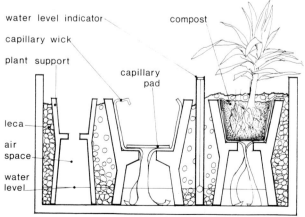

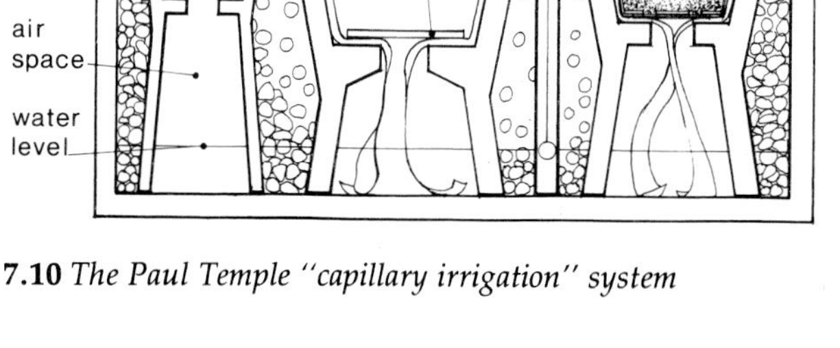

7.10 *The Paul Temple "capillary irrigation" system*

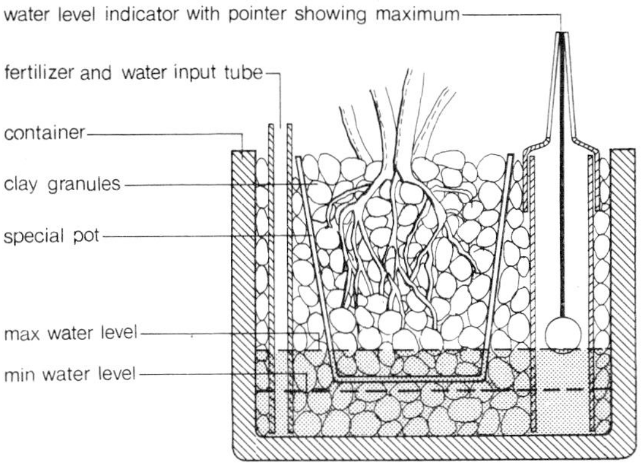

7.11 *The half-hydroculture semi-automatic watering system*

7.12 *A half-hydroculture system showing good root development*

The Mona system

This system is based on a perforated plastic sheet penetrated by truncated cones. These cones project into the reservoir in the base of the container in such a way that water is lifted through the compost to the main body of the unit (fig 7.9). Although this assembly is normally integral with special containers there is a broad cylindrical unit which can be placed independently in the base of a larger unit.

Paul Temple "capillary irrigation" system

This system has been designed to permit the use of traditional compost grown plants still in their nursery pots. As a result plants from almost any source can be used, although certain pot sizes are more convenient than others. The plant pots are dropped into an expanded polystyrene support that is cut so that the top is just below the rim of the planter (fig 7.10). The base of the plant pot then rests on a pad of capillary matting which is connected to the reservoir by a woven glass fibre strip. If a higher moisture regime is desired the ends of the glass fibre strip are laid on the upper surface of the compost. The depth of the water in the base of the container is monitored by means of a float indicator, and replenished via a filler tube. The voids which remain in the planter are filled with leca to produce a uniform surface. The main advantage of this system is that plant replacement is a rapid and simple process.

Half-hydroculture

This system is a compromise between the traditional compost grown plant and hydroculture. By employing this technique the advantages of hydroculture can be obtained in almost any container when such plants are not readily available or when plants are too large to convert to hydroculture (fig 7.11 & 7.12). The planter is approximately one third full of washed leca to provide the reservoir. The rest of the container is filled with compost which is separated from the leca by a layer of capillary matting. The water then passes from the leca layer to the compost to maintain the moisture regime while the plants develop roots into this layer to reach a more plentiful supply of water and nutrients. The water level within the leca is monitored by means of a float and pointer as in a hydroculture system, and should be allowed to fluctuate between the maximum and the minimum levels. Liquid feed can be applied to the compost although it is easier to introduce ion exchange fertiliser to the base of the container (see chapter 10).

INSITU PLANTERS

Where large masses of vegetation are required, it may well be easier to construct a planter insitu. In such situations it is possible to achieve a less frequent maintenance input by plumbing irrigation water to the container and controlling its application automatically. A drainage system should always be installed where possible, particularly if there is a positive irrigation system (fig 7.13). With large insitu planters it is advisable to provide a hard non-porous surround at least 300 mm wide to avoid any risk of damage to the surrounding surface as a result of careless maintenance.

Planters should always be of a size which can comfortably contain the plants' root system. For plants which are grown in traditional systems the compost layer should be no less than 300 mm deep and up to a maximum of 1 m deep for large plants. For plants grown in hydroculture the container should be 300 mm deep unless extremely large plants are required, when the depth should be at least 100 mm more than the largest plant pot which they are to receive.

Many of the trees which are used in North America are grown in large grp containers with a capacity of 200 to 300

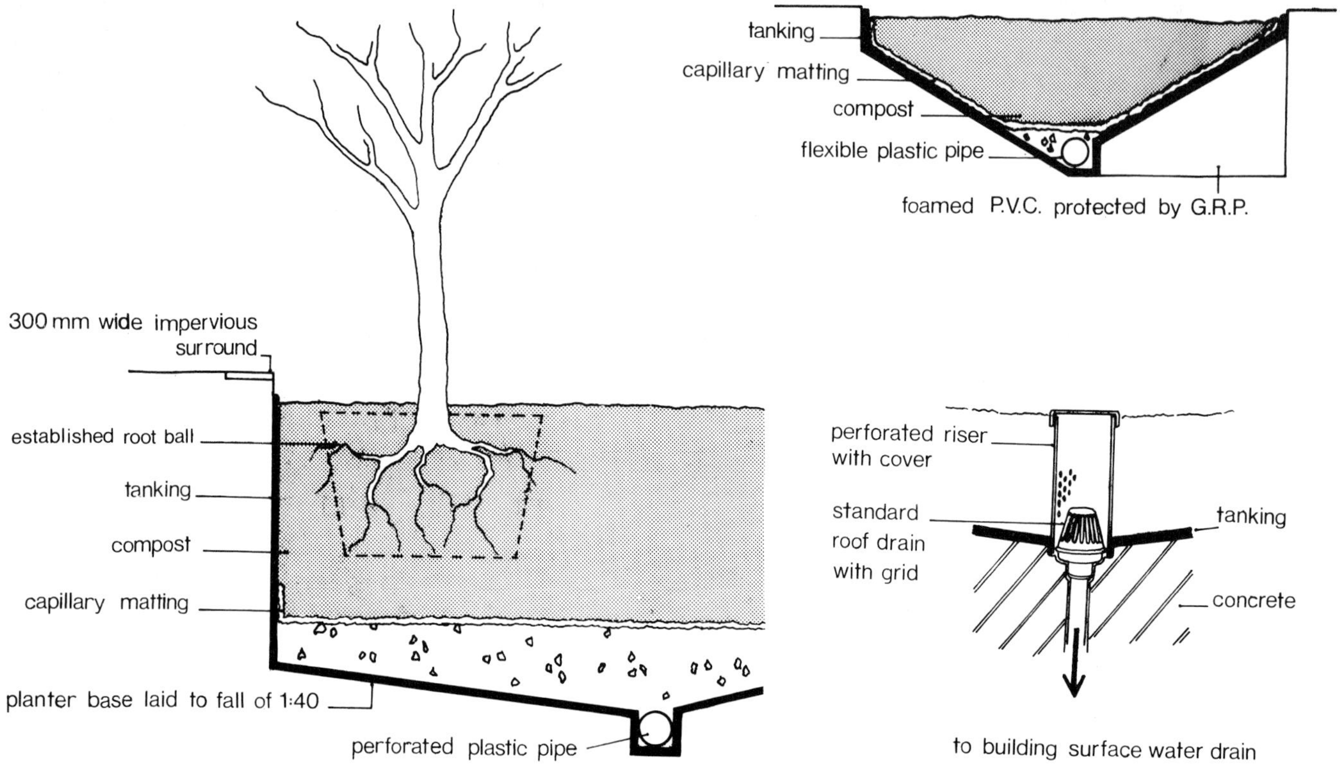

7.13 *Some design features which may be incorporated in large insitu planters*

gallons. The problems of removing the container from such a large rootball without damaging it are so great that they are usually left in place. With large insitu planters it is the usual practice to place the container on a layer of gravel at least 300 mm thick for drainage and to fill the surrounding voids with compost (fig 7.14). A filter layer of glass fibre or polypropylene matting can be used to separate the compost from the gravel but this is not common practice. This procedure ensures that the stress which is experienced upon installation is minimal as well as ensuring that there are no problems of stability.

Planter drainage
Wherever possible planters should be provided with drainage, particularly if they are to be fitted with a positive irrigation system. The components of such a system are described below:

Falls
The base of the planter should be laid to a fall of about 1:40 so that the drainage water will flow to the outlets. For small and medium sized planters such an arrangement is suitable for carrying the drainage water through the drainage layer to a single discharge point. This may take the form of a conventional plastic roof drain with grid which is sealed into the planter tanking in the appropriate manner (see fig 8.4). It may be completely covered, although it is advisable to install a large perforated riser around the cover to facilitate visual inspection from above. Any such risers will of course need to be installed in as unobtrusive a manner as possible and covered to prevent the ingress of debris.

Drainage layer
This should be laid in a layer which is 15 to 20% of the thickness of the compost layer, but not less than 50 mm or more than 100 mm thick. There are several materials which are available for this purpose including gravel, but probably the most suitable are low density aggregates such as leca.

Filter layers
The drainage layer should be separated from the overlying growth medium by a filter layer. Traditionally a layer of glass fibre matting has been used for this purpose, but the new generation of capillary mattings are admirable for this function. It is important to select only a tightly woven, fully synthetic material as those which contain natural fibres suffer from biodegradation. There are many types of matting available, such as Fibertex, Bondina, Freshmat B, and Polyfelt TS. In deep planters it is advisable to use two or even three layers of matting laid at right angles to one another to ensure their effectiveness in the event of considerable root development.

Drains
With very long and/or large planters it is possible to reduce the need for falls on the planter base by the installation of drains. These may even be placed in recesses in the planter base to increase their efficiency and linked directly to the building's drainage system. There are numerous ceramic or plastic pipes available but for ease of installation a 60 mm diameter flexible perforated plastic land drain is to be recommended. The pipes should be laid to a fall of from 1:50 to 1:100 and preferably in such a way that rodding is possible from silt traps outside the planter.

Silt traps
The drainage from any planter should pass through a silt trap before entering the building's surface water system. This not only ensures the removal of particulate matter but also provides an easy visual check on the performance of the drainage system.

Slope drainage
Some early work has indicated that an easy way of providing drainage over a large area is to produce a planter with a sloped

base. The optimum angles of such a system are unclear but appear to lie between 10% and 30% and it may be beneficial to cover the sloped base with a single layer of capillary matting to prevent the movement of fine solids. Obviously such a sloped base drainage system requires a more conventional drainage layer into which to discharge, but can represent a considerable saving in depth around the periphery of a large planter.

Open based planters
In certain situations with large scale plantings it may be economic to use open based planters which allow contact with the natural substrata. Such substrata are invariably well compacted, so that a comprehensive drainage scheme should be installed, the planter being regarded as a sealed unit.

PRACTICAL CONSIDERATIONS

Short term planting
In an increasing number of situations the plants should only be expected to have a limited display life. If they are expected to last for less than one year it is advisable to leave them in their production container to avoid the need for disturbing the rest of the display when replacement becomes necessary. For such situations a simple support compost can be used which consists of sand (33%), peat (33%) and bark (33%) with sufficient lime (about 0.75 kg/m^3) to maintain the pH between 6.0 and 7.0

In North America it is common practice to never remove plants from their production containers even if they are expected to remain in a given location for several years. The production containers are therefore stood in the display planter on sufficient packing to raise them to a level just below the rim of the container (fig 7.15). The most widely used packing material is slabs of expanded polystyrene due to its low density. Any remaining voids in the container are then filled with crushed wire netting and covered by a layer of sphagnum moss. Should the sphagnum moss pose a fire hazard then coarse bark chips measuring some 75 mm in diameter may be used in preference. Such an approach to planting obviously reduces the chance of undue stress at installation but necessitates manual watering, and can pose problems of stability.

Plant preparation for planting
To avoid the danger of high salt concentrations causing root damage in low light situations the soluble salt content in the production container should be leached to less than 500 ppm by copious watering. If this level is difficult to achieve then 1000 ppm should suffice. If slow release fertilisers or systematic insecticide granules have been placed on the upper surface of the compost then this layer should be replaced.

Planter filling
When a large planter contains a loose drainage layer care should be taken to avoid disturbance when placing the compost. For this reason the lower 150 mm of compost should be placed before the bulk of the compost is deposited. Under no circumstances should compost be delivered from a great height otherwise compaction may result which could take years to dissipate naturally.

Many modern composts achieve a low bulk density and open texture by the use of materials like peat. If such composts are compressed they lose these properties and become a hazard to root development. For this reason these composts require only a light firming followed by a very heavy watering to complete the securing process.

When plants are "potted on" it is important to ensure that compost is *not* raised above the old compost level, otherwise the stem/trunk may rot. The only exception to this may be certain palms, eg *Phoenix dactylifera*, which are claimed to develop a new root system from the trunk when planted with up to 5% of their overall height below the compost level.

Assembly location
Wherever possible it is advisable to make up planters in the production area and then allow the plants a few weeks' growth to become stabilised. This limited period of growth is often sufficient to reduce substantially any transplant stress. It is inadvisable to undertake major planting operations in the final display area if it can be avoided, due to the risk of dirt and inconvenience. If such operations are unavoidable then care should be taken to protect all surfaces within the area.

Transportation
Prefabricated planters can weigh a considerable amount when filled, and this can be a problem if the plants require regular movement for therapeutic reasons. In such situations certain makes of hand dolly or pedestrian fork lift can be used but alternatively it may be advisable to use planters fitted with castors (fig 7.16). Some techniques which reduce the effort required to move planters are indicated in fig 7.17.

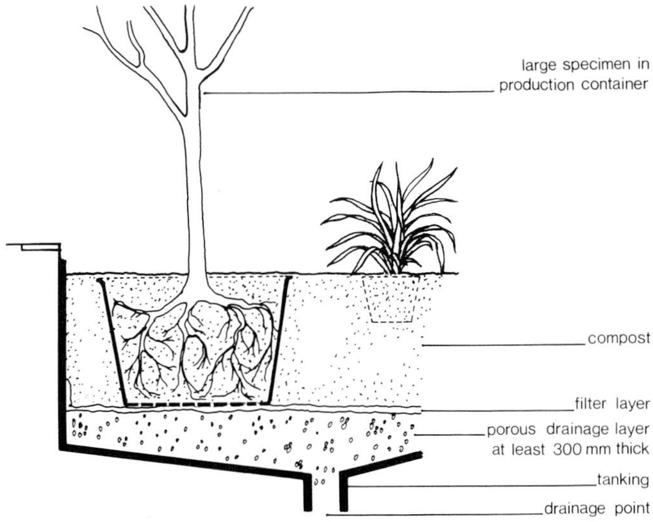

7.14 *Large trees require good drainage if the production containers are not removed*

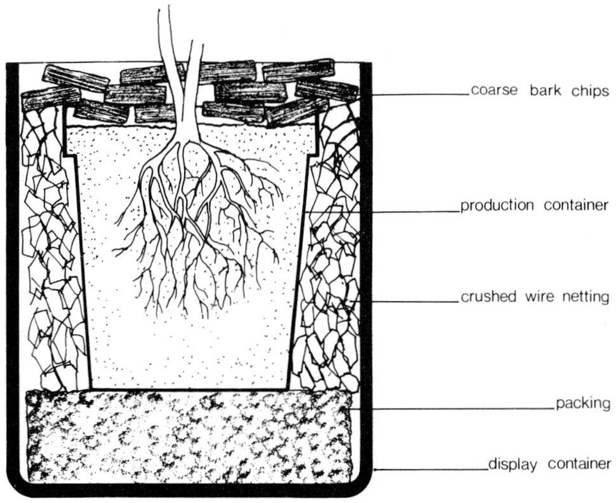

7.15 *Production containers may be stood in display planter on packing and surrounded by wire netting which is then covered by bark chips*

7.16 *A planter with castors to ease movement*

7.17 *Some techniques for moving completed planters: (top) on sacking; (bottom) by the use of a sack-truck*

Anchorage

When large specimens are used in interior schemes it is necessary to consider methods of anchorage. It is usual for large specimens to be produced with a substantial root ball which provides more than adequate support. With prefabricated planters it is possible to predict the location of the plant and so provide a guide to receive a cane. However with large insitu planters it may be necessary to consider more substantially guying systems for the short-term, using anchor points cast into the wall of the planter, although this should not be necessary if the planting has been correctly designed.

Foliar cleansing

When planting is complete it is often desirable to spray the plants to remove dirt from the foliage and level the surface of the compost. Such treatment is best done with a fine misting nozzle with care being taken to avoid any nearby furnishings.

Aftercare

After moving, all large plants should be treated with care to reduce the effects of shock, eg leaf loss. This means ensuring that the temperature is maintained at a relatively high level with little fluctuation and then modified over a period of several weeks to the ambient working regime. Wherever possible the relative humidity should be maintained at a high level. In small scale operations this can be achieved by enclosing the canopy within a polythene sheet. As can be seen from fig 4.2 (page 22) the practice of hosing down plants is of very limited value. For this reason consideration may be given to the application of an anti-transpirant, eg S600 or Wilt-pruf. This is a fairly simple procedure where the plant is sprayed with a PVC emulsion which dries on the leaves and so reduces water loss. After a few weeks the layer degrades and the stomata become fully operational once more.

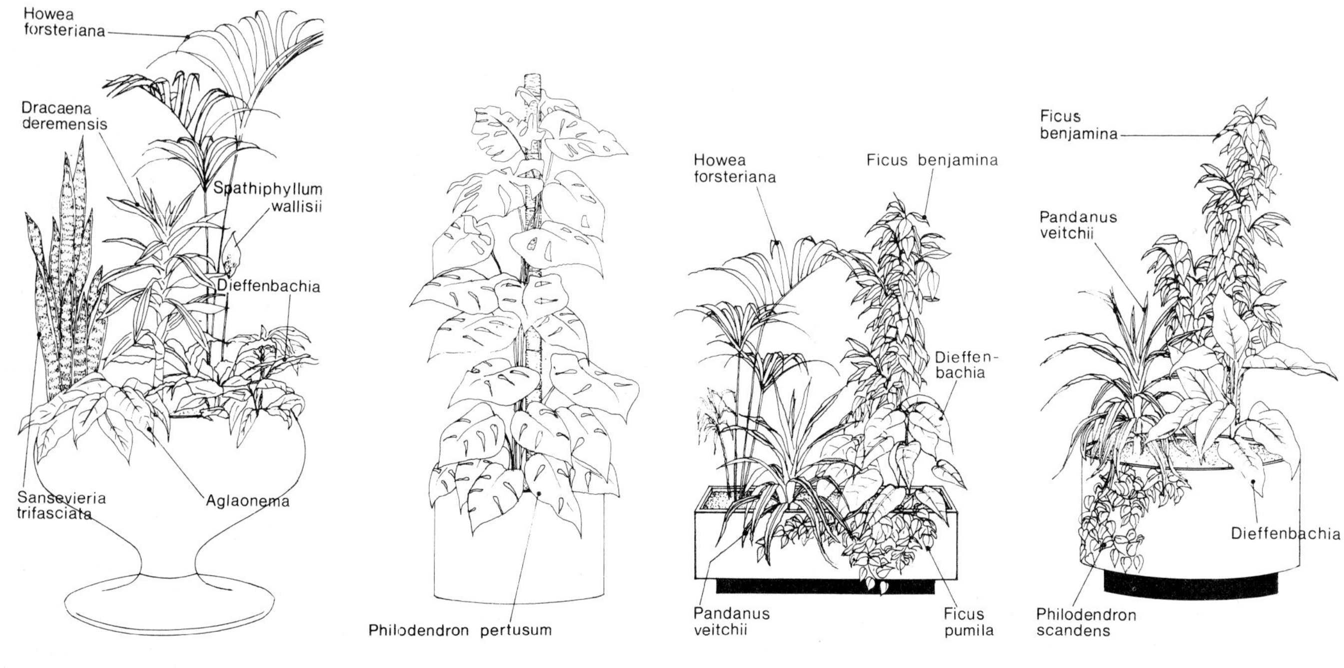

7.18 *Selection of plant arrangements. Scales differ*

8 Waterproofing for insitu planters

INTRODUCTION

When a planter is constructed insitu, it is necessary to ensure that it is watertight. Such a problem can be minimised by producing planters as a single unit, eg in concrete, in which case the only treatment which is required is the application of a coat of cold applied bitumen or acrylic emulsion, or a thin layer of insitu grp. But large planters usually consist of several components with joints. If there is little chance of movement between the components then a waterproof membrane can be produced from mastic asphalt. If there is a chance of slight movement in the structure the risk of fracture associated with mastic asphalt can be overcome by the use of a reinforced elastomeric bitumen system. For cases of even greater movement a membrane can be formed from sheets of butyl rubber or ethylene-propylene diene monomer (EPDM) which is independent of the underlying structure. A slightly more tidy solution can be produced insitu from flexible reinforced plastic, liquid hypalon, acrylic emulsion, or grp. In certain cases it may be easier to use prefabricated liners of grp or steel, although the latter will require galvanising, or sealing with a coat of cold applied bitumen or acrylic emulsion. When selecting materials for the lining of a planter it is important to remember that certain groups of materials are unsuitable for use in emergency exit zones since they fail to conform with the fire safety requirements by the Building Regulations. For this reason alone the appropriate manufacturer's advice should always be sought at the initial planning stage. Due to the importance of correct membrane installation a specialist contractor should be used for all but the application of cold applied bitumastic coats or acrylic emulsions. Specialists can also advise on any technical problems such as the venting of entrapped moisture.

COLD-APPLIED BITUMEN*

When a planter is made in one unit it may be desirable to coat the inner surface with an impervious layer to prevent moisture penetration. A cold-applied bitumen coating is ideal for protecting concrete as well as steel due to its resistance to weathering, chemical attack and mechanical damage. Some formulations of these materials are not harmful to fish and therefore may be considered non-toxic to plants. When applied correctly the bitumen coating forms a layer which is slightly flexible even at low temperatures and may serve to seal hairline cracks.

Preparation

Before applying the sealing compound the surface should be free from grease and oil. Loose surfaces such as rust, dirt and flaking paint should be removed, but where the existing rust cannot be cleared a coat of zinc phosphate or other rust inhibitor should be applied. Where possible the surface should be dry, although this is not vital.

Application

A coat of thixotropic bitumen primer should be applied to key the main coat and this will normally dry in four hours. If no primer is used then the main bitumen coats should be applied as soon as possible after the surface has been cleaned. At least two bitumen coats are normally applied by either brushing on small areas, or spraying over larger areas. The various layers can be applied as soon as the preceding layer has dried, about 24 hours under good conditions.

MASTIC ASPHALT**

Mastic asphalt is the form of asphalt which is applied to structures. It is composed of graded mineral matter and asphaltic cement in such proportions that, when heated, it can be spread by a hand float, yet when at normal room temperatures forms an impervious mass. One of its most useful functions is to waterproof basements and roofs because it is unaffected by the sulphates in the soil; being thermoplastic it can accommodate slight movements in the structure. The density of mastic asphalt varies due to slight differences in composition but is about 60 kg/m^2 (110 lb/yd^2) for a 25 mm (1 in) thick layer. Mastic asphalt is a poor thermal insulator with a thermal conductivity (K value) of about 1.23 W/m^2 deg C (8.5 Btu in/ft^2 h degF). Movement joints cannot be tolerated under mastic asphalt as any substantial movement will result in shearing.

Preparation

All surfaces to be coated must be completely dry and kept that way until the material has dried. On horizontal surfaces the asphalt should be laid over a directionally stable sheathing felt. On vertical surfaces the asphalt can be applied directly to concrete or brick but if the base is very smooth, such as concrete shuttered by steel, it is necessary to key the surface by one of the following procedures:

1 the removal of the surface layer by wire brushing
2 the application of a proprietary sand/cement plastic emulsion
3 the application of a proprietary pitch/polymer rubber emulsion.

If mastic asphalt is to be applied over a large vertical area, horizontal splayed grooves about 25 × 25 mm across at 300 mm intervals may be provided to give support. When brickwork is to be coated a good key can be achieved by raking out 5–10 mm from the horizontal joints.

Application

It is always reasonable to specify a three coat application of mastic asphalt in situations where there may later be difficulties in gaining access, as in the case of a filled planter. Therefore on all horizontal surfaces and slopes up to 30° the mastic asphalt should be laid in three coats to a total thickness of 30 mm ($1\frac{1}{4}$ in).

* The author wishes to acknowledge the assistance of Mr M. Winsor, BP Aquaseal Ltd, Rochester Kent

** The author wishes to acknowledge the assistance of Mr A. Constantine, Mastic Asphalt Council and Employers Federation, Haywards Heath, Suffolk

On vertical surfaces and steep slopes the layers should have a total thickness of no less than 20 mm (¾ in) and should continue for at least 150 mm above the substrate level. The top edge of the vertical coat should be tucked into a 25 × 25 mm chase and pointed in with a cement mortar. Where the two phases meet, an angled fillet 50 mm (2 in) thick should be applied in two layers. Any joints in successive coats should be staggered by at least 150 mm for horizontal work and 75 mm for vertical work (fig 8.1 and 8.4).

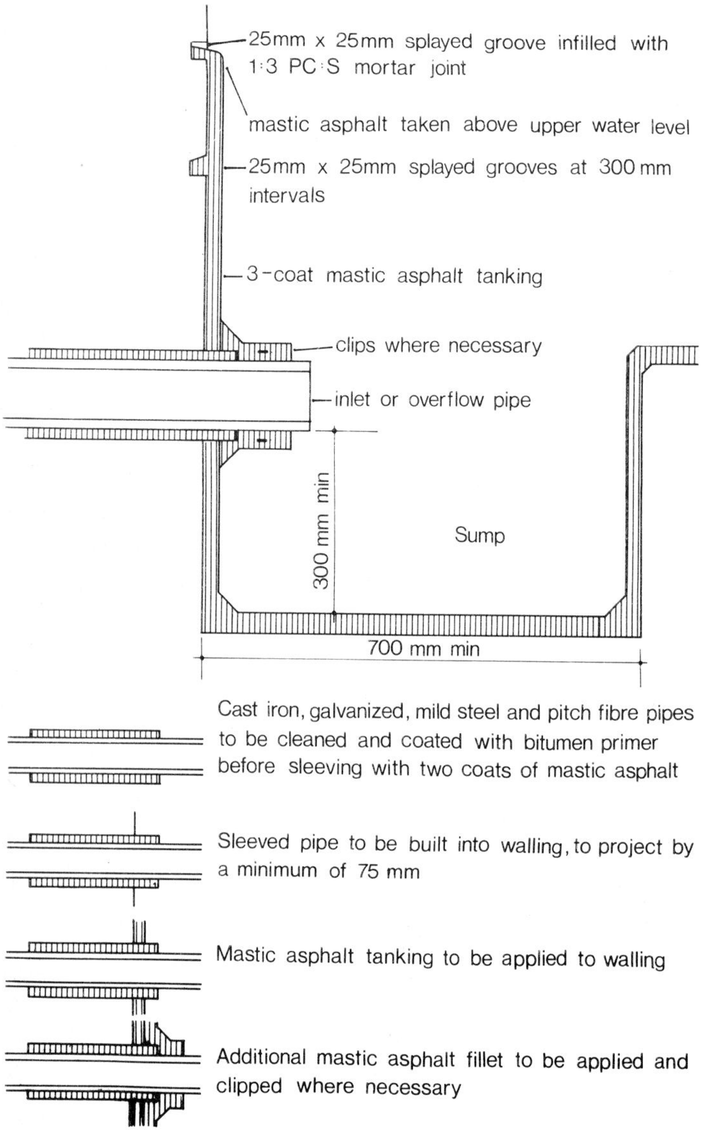

8.1 *Tanking with mastic asphalt: (top) the main features; (bottom) pipe easement*

Pipe easement

Where possible the passage of pipes through tanking should be avoided, but if it is necessary then it is best done above the substrate level. Where pipes are likely to pass through the tanking near the base of the planter it may be necessary to provide a sump so that the asphalter has room to work. When a pipe must pass through the tanking the following procedure should be adopted (fig 8.1):

1 glazed earthenware or plastic pipes are unsuitable for passing through mastic asphalt and so only cast iron, galvanized mild steel or pitch fibre pipes should be used. Before use these must be well cleaned and coated with a suitable bitumastic primer before coating with two layers of mastic asphalt

2 The sleeved portion should be cast or built into the wall so that it projects by at least 75 mm (3 in)

3 The mastic asphalt tanking can then be applied around the pipe and clipped if necessary. The tanking should then be married to the pipe by an angle fillet.

REINFORCED ELASTOMERIC BITUMEN*

This system is very similar to mastic asphalt except that it reduces the danger of fracturing. This is usually achieved by bonding two layers insitu. The bare layer usually consists of regular grades of bitumen reinforced with woven glass fibre and a sheet of polyester. Over this is laid an elastomeric bitumen waterproofing layer reinforced with woven glass fibre and a polyester sheet. The upper surface is then finished with a protective layer of fine gravel.

Application

All surfaces to be covered must be reasonably true, clean and dry before covering with a layer of crepe paper. A concrete base requires coating with cold bitumen primer before the crepe paper is laid. The base layer is secured with hot bitumen (95/25 grade) by the roll and pour technique with an overlap of at least 60 mm between adjacent sheets. When this layer has stabilised the elastomeric sheet is laid in a similar manner with staggered joints and a similar overlap.

Pipe easement

Where possible the passage of pipes through the tanking should be avoided, but if it must occur then it is best done above the substrate. Where the membrane is penetrated then the procedure which is advocated for mastic asphalt should be applied.

SYNTHETIC SHEET MEMBRANES

A strong heavy duty elastic membrane can be formed from sheets of Hypalon (chloro-sulphonated polyethylene). The sheets usually consist of a laminate of two layers of Hypalon and one layer of an organic mineral carrier which provides stability and fire resistance. The sheets have a tensile strength of at least 8 N/mm^2, an elongation at break of at least 450%. The membrane weighs about 1.8 kg/m^2 and is usually available only in light grey.

Application

The surfaces to be coated must be free from debris and should be dry. The laminated sheets are unrolled to give an overlap of not less than 50 mm which is converted to a homogeneous joint by heating with hot air or by solvent welding. The sheets are easy to work and join on site, and are bonded to the horizontal supporting surface by hot bitumen or adhesives to the manufacturer's recommendations. To ease a membrane round an acute corner a 50 mm fillet may be used to reduce undue stressing. The upper edge of a membrane is most easily secured to a vertical surface by an aluminium trim which is screwed in place and sealed with a permanently flexible sealing compound (fig 8.2).

Pipe easement

Where possible the passage of pipes through the membrane should be avoided. If this is not possible the pipe should be fitted with a preformed flexible collar which is sealed in place with a Hypalon based adhesive to the manufacturer's recommendations (figs 8.2 and 8.4).

* The author wishes to acknowledge the assistance of Mr D. Sharp, Langley (London) Ltd, London

- permanently elastic mastic
- screw
- aluminium trim
- membrane
- wedge
- adhesive or hot poured bitumen

- membrane
- waterproof sealing strip
- prefabricated collar
- waterproof sealing strip

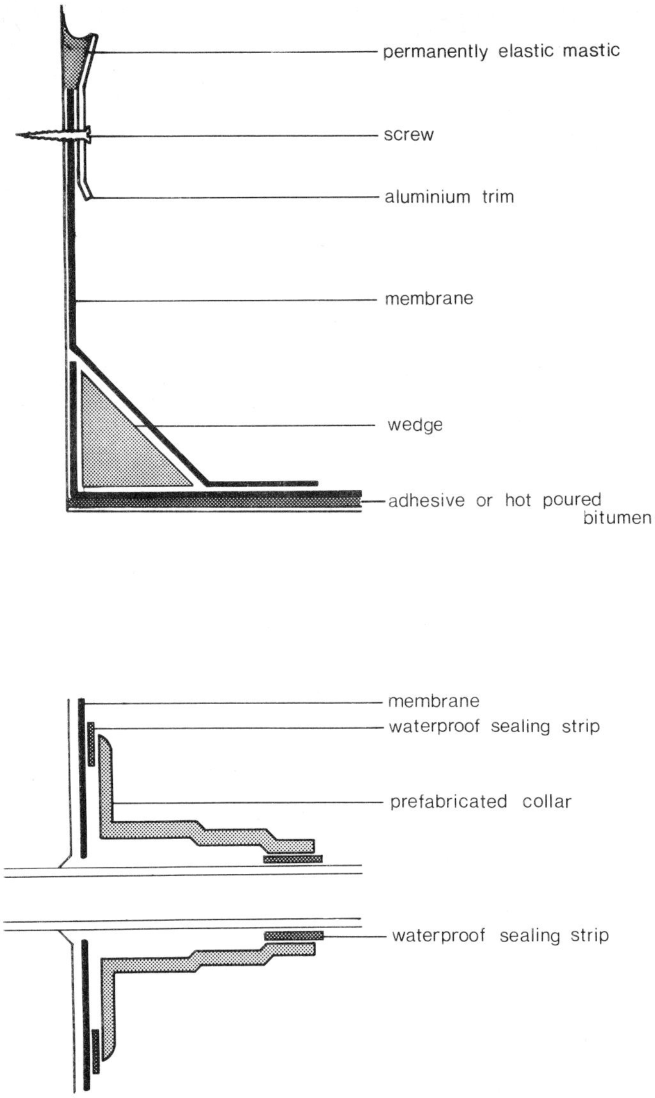

8.2 *Tanking with synthetic sheet membrane: (top) securing to a vertical surface; (bottom) pipe easement with a flexible prefabricated collar*

FLUID CONTAINMENT MEMBRANES*

In North America butyl rubber has been widely used under roof gardens with a long record of success. Other products, like ethylene-propylene diene monomer (EPDM), have similar physical properties and have the advantage of being more resilient. This system of waterproofing is independent of the structure and is therefore unaffected by movement. In most situations the desired membrane shape is constructed from rolls of fabric in the factory to reduce the need for on site activity. Seams are formed by longitudinal overlapping and vulcanising using a hot bonding machine to ensure a high quality finish. The maximum length of joint which can be prefabricated is about 75 m to give sheets in excess of 300 m² in area. Larger areas are covered by solvent welding several sheets on site although such a process can be difficult and expensive.

All modern membrane formulations are resistant to ultraviolet light and normal extremes of temperature. The tensile strength is normally about 6.8 N/mm² with an elongation of break of about 400%. For tanking the membrane is normally 1.3 mm (0.05 in) thick and weighs about 1.6 kg/m² (2.8 lb/yd²).

- hard rubber cover strip
- soft rubber fillet
- screw
- aluminium trim
- EPDM membrane
- protective underlay

- metal edge trim
- hard rubber strip
- EPDM cover strip
- waterproof sealing strip
- EPDM membrane

- preformed rubber coping
- channelled wooden batten
- EPDM membrane

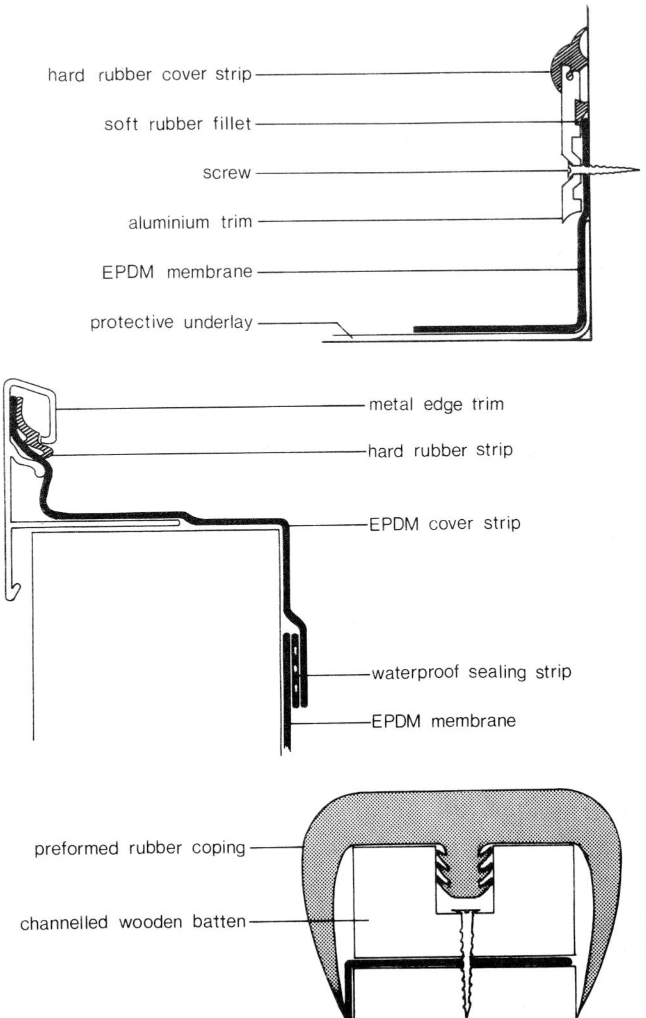

8.3 *Tanking with EPDM: (top) securing to a vertical surface with aluminium trim; (middle) securing to a parapet with a metal trim, (bottom) securing to a parapet with a wooden batten covered by a preformed rubber coping*

Preparation

When using membranes it is advisable, although not essential, to ensure that the surface to be covered is dry or adequately ventilated. If it is not then any moisture which is trapped will be unable to escape and could cause damp problems in the underlying structure. The area to be covered should always be smooth and free from debris but to protect the membrane against any rough projections it is advisable to place a protective layer of polypropylene fibre matting over the whole area before laying. To assist operations when covering vertical surfaces the matting can be secured with dabs of impact adhesive. If this system of retaining the matting is employed, then sufficient aeration should be given before placing the membrane to ensure that all traces of volatile compounds in the adhesives have evaporated. As there will almost certainly be sharp objects in the drainage layer another sheet of matting

* The author wishes to acknowledge the assistance of Mr G. Gray, Dunlop Semptex Ltd, Bishopsworth, Bristol

should be placed over the membrane and covered by a concrete screed or paving slabs for protection.

The membrane will require pinning at the top to prevent moisture from passing behind it. This is most easily achieved by the use of an aluminium trim which is screwed to the wall and sealed in the manner indicated in fig 8.3. The membrane may also be clamped under a wooden lathe and covered by a plastic extrusion (fig 8.3).

Pipe easement

Where possible the passage of pipes through the membrane should be avoided. If this is not possible the pipe should be fitted with a prefabricated collar and sealed with a flexible adhesive to the manufacturer's recommendations (figs 8.2 and 8.4).

ELASTOMERIC COATINGS*

This system can be used to produce a strong, flexible, non degradable membrane. These systems can easily be applied on site by relatively unskilled staff and can therefore be useful for repairing leaks. There are several materials available for this purpose but the most common types are produced either from layers of liquid acrylic emulsion or from layers of polychloroprene ('neoprene') covered by chloro-sulphonated polyethylene ('Hypalon'). The basic compounds are poured cold on to the surface and are spread by brush or roller. Both these compounds have a density of about 1300 kg/m^3, a tensile strength of over 3 N/mm^2 and an elongation of break of over 500%. They are available in a number of colours but the most commonly stocked are green, grey, red and white.

Application

Surfaces to be coated should be free from loose dirt and extraneous material. The surface should also be dry or fitted with vents to release entrapped vapour. Porous materials should be primed, and joints more than 3 mm wide should be filled with a sealing compound. When these stages have been completed a polypropylene nylon/terylene melded fibre or glass fibre tape some 150 mm wide should be placed as reinforcing over all joints and changes in construction, eg movement joints. The reinforcing should then be secured with an application of the liquid compound and allowed to set. The main layers of the solution can then be poured on to the surface and spread with a brush or roller. When complete the membrane should be left to cure for seven days, during which time it should not be walked on without protection.

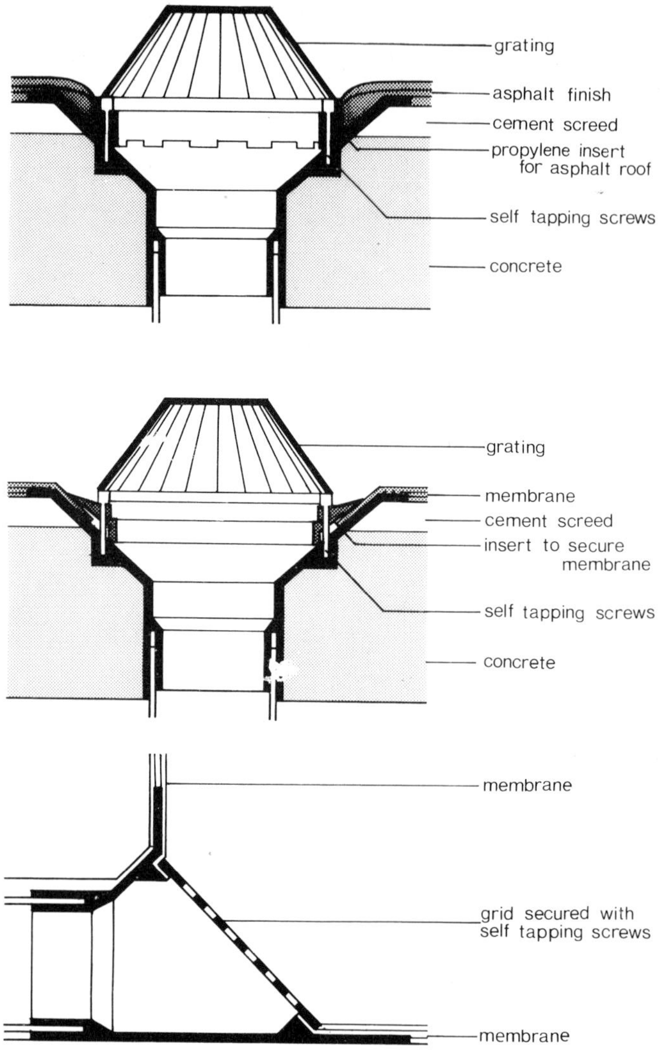

8.4 *Techniques for the easement of a drainage gully through a membrane: (top) easement through mastic asphalt; (middle) easement through a flexible membrane; (bottom) the use of a balcony outlet*

Pipe easement

The passage of pipes through the membrane is relatively easy as both the constituents will adhere to a clean surface, although a glass fibre or polypropylene/nylon/terylene melded fibre reinforcing strip should be used.

TANKING WITH FLEXIBLE REINFORCED PLASTIC*

This system is an ideal way of producing a flexible non-degradable tanking membrane with high tensile strength although its cost is relatively high. The technique usually employs a dual mix resin-based formulation which is reinforced with woven polyester fabric. The result is a homogeneous seamless membrane about 2.5 mm thick with outstanding adhesion and cohesion. Over small areas the resins are most easily mixed and applied by hand. Over large areas they can be conveyed to the point of application through two high pressure hoses from reservoir units, and mixed in an applicator gun immediately prior to deposition.

Application

All surfaces to be coated must be reasonably true, clean and dry, and throughout the application process the temperature should be between 5 and 35°C. The plastic resin is sprayed on to the substrate and the polyester reinforcing is lowered into place before being saturated with a further application of plastic. After a few hours a thin flash coat of resin is applied to produce a uniform surface.

Pipe easement

Where possible care should be taken not to pass pipes through tanking, but if it is unavoidable then it is best to do so above the substrate. Any type of pipe may pass through the membrane, although plastic pipes are not recommended except as an outer protective sleeve. The passage of high temperature pipes is

* The author wishes to acknowledge the assistance of Mr F. Kelley, Granflex Roofing Ltd, Stoke on Trent, Staffordshire

difficult as there must be a diameter tolerance, the void being fitted with asbestos or glass roving. Where the penetration of the membrane is necessary then one of the following procedures should be adopted:

1 The pipe can be fitted with a collar "welded" to the tube. The flange can then be sandwiched between a split layer of plastic membrane as far as the main body of the pipe
2 The membrane can be extended along the full length of the pipe and where appropriate can be turned back into the orifice of the pipe. Upstands can be finished by turning into a tuck-in groove prepared at the desired height.

PROTECTION OF SURFACE

During the rest of the construction operation any membrane can be damaged by impact or oils and paints. As a result care must always be taken to ensure that the tanking is protected at all times. Before the planter is filled with compost it may be advisable to protect the membrane against later digging operations by laying concrete slabs or similar materials over a polypropylene fibre matting. To produce a layer which cannot be lifted by root development a 50 mm thick screed of cement and zone six sand (1:3) may be placed on a polypropylene fibre matting over the membrane.

9 Plant substrates

INTRODUCTION

In the past there were a wide range of compost formulations in use, with many plants having a specific compost. This situation was eased considerably by Messrs Lawrence and Newell who produced the John Innes formulations to rationalise and standardise composts, but the density and scarcity of high quality loam, as well as its cost, led to the formulation of composts based on other materials. In NW Europe the material which is most widely used is peat but in North America synthesised materials like vermiculite and perlite are popular. The characteristics of the many composts which are available are wide and varied as can be seen from table 9.1.

The majority of interior plants are still grown in compost and the bigger schemes require large volumes of compost. The information in this chapter is intended to assist in the understanding of and formulation of composts for such situations.

PHYSICAL CHARACTERISTICS

All interior plants require a growth medium to supply the roots with anchorage, water, nutrients and oxygen. Such a substrate will consist of three components – a solid, a liquid and a vapour. The main consideration in this section is with traditional composts as hydroculture techniques are covered in chapter 11.

Solid phase

When a plant is grown in a container its root system is restricted and consequently the demand on the compost is greater than it would be from the same plant grown in the open ground. For this reason the recognised proprietary mixes have been formulated to provide good physical conditions for root growth. Plant substrates differ from topsoils by having a lower density and larger pore space to prevent a shortage of oxygen and to improve drainage. The total pore space varies from about 40% of the volume for a good loam soil to over 70% of the volume for certain processed materials like rockwool. Some coarse materials may initially have a high air content but require careful management to ensure that it is maintained. All mineral aggregates should be water resistant and any organic matter should not be susceptible to rapid decomposition. It is unfortunate that most proprietary compost formulations have been designed for use with an annual or biannual commercial cropping programme, and not for extended use indoors, eg it is usual for the pore space in many peat based composts to decrease by half in the first two years of use. This is largely due to "oxidation" of the peat which usually occurs at a rate of 10 to 20% of the mass per annum. This compaction of the substrate has the effect of reducing the air content, particularly when at field capacity; and as a result the plants tend to become more slower growing although they may be more resilient.

A good substrate must have the capacity to retain nutrients and release them slowly when required. The ability of a substrate to donate certain nutrients can be quantified as its cation exchange capacity (CEC). This is defined as the sum of the exchangeable cations which the substrate can absorb per unit weight. Clays are generally noted for their high CEC but some

TABLE 9.1 THE PHYSICAL PROPERTIES OF SOME COMMON COMPOST CONSTITUENTS.

Materials	Bulk density (kg/m^3)		Water retention		Void content	
	Air dry	Field capacity	Total (kg/m^3)	Percent dry weight	Total Pore space	Air space at field capacity
Bark – fir (0 to 3 mm)	230	610	380	165	70	32
Loam – clay	940	1490	550	59	60	5
Loam – sandy	1570	1955	385	24	40	2
Peat moss – hypnum	185	780	595	320	72	12
Peat moss – sedge	240	720	480	200	68	20
Peat moss – sphagnum	105	695	590	561	84	25
Perlite (1 to 5 mm)	95	395	300	316	75	45
Sand – coarse	1665	1920	255	15	36	10
Sand – fine	1500	1840	340	23	37	3
Vermiculite	110	640	530	48	80	27
Mixes – ratio 1:1						
Clay loam/sedge peat	650	1230	580	89	61	5
Clay loam/sphagnum peat	540	1165	625	116	72	10
Clay loam/coarse sand	1265	1675	410	32	47	6
Clay loam/fine sand	1315	1725	410	27	48	7
Sandy loam/sedge peat	890	1400	510	57	54	4
Sandy loam/sphagnum peat	860	1390	530	62	59	6
Fine sand/bark (0 to 3 mm)	845	1225	380	45	53	15
Fine sand/sedge peat	920	1410	490	53	54	5
Fine sand/sphagnum peat	740	1215	475	64	57	10

materials such as peat and vermiculite can have even higher values. The active constituents of most substrates have a permanent negative charge and therefore attract only cations. Anions are retained, as they combine with other chemical groups to form units with cationic properties. As a result most anions eg chloride and nitrate, are not held in any quantity and tend to be leached from the compost. With interior plants any decisions on subsequent fertiliser applications are simplified by the use of a compost with a low initial fertility, ie it is easier to raise nutrient levels than to lower them.

In the production area interior plant substrates will have a high nutrient level, often in excess of 1500 ppm. After installation the rate of growth falls rapidly and then high nutrient levels can cause damage. To avoid such dangers the nutrient salt content of the compost should be lowered to less than 1000 ppm before the plants are shipped. This reduction can be achieved by removing any pellets of controlled release fertiliser before heavy flushing with clean water. The most common symptoms of high salinity are a change in foliar colour with the development of a blue or yellow hue, and necrosis or "tip burn" in severe cases. The roots may also be damaged so that bacterial and fungal pathogens develop as "root rots" and "wilts". High nutrient levels may also cause wilting if the osmotic pressure in the compost is so high that water fails to enter the root system but this is a rare phenomena which occurs as a result of excessive fertiliser applications.

Composts usually have both an active acidity and a reserve capability, ie not only does the pH level vary but so does the amount of latent acidity which the composts contain. This means that different composts have different lime requirements, particularly those with a high peat content.

Liquid phase

With a conventional soil the irregular shaped inorganic particles do not fit closely together and so give voids. The organic materials used in composts have a natural sponginess which ensures the presence of pores which contain air and/or water. A film of water is attached to the constituents of the compost by molecular attraction and as this is lost it is replaced by air. As a saturated substrate drains, the film of water around each particle is reduced in thickness and the attraction between the remaining water and the compost is increased. Ultimately an equilibrium is reached where the water ceases to move, and the substrate is then said to be at "field capacity", ie retaining its maximum amount of water, although even at "field capacity" a good compost should still contain at least 15% by volume of air. A plant in a compost at field capacity can absorb water with little effort but as the water content falls so its bond with the compost increases, and water uptake becomes more difficult. Eventually a point is reached where the attraction of the compost becomes so great that uptake ceases, with the result that the foliage wilts. The point at which this occurs is called the "permanent wilting point" and a plant taken beyond this point will not recover even when placed in a humid environment. With a good compost it is usual for 75 to 90% of the total available water to be removed before plant growth is seriously affected by moisture stress. Some of the remaining moisture is still available but there is a continued reduction in the rate of growth. From the above it follows that between "field capacity" and "permanent wilting point" there is water which the plant can abstract from the compost. The actual amount of water which is available depends upon the composition of the compost and is very variable, as can be seen from table 9.2. From this table it can be seen, for example, that sand has a lower maximum water content than clay, although it tends to be held with less tenacity. This means that the sand contains a smaller volume of water that is more readily available but quickly exhausted. A similar situation exists with organic materials, which usually have a high moisture retention capability. It has been found that the fastest growth is achieved with an open compost provided that the water content is frequently restored.

TABLE 9.2 SOME TYPICAL MOISTURE CONTENTS OF COMMON SUBSTRATE CONSTITUENTS

Material	Moisture content (% of total weight)		Available water (mm/m)
	Field capacity	Permanent wilting point	
Coarse sand	13	9	85
Sand	18	12	150
Loam	20	12	170
Clay	38	28	210
Peat	85	58	450
Leca	10	3	25

Gaseous phase

To maintain optimum growth rates all roots require a continuous supply of oxygen to respire carbohydrates and a flow of air to remove the waste gases produced by this process. The carbon dioxide level in the pore spaces of most composts is between 10 to 100 times higher than that in the surrounding air. The exact composition of the gas within a substrate is very variable and depends upon such factors as the compost formulation, the level of bacterial activity and the irrigation programme. Although much of the gaseous exchange occurs by simple diffusion, another important method is displacement when the substrate is flooded during irrigation. As the substrate drains, fresh air is drawn into the medium and soon saturated with water vapour.

Conclusion

It should be remembered that interior planting schemes are not natural and therefore have special problems of their own. The composts which are required for such schemes must be free draining because of the continual dangers of over watering. This danger is particularly pronounced at low light levels where transpiration has almost ceased. The low light levels also mean a reduction in the rate of growth so that the high nutrient levels required during production are no longer necessary or desirable. Such high nutrient levels can cause root damage and even drought symptoms due to the development of high osmotic pressures in the soil. This problem can be overcome by reducing the nutrient (but not the lime content) of a compost to be used in a dark location to at least a half, if not a third, of that which would be normal for a production situation.

BULK COMPOST MATERIALS – ORGANIC

Peat

Peat is by far the most widely used material for compost. In its raw state it is almost completely devoid of nutrients but has a high cation exchange capacity of up to four times that of clay. Peat is formed by the partial decomposition of plants growing in areas with high rainfall, high humidity and low summer temperatures. There are many sources of peat in Northern Europe and North America but unfortunately there is no standardised international method of classification available, although for horticultural purposes the following are accepted:

1 Sphagnum Sphagnum moss peats come from peat bogs and should consist of at least 75% of partially decomposed sphagnum moss. The leaves of the moss usually consist of a single layer of cells which gives them a high rate of water absorption and retention. The general characteristics of sphagnum peat is a spongy fibrous texture, a high porosity with high water retention, a low inorganic content and usually a low pH. Such peat deposits occur naturally in Germany, Canada and Ireland, and have similar properties to the hypnaceous moss peats of the USA.

2 Sedge These are formed mainly from sedges and reeds during the silting up of shallow lakes. As a result they typically hold more nutrients than sphagnum peats, have a higher CEC per unit weight, and are more humidified and decomposed. They have a lower porosity than sphagnum moss peats, a less durable structure and are particularly difficult to re-wet, although these problems can be overcome by careful management.

Shredded bark

The quantity of bark which is available for use in composts is considerable and increasing each year. It has the advantage that its rate of decomposition is about one third of that of peat. However, in certain cases it can suffer from nitrogen deficiency and the generation of toxic compounds, although these problems usually moderate after the first six months. To avoid problems of toxicity from compounds arising from natural resins and turpins, only those barks which are specifically marketed for composts should be used unless expert advice is sought. Most of the barks used in Britain are from larch and pine, whilst in North America douglas, red and white fir are common sources. The best barks have a loose open structure which provides good drainage, although in extreme cases this can reduce the volume of water available to the plants. For this reason bark should not be used as the main bulk constituent of a compost. When well decomposed, barks have a high CEC which can exceed that of peat.

Before bark can be used as a growth medium it requires composting with additions of nitrogenous fertiliser and superphosphate for about three months. Normally the bark of hardwoods will decompose more rapidly than that of softwoods with the result that 4 kg/m^3 of ammonium nitrate are needed to compost the former against 2 kg/m^3 for the latter. These are very high levels of free nitrogen which can be harmful to some plants, so the material should be stored for several months to ensure that the nitrogen is converted to an organic form. The bark can still be decomposing rapidly 160 days after preparation and during this period additional fertiliser may be required to prevent nitrogen deficiency. Most hardwood barks are acid, with pH values of 3.5 to 6.5. This can rise quite rapidly due to the high level of calcium which they contain naturally, although this is not always the case with softwoods.

BULK COMPOST MATERIALS – INORGANIC

Sand

Sand is an inert material with poor water retention which is frequently used to change the physical properties of a compost, eg to increase the rate of drainage. Sand also has a high bulk density of about 1600 kg/m^3 which can provide stability for larger plants. There are several established definitions available for sand but few relate to the formulation of composts. For such a use the recommendations on particle size have varied from 0.1–0.4 mm to 0.5–3.0 mm or more, although for long term interior planting the coarser grades are usually preferred. An important factor in the selection of a sand is to avoid any with a calcareous origin as they can raise the compost pH to an unacceptable level.

Clay

Powdered clay is still occasionally used to provide additional nutrient buffering in a compost. Where there is a high peat content its main function is to regulate the supply of phosphorus and minor elements. Being a powder the clay fraction can adversely reduce the pore size of the compost if it constitutes more than 10% of the total volume.

Loams

The main use for loams is in John Innes Compost where they provide a nutrient buffer and a supply of trace elements. Unfortunately natural loams are variable in composition and need selecting with care. Loams are a cheap raw material but normally require "partial sterilisation" before use to destroy the weed seeds which they contain. In most loam soils the inorganic particles occupy about half the total volume and have an organic content which varies from 1 to 5% of the total weight. The best material is a medium clay loam (20% clay) with a pH of 5.5 to 6.5 which has supported permanent pasture for at least five years. Before it can be used the loam should be lifted as 100 mm deep turves and stacked with animal manure for at least six months, after which the pH should be corrected to a minimum of 6.3.

BULK COMPOST MATERIALS – PROCESSED

Perlite

This is a natural alumina silicate which when crushed and heated to 1000°C expands to give a white, lightweight aggregate with a closed cellular structure. Perlite is stable, with a density of 130 kg/m^3 (8 lb/ft^3), a low water retaining capability and no CEC function. As a result it should only be used to "lighten" peat based composts.

Expanded polystyrene

In the production of raw polystyrene beads a foaming agent may be added, which is later activated by heating with steam, so that they expand to give soft spheres. Expanded polystyrene is a totally inert material with a closed cell structure which does not decompose. It seldom constitutes more than 25% of the total volume of a compost and is used primarily to reduce water retention.

Vermiculite

This is a complex metal silicate which is found naturally as a thin plate-like material called mica. The graded mineral is exfoliated by heating to 1000°C for one minute. This causes moisture trapped in the mineral to be converted to steam so that it expands to twenty times its former volume. In this form vermiculite has a high porosity, a good air/water relationship and a bulk density of 80 kg/m^3 (5 lb/cu. ft^3). It is available in a number of grades, the most common being 4–6 mm in diameter. It has a high CEC which compares with that of peat but over a year or two tends to collapse with a resultant loss of voids. Vermiculite from certain sources can contain magnesium limestone which will raise the pH of a compost and these should be avoided.

NUTRIENTS

Most of the bulk materials which are used in compost have a low nutrient content and some, like peat, also have a low pH value. As a result it is necessary to incorporate nutrients in the compost as well as those calcium compounds necessary to raise the pH. It is possible to correct a nutrient imbalance in a compost by the use of liquid feed but unfortunately this requires regular skilled labour, and so slow and controlled release fertilisers are now becoming popular.

Bulk fertilisers

There are many bulk fertilisers on the market and probably the main division within these is into organic and inorganic materials. The organic fertilisers are produced from natural animal and vegetable sources, and rely upon bacterial activity to make their nutrient content available to the plant. As the activity of bacteria is regulated by soil temperature their behaviour can be erratic in some situations. Inorganic sources are mined or produced artificially and have a more reliable performance, which makes them more desirable for use indoors.

Due to low growth conditions in buildings, fertilisers should be used at less than half the normal rate and a nitrogen, potassium and phosphorous mix (NPK) with a formulation ratio of 1:1:1 or 3:1:3 is probably best. The only need for caution with specific inorganic fertilisers is the use of superphosphate, as some plants are sensitive to the fluoride which is a by-product of its manufacturing process.

Slow-release fertilisers

These are usually organic based materials whose nutrient content is made available to plants as a result of bacterial activity. Consequently the availability of the nutrients is related to the prevailing temperature. Their mode of operation also means that the rate of nutrient release is initially high but declines with time. However, despite these limitations they are more efficient than inorganic fertilisers when used in situations which are prone to leaching.

TABLE 9.3 SOME COMMON CONTROLLED RELEASE FERTILISER FORMULATIONS.

Trade name	Constituents N .P .K	Formulation title	
Osmocote	15.12.15	3–4 month	regular
	18.11.11	3–4 month	high nitrogen
	40. 0. 0	3–4 month	nitrogen
	18.11.10	8–9 month	regular
	17.11.11	8–9 month	fast start
	38. 0. 0	8–9 month	nitrogen
	17.10.10	12–14 month	regular
Nutricote	16.10.10	100 day	
	13.13.11	140 day	
	43. 0. 0	180 day	
	16. 0.16	360 day	

There are several slow release fertilisers on the market, including such products as Vitax Q4 and Plantosan. Slow release nitrogen fertilisers such as Gold Nord SCU and Nutriform are available, but these are of little value for interior planting.

Controlled release fertilisers*

These are designed to extend the period over which nutrients are released into the compost and to do so in a controlled manner. There are many formulations available but the most common consist of a nutrient pellet coated with an acrylic or epoxy resin, or more recently a polyethylene skin. The coat is perforated and the osmotic potential across this layer causes moisture to be drawn into the pellet to displace the nutrient core. The rate of chemical release is controlled by temperature rather than pH or microbial activity and then slowly spreads into the substrate. This is useful as it means that release is limited when temperature and therefore plant growth rates are low.

Probably the best known formulation is Osmocote which is available in a range of analyses. A more recent product is Nutricote, which employs an accurately perforated polyethylene skin to effect control (table 9.3).

Fritted trace elements

An important source of trace elements are the impurities in fertilisers and irrigation water. The actual amounts are very variable and so it is difficult to quantify the value of these sources. One of the main difficulties with supplying additional micro nutrients is the narrow limit between deficiency and toxicity. Any application must be accurate, incorporation thorough, and any subsequent additions undertaken with care.

Micro nutrients are best added as fritted trace elements (FTE) or frits which are formed by heating sodium silicate and the desired salts together at 1000°C. The molten material is then poured into water where it cools and shatters before being ground into a fine powder. This fine chemical impregnated "glass" then slowly "dissolves" into the compost and releases the entrapped chemicals. There are many types of FTE available but the most widely used is:

FTE 253A – 2% B 2% Cu 12% Fe 5% Mn 0.13% Mo 4% Zn

Another formulation for plants which are sensitive to high boron levels and require more copper and molybdenum is:

WM 255 – 1% B 4.3% Cu 13.8% Fe 5.4% Mn 1% Mo 4.3% Zn

Potassium frits are also available to provide a long term source of free potassium.

* The author wishes to thank Mr L. Lane, Hasin Marketing Ltd, Princes Risborough, Bucks., for his technical assistance.

Chelated micro elements

If there are problems with micro elements becoming bound in the compost it is possible to produce the element mixed with another chemical which safeguards its integrity. Several materials are available for this purpose, such as naturally occurring citrate and tartaric acids, and synthetic ones based on polyamino polycarboxylic acid. Their main value is to prevent a deficiency of iron, although they can be used to reduce the toxic effect of copper, zinc and manganese. Two of the best known formulations are Librel and Sequestrine which are usually applied at a rate of up to 100 g/m^3.

pH MODIFICATION

The best composts for plant growth have a pH value of 5.5 to 6.5. Unfortunately this level is seldom achieved naturally and so it is necessary to modify pH by the addition of other materials. The usual problem is raising the pH, for which purpose one of the following compounds may be used:

1 *Calcium hydroxide* – slaked lime is not generally used, and any compost which contains this material should not be used for at least one week after mixing due to its "harshness"

2 *Calcium carbonate* – chalk or ground limestone. Due to their stable nature this group of materials provide a long term benefit.

The actual amount of these materials required to correct a compost pH should be determined empirically but an approximate rate is indicated in table 9.4. Dolomite limestone should always be used with plants that have an aversion to fluoride, as the calcium from this source bonds more freely with the fluoride to render it harmless.

If the pH of the compost should rise excessively due to the use of hard water it may be reduced by fertilising with ammonium sulphate or ammonium nitrate. Should these prove to be inadequate then ferrous sulphate may be used. These are drastic procedures and should be used with extreme caution.

TABLE 9.4 THE APPROXIMATE TIME REQUIREMENTS OF COMMON PEAT BASED COMPOST FORMULATIONS

Compost	Lime required to raise pH by 1 unit*
75% Finnish sphagnum peat 25% fine sand	0.9 kg/m^3 (1 lb 8 oz/yd^3)
75% Irish sphagnum peat 25% fine sand	1.1 kg/m^3 (1 lb 14 oz/yd^3)
75% English sphagnum peat 25% fine sand	2 kg/m^3 (3 lb 6 oz/yd^3)
75% English sedge peat 25% fine sand	2 kg/m^3 (3 lb 6 oz/yd^3)

* Assuming equal quantities of calcium carbonate and dolomite limestone (calcium magnesium limestone)

MIXING

For ease of operation it is normal to measure the bulk components of a compost by volume and the chemical component by weight. Such a policy is quite acceptable but means that the chemical content of one compost is unlikely to be suitable for another combination of bulk constituents. To ensure the complete incorporation of the minor ingredients the compost should be mixed dry and then wetted. The mixing time should always be sufficient to permit complete incorporation without pulverising the coarser ingredients.

The mixing of composts can be a laborious and time consuming operation. For small quantities (under 1 m^3) it is possible to mix the compost by hand on site. For greater volumes a clean concrete mixer which has not been used with cement or lime can be used. For extended operations there are several compost mixing machines now on the market which rapidly process batches of 1 m^3 or more. The characteristics of some common mixing techniques are described in table 9.5.

TABLE 9.5 THE CHARACTERISTICS OF SOME COMMON TECHNIQUES FOR MIXING COMPOST

	Volume per load	Time to mix one load	Mixing rate per hour	Order of material loading	Level of ingredient damage
1 Custom built mixers (eg Adelphi)	1 m^3	10 min	6.0 m^3	Any order	Moderate
2 Hand mixing	1 m^3	2 h	0.5 m^3	In layers	Low
3 Manure spreader	2 m^3	2 h	1.0 m^3	In layers	High
4 Small concrete mixer*	0.15 m^3	12 min	0.75 m^3	As sub unit of total amount	Low
5 Medium concrete mixer*	0.5 m^3	20 min	1.50 m		Low
6 Large concrete mixer*	4.0 m^3	1 h	4 m^3		Low

* Concrete mixers should always be clean to avoid contamination with lime and cement

STERILISATION

A planting scheme will always be more successful if any substrate which is used is free from weeds and pathogens. With most modern compost formulations it is seldom necessary to sterilise unless materials are stored outside for a long time. When topsoil is used there will always be an infestation of weeds and occasionally pests and disease organisms. Many techniques are used to sterilise soil, such as steam, steam-air mixtures, flame pasteurising, and chemicals. Steam has the advantage that it can be used under almost any conditions whereas chemical fumigants function slowly at temperatures below 15°C and are usually inappropriate below 12°C. Most of these techniques do not eliminate all organisms and so are referred to as "partial sterilisation". Of the techniques available those which are most widely used are described below.

Steam

Probably the best technique for "partial sterilisation" is to pass steam through a compost to raise its temperature to at least 85°C for at least 30 minutes. Low pressure steam is normally used, which condenses when it enters the compost and raises the temperature to 100°C. Steam and air mixtures are now becoming more popular as the air carries the steam rapidly through the compost with a saving in time and energy. Some soil pathogens are not killed until temperatures of 125°C have been reached, and so the process is only partially effective, although all weed seeds will be destroyed.

The only difficulty with steam sterilisation is that certain organisms (Actinomycetes) which release ammonia from organic nitrogen survive, whilst those which should convert the ammonia to nitrates (Nitrosomonas and Nitrobacter) do not. As a result toxic concentrations of ammonia can develop after one or two weeks. For this reason no form of nitrogen, and especially organic sources, should be added until after pasteurisation. A similar toxicity problem can occur with other materials, like phosphate, potash, zinc and copper, which become more soluble with heating but can be overcome by heavy leaching before use.

Chemical fumigants

These are volatile chemicals which diffuse through a compost and destroy pests. They are usually more active against insects and weed seeds than pathogenic fungi, such as Verticillium, Fusarium and Rhizoctonia. The treatment period for most chemical fumigants is from one to three days and must be followed by an aeration period of two to fourteen days. The only real problem with chemical fumigants is that they can be harmful to plants and people if used incorrectly.

Chloropicrin

This is a form of tear gas and so can be easily detected by smell. The liquid is applied to a loose compost at a rate of 100 cm^3/m^3, and to a large mass by pouring 4 cm^3 of chemical into 150 mm deep holes at 300 mm centres. The compost is then covered for two to three days, before being aerated for 10 to 14 days.

Methyl bromide

This is an odourless and colourless gas which is harmful to all fungi, insects and weed seeds. It is extremely effective but is harmful to people and should only be applied by a licensed contractor. The liquefied gas is pumped into compost at a rate of 0.5 kg/m^3 or 1 $kg/10m^3$, and the compost is then covered by a polythene sheet. After four to five days the polythene is removed and the compost ventilated for four to ten days to allow the gas to vaporise.

COMPOST MIXES

The following mixes are all in widespread use and the nutrient concentrations are given at the normal rate. For interior use the fertiliser rates should be reduced to at least half, if not a quarter, of those given below. Any of these mixes will be ready for immediate use or can be stored indefinitely. The quantities of ground limestone and Dolomite limestone which are specified throughout are based upon the lime requirement of Irish sphagnum peat. If a peat with different lime requirement is used the amount of liming material must be varied accordingly. The moistening of dry peats can be difficult even when wetting agents have been added, so materials such as sand are useful to facilitate this process. It should be remembered that the following formulations have been designed for annual or biannual commercial cropping programmes and should be selected with care for long term interior use.

Improved soil mixes

The following mixes are based on natural loam soils.

Heavy soils: clay or clay loam	20% by volume clay/loam 40% by volume sphagnum peat 40% by volume horticultural perlite
Medium Soils: silt loam or sandy clay loam	33% by volume silt/loam 33% by volume sphagnum peat 33% by volume horticultural perlite
Light Soils: sandy loams	50% by volume sandy loam 50% by volume sphagnum peat

To this mix add

	Per cubic metre	Per cubic yard
John Innes Base*	2.0 kg	3 lb 8 oz
Ground limestone†	2.4 kg	4 lb 0 oz
Dolomite limestone†	2.4 kg	4 lb 0 oz
Superphosphate	1.5 kg	2 lb 8 oz
Fritted trace elements FTE 253A	0.2 kg	6 oz

* This material can be replaced by Osmocote 17:10:10 Regular or Nutricote 16:10:10 360 day at 1.5 kg/m^3 (2 lb 8 oz/yd^3)

† For interior plants the medium should be acid. If the loam has a high pH, calcium sulphate (gypsum) should be substituted for the ground limestone.

John Innes compost

This is a loam based potting compost.
60% by volume loam
25% by volume sphagnum peat
15% by volume sand and grit (lime free up to 3 mm).
To this mix add:

	Per cubic metre	Per cubic yard
1 Hoof and Horn*	1.2 kg	2 lb 0 oz
2 Superphosphate	1.2 kg	2 lb 0 oz
3 Potassium sulphate*	0.6 kg	1 lb 0 oz
4 Calcium carbonate	0.6 kg	1 lb 0 oz

* These materials may be replaced by Osmocote 17:10:10 Regular or Nutricote 16:10:10 Regular at 1.2 kg/m³ (2 lb/yd³) and FTE 253A at 0.2 kg/m³ (6 oz/yd³)

Items 1, 2 and 3 may be purchased ready mixed as "John Innes Base" Fertiliser.

Note: For a higher nutrient regime the base fertiliser rates can be doubled or trebled although this is not necessary for interior planting.

GCRI potting compost II

The following mix is a general peat based compost.
75% by volume sphagnum peat
25% by volume fine sand (lime free)
To this mix add:

	Per cubic metre	Per cubic yard
Urea formaldehyde*	0.5 kg	1 lb 0 oz
Superphosphate	1.5 kg	2 lb 10 oz
Potassium nitrate*	0.75 kg	1 lb 5 oz
Ground limestone	2.25 kg	4 lb 0 oz
Dolomite limestone	2.25 kg	4 lb 0 oz
Fritted trace elements WM 255	0.375 kg	10 oz

* These materials can be replaced with Osmocote 17:10:10 Regular or Nutricote 16:10:10 360 day at 3.3 kg/m³ (5 lb 8 oz/yd³)

The University of California system

At the University of California a complete range of composts were formulated which are based on either sand or peat, or a mixture of both. There are five possible bulk mixes to which can be added one of six base fertilisers. In theory this gives a possibility of thirty different composts, although few are in regular use and the following are probably the most common.

U. C. Mix C
50% by volume peat moss
50% by volume fine sand (lime free 0.1 to 0.4 mm).
To this mix add fertiliser II (C): with both organic and inorganic nitrogen.

	Per cubic metre	Per cubic yard
Hoof and horn*	1.5 kg	2 lb 8 oz
Potassium nitrate*	0.15 kg	4 oz
Potassium sulphate*	0.15 kg	4 oz
Single superphosphate	1.5 kg	2 lb 8 oz
Dolomite limestone	4.5 kg	7 lb 8 oz
Calcium carbonate	1.5 kg	2 lb 8 oz

* These materials can be replaced with Osmocote 17:10:10 Regular or Nutricote 16:10:10 360 day at 2.4 kg/m³ (4 lb/yd³) and FTE 253A at 0.3 kg/m³ (8 oz/yd³)

UC Mix D
75% by volume peat moss
25% by volume fine sand (lime free 0.1 to 0.4 mm).
To this mix add either fertiliser I (D) or fertiliser II (D).

Fertiliser I (D): low inorganic nitrogen mix

	Per cubic metre	Per cubic yard
Potassium nitrate*	0.15 kg	4 oz
Potassium sulphate*	0.15 kg	4 oz
Superphosphate*	1.2 kg	2 lb 0 oz
Dolomite limestone	3.0 kg	5 lb 0 oz
Calcium carbonate	2.4 kg	4 lb 0 oz
* These materials can be replaced with		
Osmocote 17:10:10 Regular, or Nutricote 16:10:10 360 day	0.6 kg	1 lb 0 oz
FTE 253A	0.15 kg	4 oz
Superphosphate	0.6 kg	1 lb 0 oz

Fertiliser II (D): both organic or inorganic nitrogen

	Per cubic metre	Per cubic yard
Hoof and horn*	1.5 kg	2 lb 8 oz
Potassium nitrate*	0.15 kg	4 oz
Potassium sulphate*	0.15 kg	4 oz
Superphosphate	1.2 kg	2 lb 0 oz
Dolomite limestone	3.0 kg	5 lb 0 oz
Calcium carbonate	1.2 kg	2 lb 0 oz
* These materials can be replaced with		
Osmocote 17:10:10 Regular, or Nutricote 16:10:10 360 day	1.5 kg	2 lb 8 oz
FTE 253A	0.15 kg	4 oz
Superphosphate	0.6 kg	1 lb 0 oz

Cornell potting composts

House plant mix

A high moisture retention compost suitable for *Cissus spp*, Ferns, *Ficus spp*, *Hedera spp*, *Sansevieria spp*, etc.
50% by volume sphagnum peat
25% by volume Vermiculite (No. 2 grade)
25% by volume Perlite (medium grade).
To this mix add:

	Per cubic metre	Per cubic yard
Potassium nitrate*	0.6 kg	1 lb 0 oz
Superphosphate	1.2 kg	2 lb 0 oz
10:10:10 fertiliser*	1.6 kg	2 lb 12 oz
Dolomite limestone	4.9 kg	8 lb 4 oz
Iron sulphate	0.4 kg	12 oz
Fritted trace elements	0.07 kg	2 oz

* These materials can be replaced by Osmocote 17:10:10 Regular or Nitricote 16:10:10 360 day at 1.6 kg/m³ (4 lb 8 oz/yd³)

Epiphyte mix

A well drained compost, this mix is suitable for *Bromeliad spp*, cacti, *Dieffenbachia spp*, *Philodendron spp*, *peperomia spp*, etc.
33% by volume sphagnum peat (screened 12 mm mesh)
33% by volume pine, larch or douglas, red or white fir bark (3–6 mm)
33% by volume Perlite (medium grade)

To this mix add:

	Per cubic metre	Per cubic yard
Potassium nitrate*	0.6 kg	1 lb 0 oz
Superphosphate	2.7 kg	4 lb 8 oz
10:10:10 fertiliser*	1.5 kg	2 lb 8 oz
Dolomite limestone	4.2 kg	7 lb 0 oz
Iron sulphate	0.3 kg	8 oz
Fritted trace elements	0.07 kg	2 oz

* These materials can be replaced by Osmocote 17:10:10 Regular or Nutricote 16:10:10 360 day at 2 kg/m³ (4 lb 8 oz/yd³)

10 Hydroculture

INTRODUCTION

Hydroponics or water culture has been practised for over three centuries, but mainly as a research technique. Recent technical developments have produced a form of hydroponics, called hydroculture, for use with interior plants. The main benefit of the system is that the frequency of maintenance required by the plants can be drastically reduced. The plants are grown in an inert supporting medium whilst deriving their water and nutrients from a solution in the base of the container (fig 10.1).

Although a range of support materials is available, including Perlite, lytag and gravel, the most popular is leca (lightweight expanded clay aggregate). This is produced by rolling small clay pellets in a rotary kiln at temperatures up to 1200°C. The heat causes the moisture in the clay to vaporise and so produce an open honeycomb structure which is baked by further heating. The pale brown granules are screened to remove waste debris produced during the manufacturing process. For hydroculture any fine debris is removed by passing over a 5 mm mesh; and occasionally, to produce a more uniform product, that material which passes over a 15 mm mesh is also removed. Smaller grades of Leca, the most popular form of which is called Agrex, are used to assist root development in smaller plants. Leca granules have a closed cell composition and therefore do not absorb water; the result is a low bulk density even after soaking in water. Moisture is able to move round the granules by surface tension whilst the large voids between the leca are filled with saturated air. The high levels of relatively oxygen rich saturated air in the substrate is probably one of the major factors contributing to the success of this technique.

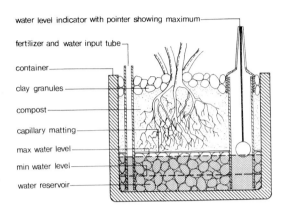

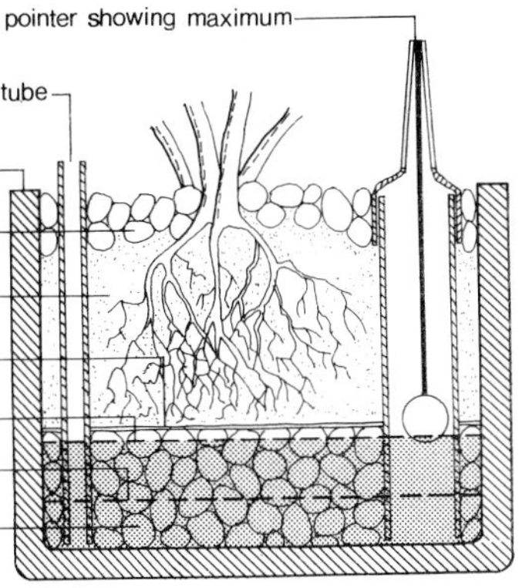

10.1 *Diagram of a hydroculture planting system*

PLANT PRODUCTION

Plants can be grown in hydroculture from the earliest stage by germinating seeds or rooting cuttings in loose open materials like Perlite, grit or cubes of polyurethane foam. The rooted cuttings are then placed with leca into special plastic pots which have slitted or mesh sides to allow for the circulation of the hydroculture nutrient solution. However it is still common for traditional compost grown plants to be converted to hydroculture by washing the compost from the roots and repotting them in leca (fig 10.3). The conversion process is a rapid way of obtaining large plants in hydroculture but in some cases the failure rate can be significant, eg with large specimens of *Ficus spp.* and *Yucca spp.*, the failure rate is usually in the order of 5%. This is usually due to the damage which is done to the root system during the conversion process and the subsequent need of the plant to replace this tissue. The new roots which develop are invariably fleshy and light in colour due to the clean open material through which they are growing, ie there is less requirement for mechanical penetration than with a compost. It has also been noted that some species develop a better root system if light is totally excluded from the support medium, so that with mesh pots additional screening can be beneficial.

The advantages of producing plants in hydroculture from the earliest stage are the simplicity of production management and the increased range of plants which can be grown successfully. This is important as several species such as *Codiaeum variegatum* do not grow rapidly after conversion.

Growing on

After planting the pots are usually placed in raised troughs which are lined with polyethylene sheets or assembled from precast concrete units (fig 10.4). The troughs contain about 50 mm of water which is usually circulated by pumps to aerate and mix the nutrient solution, as well as sometimes operating the water level control mechanism (fig 10.5).

It has been found that the roots of certain species develop both above and below the water level whilst others will not develop roots in standing water. The various root systems often appear to have zones with different functions and oxygen demands. Due to this differentiation care should be taken to ensure that, when a plant is placed in its final display location, the maximum water level is not above that which was experienced during production. Fortunately it would appear that roots which are deeply submerged during production show no distress should they be above or below the fluctuating water levels when in a display container.

The development of submerged roots in the nutrient solution can be restricted by the low insolubility of oxygen, with its maximum of 8 ppm (by weight). Research has shown that growth is optimised at twice this level which demonstrates the potential advantage of aerating the solution. It is generally acknowledged that jetting the circulated nutrient solution back into the production troughs can stimulate root growth in some species by up to 20%. Such an expensive procedure is not always necessary as root development in many species is sufficiently rapid without the benefits of aerated water.

10.2 *The stages in converting a plant to hydroculture:* **a**, *surplus compost is shaken off;* **b**, *any remaining compost is washed off;* **c**, *the clean root system is tidied up*

10.3 *Final stage: roots are shaken down with leca into a mesh pot*

10.4 *The plants are often produced in raised troughs lined with polyethylene. Hydro bv, Malden*

10.5 *Some companies use concrete troughs in which the nutrient solution is circulated by pumps. Thomas Rochford Ltd.*

Nutrition

The basic nutrient requirements of plants were established over a century ago. Improvements have come through the recognition of various minor elements essential for growth, and techniques for their preparation in a readily assimilable form. The administration of nutrients has been simplified by the realisation that plants can be grown successfully in a solution where fertility is maintained as a consequence of controlling the pH and overall conductivity by introductions from a stock solution. It has also been found that growth is not greatly suppressed even when concentrations of nitrogen fall as low as 10 ppm presumably because of the very limited diffusion shell around the roots. The upper nutrient solution concentration is limited by osmotic effects at 1.5 atmospheres, beyond which plant growth is reduced. A balanced nutrient solution can be produced from pure chemicals to the formula described in table 10.1. For simplicity, in commercial production units the nutrients are often supplied in the form of dilute foliar feeds. For example, Thomas Rochford Ltd use Poliverdol diluted at 1:5000 with Iron Sequestrene to correct for an apparent lack of iron. There is some suspicion that additional magnesium may also be necessary as this element is difficult to include in foliar feeds. As the nutrient balance within the solution is disturbed by preferential absorption it becomes necessary to analyse the solution and correct for specific shortcomings. Even so it is common to replace the whole nutrient solution every four to six weeks. If the plants are only being converted the nutrients can be supplied by ion exchange fertilisers although this is an expensive alternative.

TABLE 10.1 A FORMULATION FOR A NUTRIENT SOLUTION BASED ON WORK UNDERTAKEN AT THE UNIVERSITY OF CALIFORNIA

	Chemical source	Stock solution (per litre)	Stock solution dilution rate	Final concentration (ppm)
Macronutrients	Monobasic potassium phosphate (KH_2PO_4)	136 g	1:1000	136
	Potassium nitrate (KNO_3)	101 g	5:1000	505
	Calcium nitrate ($Ca(NO_3)_2 \cdot 4H_2O$)	236 g	5:1000	1180
	Magnesium sulphate ($MgSO_4\ 7H_2O$)	247 g	2:1000	494
Trace elements	Iron chelates (10% Fe)	20 g	4:1000	80
	Boric Acid $H_3B\ O_3$	2.86 g	1:1000	2.86
	Manganese $MnCl_2 \cdot 4H_2O$	1.81 g	1:1000	1.81
	Zinc sulphate $ZnSO_4 \cdot 7H_2O$	0.22 g	1:1000	0.22
	Copper sulphate $CuSO_4 \cdot 5H_2O$	0.08 g	1:1000	0.08
	Sodium molybdate $Na_2MoO_4 \cdot 2H_2O$	0.27 g	1:1000	0.027

For large installations in dry conditions there is a need to make good the water lost from the nutrient solution by evapotranspiration. This can cause problems due to the possible accumulation in the water supply of contaminants such as sodium chloride. pH does not appear to be very critical but should be monitored to ensure that there is no precipitation of calcium phosphate which could block plumbing or coat roots.

Pest and disease

One advantage of hydroculture is that the support medium is reasonably sterile. Although diseases do appear, little information is available on their epidemiology as few cases of root infection have been studied. All the normal pathogenic bacteria appear to function, although their rate of spread appears to be slow and their damage is seldom severe.

In the absence of clay or organic matter, which usually "fix" soil applied pesticides, low concentrations in the nutrient solution can be most effective against insects which suck sap directly from the vascular system, and in some cases a full strength application can be phytotoxic. Chemicals may be effective against aphids at concentrations as low as 10 ppm, although much higher levels are necessary for red spider and white fly. In practice the concentration of systemic drenches can be reduced to 20% or even 10% of the normal rate for most pests and 3% for aphids.

DISPLAY

When the plants are ready for use they are transferred to an ornamental planter which already contains leca up to the minimum water level. This reduces the possibility of asphyxiating the established root system by permanently flooding the base of the production container. The surrounding void in the planter is then filled with leca. If a planter is to be moved to a display location it is usual to minimise the weight by omitting the nutrient solution until after installation. The water level within the container is usually monitored by a float and pointer, and allowed to fluctuate between the maximum and minimum levels supposedly to encourage good root development (fig 10.6 & 10.7 & 10.8). The real significance of this procedure is probably to ensure that the root systems of those plants which fail to develop below the water level are coated with nutrients at regular intervals without becoming waterlogged. One major advantage of the hydroculture technique is that once the surface layer of leca has dried there is little tendency for more water to pass through this zone. This means that the rate of water loss from the surface of the substrate is about 20% of that from a moist compost, and so the only significant source of water loss from the system is by transpiration. This low rate of water loss results in a considerable decrease in the frequency of irrigation so that under normal interior conditions the water level needs to be restored every two to three weeks. The loss of water from the surface of the substrate can cause the formation of a white crystalline deposit on the leca at the surface but this is completely harmless and formed largely by halogens present in the water supply.

10.6 *The water level in the container is monitored by a float, whilst feed and water is normally introduced through a separate open-ended tube*

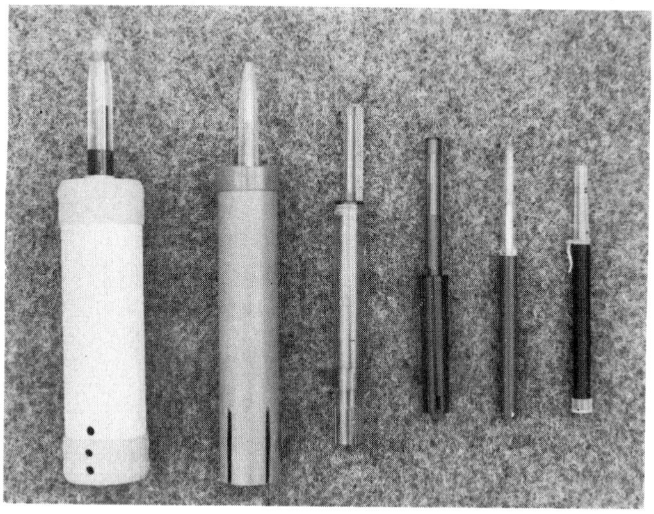

10.7 *There is a range of water level indicators available. The larger are for use in freestanding planters; the smaller for table top planters*

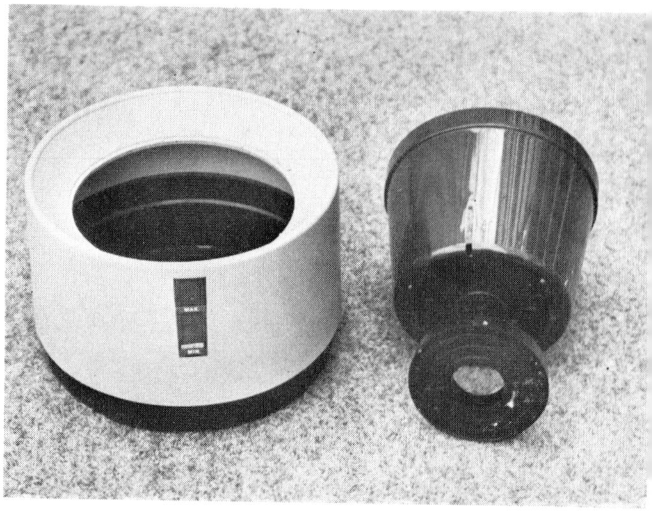

10.9 *Some small retail planters carry a removable cartridge which contains ion exchange fertiliser*

10.8 *Roots develop through the openings in the production containers and ramify through the planter*

Ion exchange fertilisers*

One of the main reasons why hydroculture is now available as a low maintenance system for interior landscape is the development of ion exchange fertilisers. These consist of a mass of small brown resin beads which contain plant nutrients. At present the only company which has successfully produced an ion exchange fertiliser is Bayer AG (W. Germany)*. The bulk of their sales is of a moist form called Lewatit HD5, which contains 50% water by weight to improve the physical properties of the resin. The moisture can cause it to aggregate so a dry form of the fertiliser called Lewatit HD5 R is now marketed specifically for reloading the special cartridges which fit in some small retail planters (fig 10.9).

The concept of an insoluble material which is capable of carrying ions that can be exchanged with others in the surrounding solution was appreciated in the last century. The modern ion exchange fertilisers are based on cross-linked

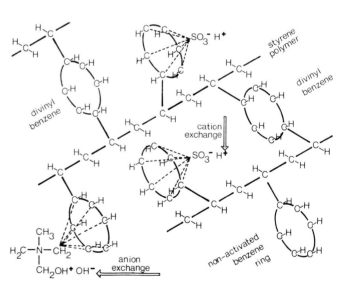

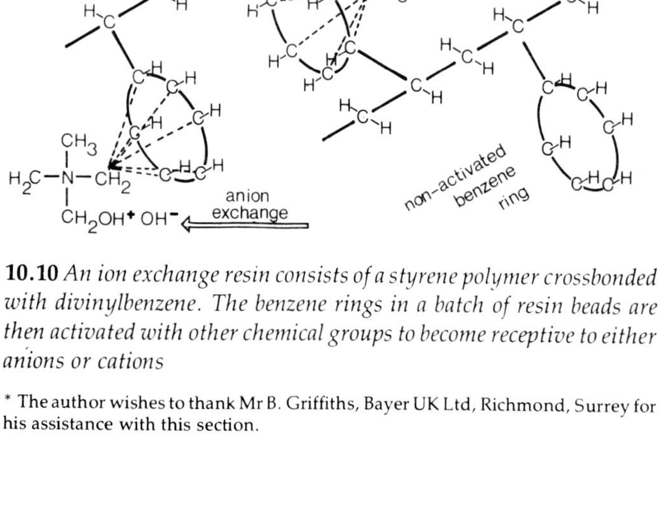

10.10 *An ion exchange resin consists of a styrene polymer crossbonded with divinylbenzene. The benzene rings in a batch of resin beads are then activated with other chemical groups to become receptive to either anions or cations*

* The author wishes to thank Mr B. Griffiths, Bayer UK Ltd, Richmond, Surrey for his assistance with this section.

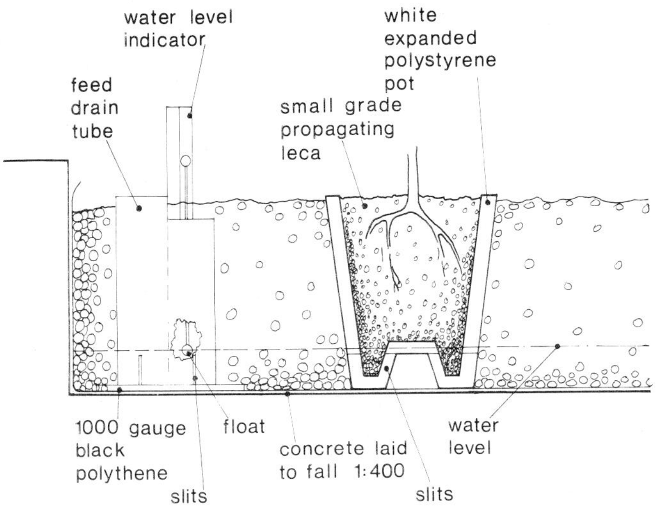

10.11 *The Luwasa system of hydroculture employs a combination water level indicator and a feed/drain tube*

polystyrenes produced by the addition of divinylbenzene to a styrene polymer (fig 10.10). The resin is manufactured to give a gel-like structure with pores in the order of 0.5 to 2 nm, which facilitate the entry of ions. For ease of production ion exchange fertilisers are retailed as a mixed bed, ie different samples of undercharged resin are placed into different charging solutions to become activated and mixed in the desired ratios before marketing.

Ion exchange is a self equilibrating process where the charge on the ions entering the resin equals the charge of the ions leaving. The selective coefficient of a particular ion is dependent on several factors such as the nature of the functional groups, the nature of the exchange ions and the non exchange ions, the form of the resin and the strength of the solution. Specific resins usually have a preference for a particular type of ion and establish an equilibrium with the surrounding solution. Any change in the concentration of the ions in solution will affect the concentration of the ions in the resin:

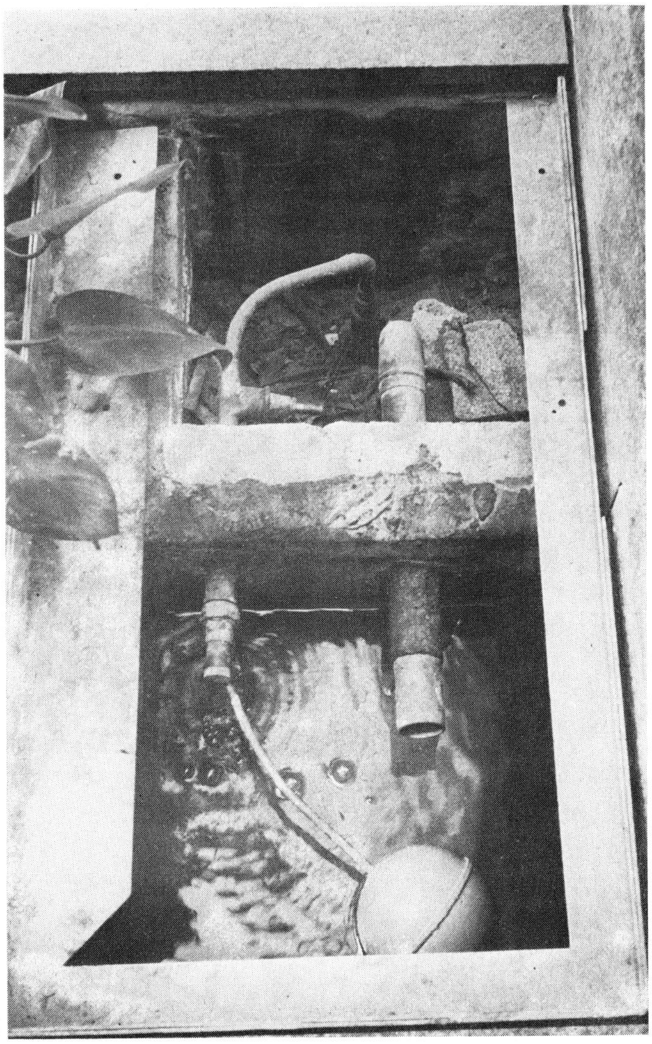

10.13 *A possible assembly of a small scale hydroculture circulation system*

10.12 *A conventional ball cock can provide water level control for a small hydroculture system as well as a site for a circulation pump*

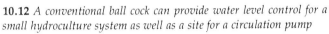

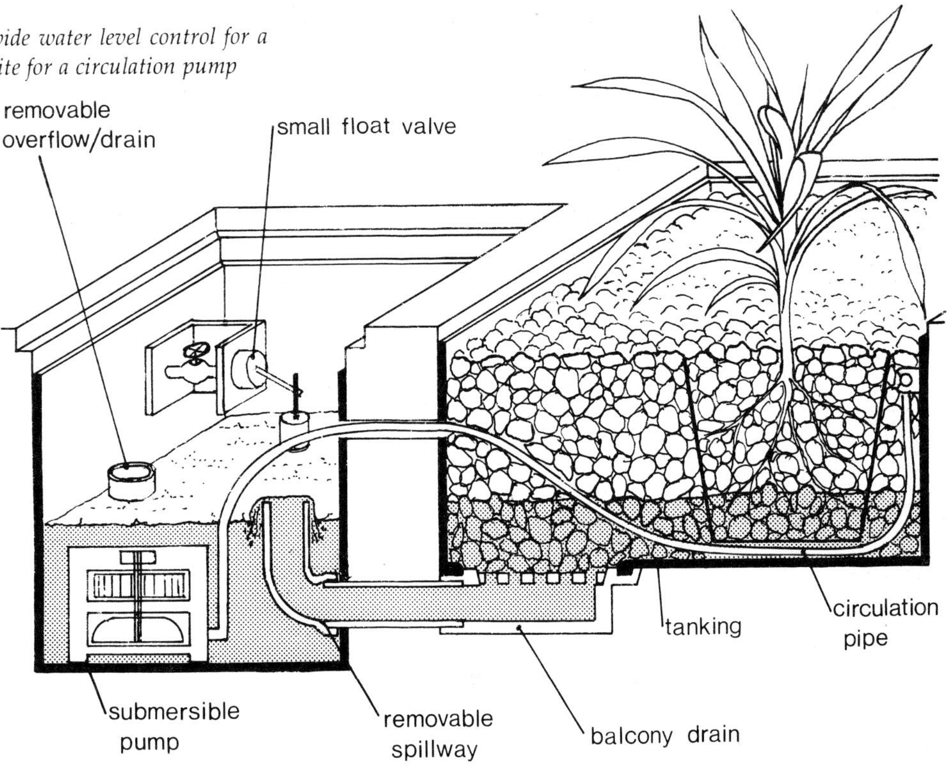

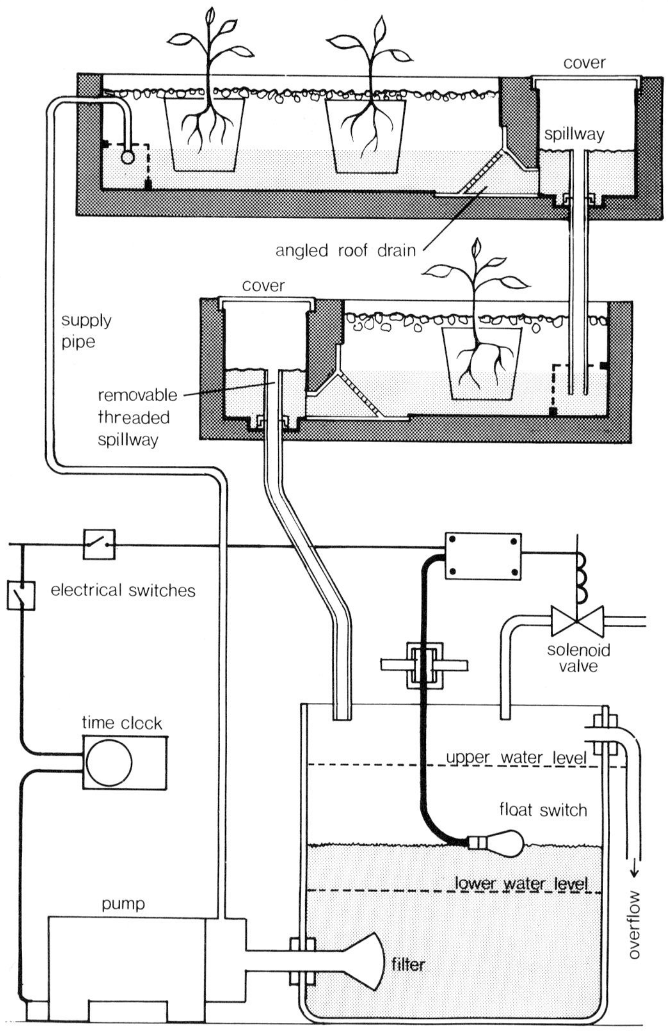

10.14 *A possible assembly of a large scale hydroculture circulation system*

$$K = \frac{\text{(Conc. of ion A in resin)} \times \text{(Conc. of ion B in solution)}}{\text{(Conc. of ion B in resin)} \times \text{(Conc. of ion A in solution)}}$$

When ion exchange fertilisers are added to a solution of tap water a relatively large number of ions pass from the resin into the solution in exchange for other ions present in the water, such as sodium and calcium. This means that at each watering there is a recharge of the ions in solution to re-establish an equilibrium with the resin. With very pure water it may prove necessary to add a small quantity of liquid feed to provide free ions to activate the process. As the level of useful salts in solution is reduced by the plant, so more passes from the resin to re-establish the equilibrium. It follows from this that as the reserve of useful ions within the resin falls so there must be a slow decline in the level of useful ions available in solution. Plant growth is then reduced until a deficiency of one of the nutrients becomes limiting and a further application of fertiliser becomes necessary.

The value of ion exchange fertilisers is considerable, although their effectiveness is due in the main to the ability of plants to function over a considerable range of nutrient concentrations. The main value claimed for the resin is to supply in a free ionic form certain plant nutrients that are relatively difficult to maintain in a long term nutrient solution. One disadvantage of ion exchange fertilisers is that at present they are expensive. Most ion exchange resins can be recharged when they are exhausted but it is unlikely that such a technique will be practical with a mixed bed fertiliser.

The rate of application is not critical but according to size each plant should receive from 25 to 30 cm^3 of Lewatit HD5 every six months. With large planters it is normal to give an initial application of 0.5 l/m^2 followed by a six monthly application of 0.15 l/m^2.

Luwasa (Hydroculture) Ltd do not normally use ion exchange fertilisers but supply nutrients in the form of a concentrate which is diluted to 1:1000 and poured into the planters. The solution level is then maintained in the normal hydroculture manner by the use of a floating indicator. As the system is not buffered by an ion exchange fertiliser it is necessary to empty the trough every six months, normally through the tube provided in the water level indicator (fig 10.11). A fresh liquid feed solution is then produced and poured into the planter.

AUTOMATIC HYDROCULTURE SYSTEMS

Small scale

The low maintenance requirement of a hydroculture system can be reduced still further by automating the control of the solution level. This can easily be done by the installation of a ball-cock into the end of the planter. However, due to their construction ball-cocks usually operate best when subjected to extreme fluctuations in water level. As a result when a simple single level trough is being automated it is best to have the pump unit linked closely with the ball-cock in a supply tank and separated from the trough by a spillway as shown in fig 10.13.

Large scale

A feature of large hydroculture systems is that it is often necessary to maintain the nutrient solution at different heights in a

10.15 *A large hydroculture system where the nutrient solution is pumped from a tank in the basement to return via a cascade (Alexander Howden House, London)*

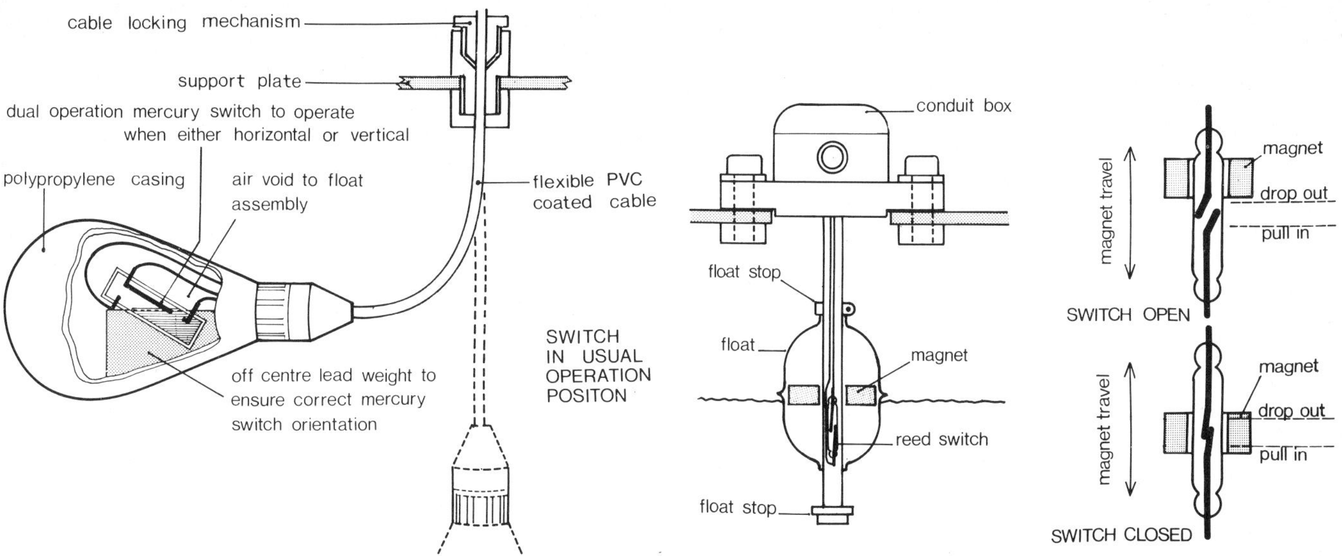

10.16 *Float switches can be used to regulate the water level in a large hydroculture reservoir: (left) a Flygt switch; (right) a Cobham float switch*

building. As a result it may be reasonable to employ pumps to achieve the necessary lift with a gravity cascade system for return (fig 10.14 and 10.15). Submersible pumps are proving to be of considerable advantage for this function due to their ease of installation.

Whenever it is necessary to pump water about a system it should be remembered that water under pressure will enter a system more rapidly than it can exit under gravity through a similar sized pipe. As a result it is recommended that the return pipe should be at least twice the diameter of the supply pipe.

When water is pumped to a trough and returned via a spillway a surcharge is produced due to surface tension effects. This retarding of the flow means that water will continue to leave the system for several minutes after the supply ceases. The depth of water so retained will depend upon the design of the spillway but can be assumed to be about 2 mm overall. There will also be a volume of water in the supply pipes which will fall back when pumping ceases. As a result of these factors it is important that adequate storage facilities be provided. The traditional technique of controlling water levels in the reservoir by a ball-cock is unsuitable for such systems as they cannot operate over the extreme fluctuations in water levels which are necessary for establishing circulation. The best solution for regulating the water level in such a situation is a float switch linked to solenoid valves on the water supply (fig 10.16).

11 Irrigation

by Philip Cooper and Stephen Scrivens*

INTRODUCTION

One of the most important factors regulating the growth and development of plants is the availability of water. With interior planting, light is usually the primary limiter, but erratic substrate moisture levels due to poor irrigation procedures, can reduce the rate of growth and may even result in death. There is, however, no need for this to occur as the technology exists for regulating substrate moisture levels. The information in this chapter covers the irrigation of plant substrates with particular reference to interior plantings.

WATER QUALITY

There should be few problems associated with the quality of water used for interior plant irrigation as it is usually derived from a mains supply. The continued use of very hard water can slowly raise the compost pH but this can be countered by the use of fertilisers which are acidic in operation, such as ammonium nitrate and ammonium sulphate. The only real hazard for interior planting is the high salt concentration (table 11.1) which can be produced when irrigation water evaporates and deposits chemicals. To avoid such problems the dissolved salt concentration should be under 200 ppm and never over 500 ppm. If the development of a salt level over 1000 ppm is inevitable the planter should be flushed by heavy watering every three months. To ensure that this procedure does not remove the nutrients from the compost a controlled release fertiliser should be used. Specific salts can affect different plants in different ways, eg *Dieffenbachia picta* can become chlorotic and dull when copper levels reach 8 ppm and zinc can reduce growth in most plants at concentrations over 30 ppm.

Fluoride is sometimes added to drinking water at concentrations of 1 ppm, although levels over 3 ppm are used in some areas. This fluoride can accumulate and cause damage in some species when tissue concentrations reach 15–100 ppm of dry matter although non sensitive plants can contain 200–400 ppm of dry matter without damage. This situation is aggravated by the use of superphosphate and perlite which both contain traces of fluoride. The more common symptoms of fluoride damage are "die back" from the leaf tip or dead patches on the main leaf blade. The more susceptible plants are indicated in the plant selection table. Fluoride damage can be reduced by aerating irrigation water, and avoiding the use of superphosphate and perlite. As fluoride is not easily leached the best remedial action is to replant damaged plants in a compost which is high in dolomite limestone to raise the compost pH to 6.0 to 6.5, under which conditions the calcium and fluoride react.

TABLE 11.1 TYPICAL SALT CONCENTRATIONS FOUND IN IRRIGATION WATER

Conductivity readings (milli mhos/cm³)	Total salt concentration (ppm)	Evaluation
Up to 0.25	Up to 175	Very good
0.25 to 0.75	175 to 500	Good
0.75 to 1.50	500 to 1000	Fair
1.50 plus	1000 plus	Poor

Water purification

Continuous irrigation with hard water can modify the pH of a substrate to the point where growth is modified. Similarly the cleaning of foliage by spraying with hard water can lead to the production of a white calcium deposit. To avoid these problems it is often advantageous to provide a soft water supply for a large scale planting. There are several purification systems available but most are unsuitable as they replace the calcium salts in the water with common salt which may then accumulate in the substrate. Probably the best technique for water purification is reverse osmosis but this is a comparatively slow and expensive process.

Water temperature

Irrigating a growth substrate with hot or cold water has a short term effect on substrate temperature with the greatest change occurring in the surface layers and decreasing with depth. If a substrate is completely moistened with either hot or cold water the change in substrate temperature is most pronounced for the first 40 minutes, after which it will have fallen to that of the surrounding environment (fig 11.1). Provided that such temperature fluctuations are less than 10 deg C there does not appear to be any serious long term effect, although a drastic reduction in root temperature can reduce absorption by the roots so that the plant may even wilt.

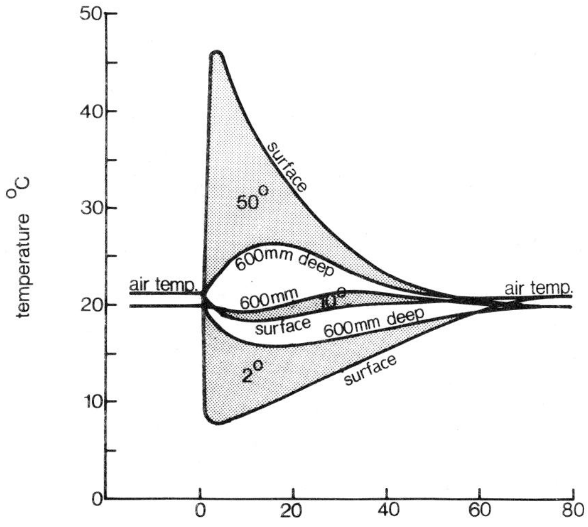

11.1 *Graph showing the limited effect of irrigation water temperature upon that of a peat based compost, at the surface and at a depth of 600 mm*

*Mr P. Cooper is with Irrigation Specialists, The Aerodrome, Wellesbourne, Stratford upon Avon

WATER LOSS

Water is lost from a planter by evaporation from the substrate and transpiration from the plants. In normal external situations the rate of water loss from a complete layer of vegetation is very similar to that from a moist compost, which in turn is similar to that from an open water surface. In the low light conditions which exist indoors the rate of loss from the foliage is minimal so that the largest single source of water loss is from the substrate. Evaporation from a wet compost will continue whilst the supply lasts and then the surface suddenly dries.

Water may be applied to a compost from above or below. Entry from below is often referred to incorrectly as capillarity and occurs as a result of surface tension lifting water round the substrate components. Entry from above is governed by the rate of infiltration and should water be applied faster than this rate run-off will occur. When water is applied to the surface of a compost it brings each successive layer to saturation before further downward movement occurs. Any attempt to moisten a compost "lightly" will only reduce the depth of penetration. The lower drier layers still exert a suction on the upper layers but further downward movement will not occur as there is no free water available. It is the suction from the lower layers which draws water uniformly through a substrate and this explains the very high moisture content which is produced when a saturated compost is suspended over a void, eg when a production container is stood on open gravel.

Estimation of water loss

The loss of water from both compost and plants will depend upon the difference in temperature between the system and the air, the relative humidity of the air and the ability of the system to donate water. In the open during bright sunlight the rate of water loss from a complete vegetation cover is equal to that of an open water surface. However, the main source of water loss from a plant is transpiration due to warming by radiant energy. The absence of such heating at night and variations in seasonal day length means that this simple theoretical relationship must be modified. The following modification factors are suitable for plants which are grown outside in a temperate climate, and give a rate of loss due to transpiration expressed as a percentage of the loss from an open water surface.

May to August	80%
September to October	70%
March to April	70%
November to March	60%

Unfortunately the loss of water from plants indoors is more complex and exceedingly difficult to predict because of the isolated nature of most interior planting and the variability of light levels. When plants are placed in low light situations the transpiration loss can be minimal, particularly as most interior plants have a thick cuticle. But the rate of loss from a moist compost is still similar to that from an open water surface, which is usually less than 1 mm per day.

The low rate of water consumption associated with planters fitted with reservoir based irrigation systems is due to their reliance on a surface tension lift through the body of the compost. This invariably fails after 150 mm so that the upper 50 mm of the planter is filled with dry compost which acts as an effective barrier to further water loss from below. A similar situation exists with hydroculture systems except that the open nature of the supporting medium results in a water loss amounting to about one fifth of that associated with an open water surface. When the transpiration and evaporation com-

11.2 *A wall-mounted reel offers a neat solution to pipe storage*

11.3 *A mains pressurised irrigation trolley*

ponents are considered together it is usually found that in a permanent shade situation the rate of water loss is often equivalent to be less than 1 mm per day over the area of the planter. In a bright situation where direct sunlight impinges on the foliage for even a small part of the day the loss can be four or five times this level.

HAND WATERING

It is almost inevitable that when plants are used in buildings there will be a need for some degree of hand watering. This is normally a highly labour intensive operation but it can be greatly reduced by the use of special equipment.

Where hand watering is necessary, suitable supply facilities should be provided as often as possible to reduce the carrying distance, and there should never be less than one water point per floor. Usually the best arrangement is a spacious cupboard containing a large deep sink with a hot and cold mixer tap. All hosepipes should have quick fit couplings and should carry a lance with a hand operated valve and a spray nozzle. In certain situations a wall mounted hose reel can offer a neat storage solution (fig 11.2).

Traditionally water has been carried in watering cans but there is a range of mobile water carriers which reduces the effort required to transport and administer water. These usually contain 50 to 100 gallons of water which is discharged by means of internal pneumatic pressure or an electric pump (fig 11.3).

INTEGRATED SYSTEMS DESIGN

When large scale plantings or planting in inaccessible localities are proposed consideration should be given to the installation of a comprehensive irrigation system. Fully automatic irrigation systems still meet resistance despite the technology and expertise which is now available but even a manually controlled system can offer a considerable reduction in labour input. The procedures for designing a fully or partially automatic system are relatively simple and are described below.

Water storage vessels

Due to the relatively limited water storage capability necessary for most interior planting it is reasonable to restrict the choice of storage vessels to uPVC tanks due to their durability and availability.

Filters

All water to be introduced to an irrigation system with fine apertures, eg drip nozzles, should be filtered to avoid blockages. There are many types of filters available, including elaborate back-flushing systems, but the most simple and efficient for interior planting are high pressure screen filters with pleated element cartridges (fig 11.4). High flow rates can be accommodated by installing several units in parallel. For very large flows sand and screen filters, or more complex self cleansing centrifuge separators, can be used. Filters should not restrict flow as this may result in a reduction in water pressure.

Pumps

In most building situations the existing water supply is adequate for operating an irrigation system, although in some cases it is necessary to pump from a storage tank or to boost mains pressure to achieve the desired flow characteristics. For ease of control the only pumps worth considering are electric centrifugal units, and these can be single stage end suction, vertical multi stage, or submersible. When a pump is installed it should be capable of fulfilling the following functions:

Delivery volume The quantity of water required is determined by the number of outlets and their individual emission rates.

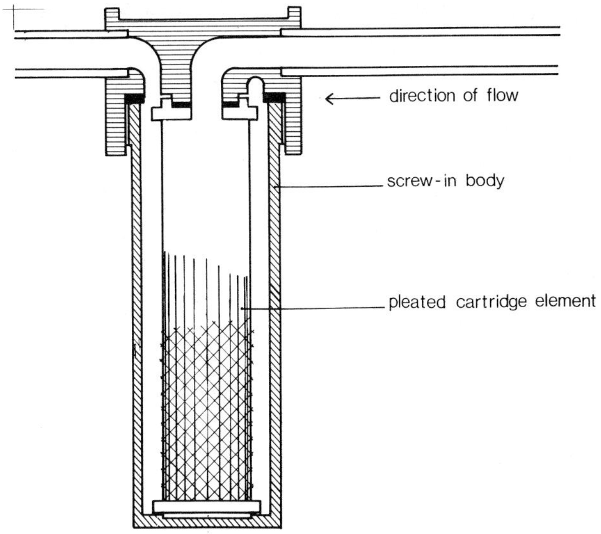

11.4 *A high pressure screen filter with pleated cartridge element*

Developing sufficient pressure head The developed head must be sufficient to convey water to the emitters with sufficient pressure to permit them to operate. The total pressure head must therefore allow for:

1 Any difference in level between the pump and the discharge points
2 Friction loss in the delivery network
3 Operating pressure in the delivery network
4 The suction head, ie the force needed to lift the water the vertical distance from the water surface to the centre of the pump impeller.

To reduce possible operating difficulties the suction head should be reduced to a minimum by installing pumps with the suction side flooded, ie with the pump unit below the water level, although with submersible pumps this factor does not arise. It is also important that the required quantity of water can enter the body of the pump if its full potential is to be realised.

If there are no problems with suction head then the following section may be omitted.

A pump will work satisfactorily up to a given height above the water level and then fail. The height at which this occurs is determined by two aspects of the pump's operation. The first is the resistance which has to be overcome to establish a stable flow through the supply pipe and into the impeller, and is called the Net Positive Suction Head (NPSH) Required. The second is the ability of the pump to donate water to the delivery point under pressure and is called the NPSH Available. The choice of pump and the method of installation must be reconciled so that the NPSH Required does not exceed the NPSH Available otherwise the pump will not work. Most pump manufacturers provide pump graphs which show the NPSH Required by a given pump at various flow rates, and the NPSH Available may be determined by the formula:

$$\text{NPSH Available} = ((P - Vp)\frac{0.7}{SG} \pm Hs) - Hf \text{ (metric)}$$

$$\text{or} = ((P - Vp)\frac{2.31}{SG} \pm Hs) - Hf \text{ (imperial)}$$

where P = Barometric pressure
Vp = Vapour pressure
SG = Specific gravity
Hs = Suction Lift
Hf = Friction loss in suction line

This can usually be simplified to
(9.75 ± Hs) − Hf (metric)
or (32 ± Hs) − Hf (imperial)

Pressure regulators

The pressure of water entering an irrigation scheme can be variable and so it is advisable to install pressure regulators to prevent the nozzles from blowing off. It is possible to effect an amount of control by the use of a partially closed valve, but this technique fails to compensate upwards when pressures are low. There are several pieces of equipment of varying complexity which can regulate pressure, but the most efficient usually rely upon a spring damped diaphragm to give a pressure control which is accurate to ± 10% (fig 11.5).

On steeply sloping sites or sites with different levels there may be irregular flow rates due to pressure differential and these can be overcome by flow rate controllers. The control of flow rates can be more easily achieved than pressure control by the use of a simple Dole Valve. This consists of a flexible rubber dish with an orifice at the centre whose dimensions vary in response to the pressure of the water which passes through it (fig 11.6). Such a unit is fitted at the start of the final distribution line to give a flow control which is accurate to ± 10%.

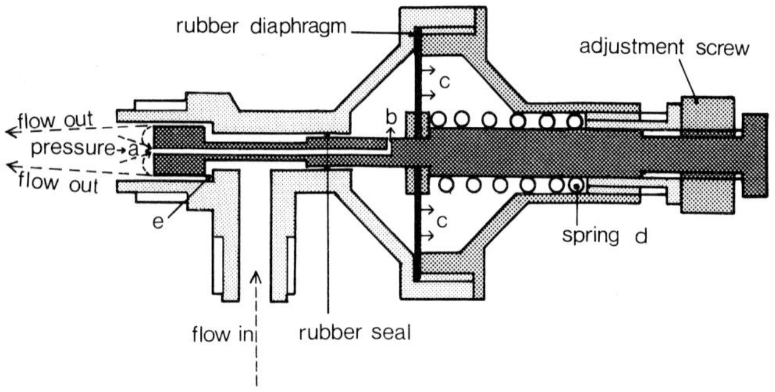

11.5 *A diaphram pressure regulator. The pressure of the water passing through the assembly is transferred through the pipe at (a) to the cavity at (b) where it moves the diaphram (c) against the spring (d) and so increases or decreases the gap at (e) depending upon the setting of the adjustment screw*

Pressure meters

The efficiency of an irrigation system is dependent upon the pressure under which it operates and so it is necessary to monitor the water pressure at at least one point in the system. For ease of adjustment the meter should be located immediately prior to the supply leaving the ancillary equipment housing. Where distribution pipes are to be located at different levels within a building it is desirable that the pressure should be monitored at each level so that adjustments can be made. The pressure meter itself does not need to be connected directly to the distribution pipe but can be attached remotely by a length of small bore tube.

System isolation

Water authorities will not always accept a situation where water in an irrigation system could in theory be drawn back into a mains water supply to pose a potential health risk. It is often suggested that the irrigation system should be separated from the mains supply by a header tank fitted with a ball cock, but this invariably reduces the water pressure in the system. For this reason the best technique for isolating a system is to install a non return valve (fig 11.7). Where possible these units should

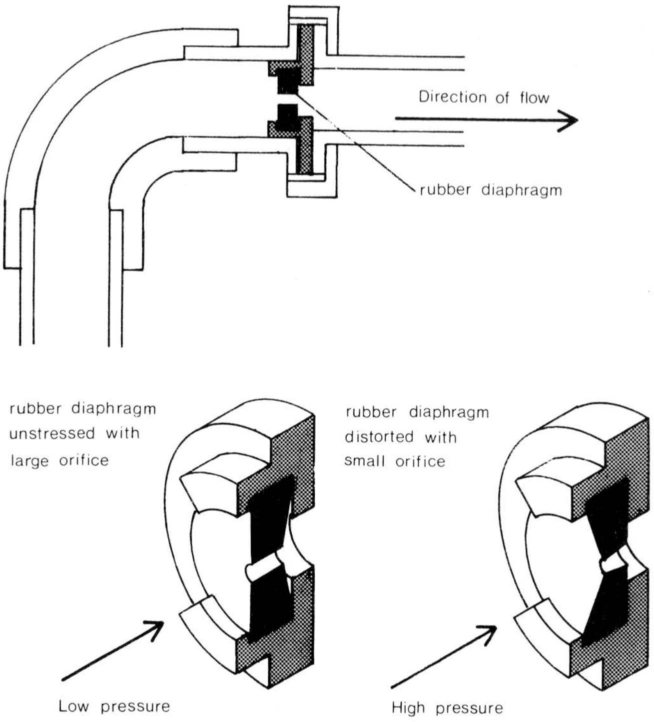

11.6 *A Dole flow regulating valve with its variable orifice*

be installed on the supply side of the irrigation control system and placed as low as possible as optimal performance is achieved when under load. Occasionally a poorly installed non return valve can exhibit poor flow characteristics but in general this approach offers the easiest method of isolating a system.

Diluters

If plants are to grow in compost for any length of time they will require small quantities of nutrient feed, which may be introduced from a diluter at the start of the system. The range of equipment is considerable and is able to process from 100 to 25 000 litres of feed per hour at dilutions between 1:25 to 1:2000, from a reservoir of 10 to 150 litres.

PIPE SELECTION

For durability and ease of installation most irrigation supply lines are composed of either black UV resistant polyethylene or rigid uPVC. Polyethylene pipe usually comes in rolls up to 100 m in length and can easily be turned through curves with a

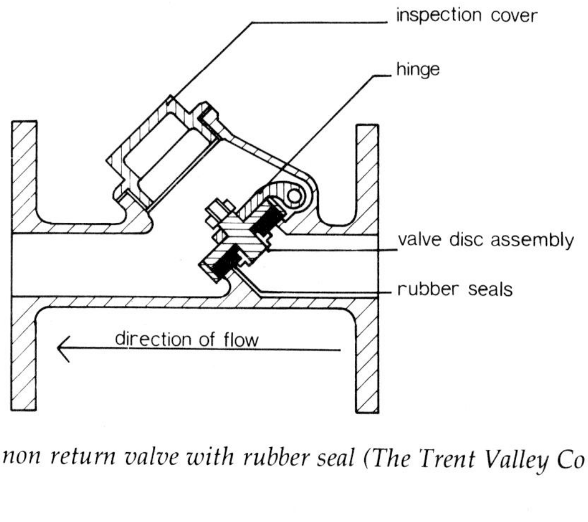

11.7 *A non return valve with rubber seal (The Trent Valley Co Ltd)*

radius as low as 500 mm without distortion. In contrast uPVC comes in lengths of 6 m and 9 m, and requires compatible fittings such as tees, bends, etc. It is usual for uPVC tubes over 25 mm in diameter to be socketted at one end, but pipes of less than this diameter have plain ends and are joined by separate junctions. Polyethylene pipes are usually joined with compression fittings of either gunmetal or plastic, whilst PVC pipes are cemented with special uPVC solvent cement after wiping with a cleaning fluid.

The pipe sizes associated with irrigation work range from 12 mm (½ in) to 75 mm (3 in). Pipes may be described by reference to their internal or external diameter according to the material, but when calculations are made on the capacity of a system it is the internal diameter which is of importance. As water passes through a pipe there is a pressure loss due to friction and the larger the flow through a given pipe size the greater will be this loss. The loss of pressure due to friction is most simply described as a loss of head measured in terms of metres per 100 m or feet per 100 ft (10.19 m head = 1 bar and 2.31 ft head = 1 psi). Other parts of the system such as bends, tees, etc., all contribute to the overall loss in pressure and are most easily covered by the addition value of 10% of the total pipe friction loss. The maximum drop in pressure in the supply pipe due to friction should not be more than 20% of the desired operating pressure with a mains supply, or 25% with a pumped supply. In the design of an irrigation system it is also necessary to avoid exceeding the maximum recommended flow velocity of 1.5 m/sec (5 ft/sec).

Using mains water

A simple method for determining pipe sizes to carry mains water of known pressure is to use a friction factor as determined in the following manner:

METRIC

$$\text{friction factor} = \frac{(\text{operating pressure} \times 10.19) \times \%\ \text{pressure variations (assume 20\%)}}{\text{length of pipe in 100 m units}}$$

IMPERIAL

$$\text{friction factor} = \frac{(\text{operating pressure} \times 2.31) \times \%\ \text{pressure variations (assume 20\%)}}{\text{length of pipe in 100 ft units}}$$

The friction factor can then be related to the friction loss tables which show the relationship between flow, friction loss and velocity. The pipe size can then be selected so that at the required flow rate there will be a velocity of less than 1.5 m/sec or 5 ft/sec. Sizing the pipe in this manner will ensure that the friction loss does not exceed 20% of the available pressure.

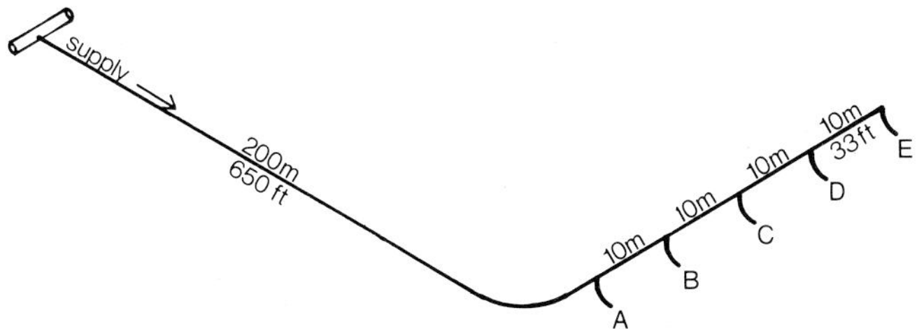

11.8 *Example: irrigation circuit friction loss*

Example (fig 11.8)

Assume: Flow requirement = 5 sprayheads at 0.1 l/sec (2 gal/min)
= 0.5 l/sec (10 gal/min)

System pressure = 2 bar (29 psi)

Total circuit length = 200 m or (650 ft)

METRIC

$$\text{friction factor} = \frac{(2 \times 10.19) \times 0.20}{2.00}$$

$$= 2.03.$$

TABLE 11.2 FRICTION LOSS THROUGH LOW DENSITY POLYTHENE PIPES. Pressure drop in metres per 100 metres. Shaded figures indicate water velocities below 1.5 m/sec (5 ft/sec)

	Internal Pipe Diameter					
Flow (l/sec)	12 mm ½ in	18 mm ¾ in	25 mm 1 in	32 mm 1¼ in	38 mm 1½ in	50 mm 2 in
0.01	0.20					
0.02	0.58	0.08				
0.03	1.30	0.17	0.05			
0.04	1.90	0.25	0.07			
0.05	2.9	0.38	0.11			
0.06	3.8	0.54	0.15	0.05		
0.07	5.2	0.63	0.18	0.06		
0.08	6.3	0.79	0.23	0.07		
0.09	8.0	0.91	0.27	0.08		
0.1	10.0	1.2	0.33	0.10	0.04	
0.2	33	3.7	1.1	0.34	0.10	0.04
0.3	60	7.5	2.3	·0.70	0.24	0.09
0.4		12	3.4	1.10	0.34	0.14
0.5		17	5.0	1.5	0.53	0.21
0.6		25	7.2	2.4	0.78	0.30
0.7		31	9.0	3.0	0.99	0.38
0.8			12	3.7	1.3	0.48
0.9			14	4.4	1.5	0.63
1.0			17	5.0	2.0	0.73
1.2			22	7.2	2.5	1.0
1.4				10	3.5	1.4
1.6				12	4.1	1.6
1.8				14	5.0	1.9
2.0				17	6.0	2.4
2.2				21	7.7	2.8
2.4				24	8.7	3.2
2.6					9.3	3.7
2.8					111	4.3
3.0					113	4.8
3.5					116	6.2
4.0					221	7.8
4.5						10
5.0						14

TABLE 11.3 FRICTION LOSS THROUGH LOW DENSITY POLYETHYLENE PIPES. Pressure drop in feet per 100 feet. Shaded print indicates water velocities below 5 ft/sec (1.5/sec)

	Internal pipe diameter					
Flow (US gall/min)	½ in 12 mm	¾ in 18 mm	1 in 25 mm	1¼ in 32 mm	1½ in 38 mm	2 in 50 mm
0.2	0.28	0.04				
0.4	0.90	0.12	0.03			
0.6	1.9	0.25	0.07	0.02		
0.8	3.1	0.39	0.11	0.03		
1	4.7	0.59	0.17	0.05	0.02	
2	14	1.6	0.47	0.14	0.05	0.02
3	32	3.5	1.0	0.32	0.11	0.04
4	48	5.4	1.6	0.48	0.17	0.07
5	74	8.0	2.4	0.74	0.20	0.10
6	100	11	3.2	1.0	0.34	0.13
7		14	4.3	1.4	0.45	0.17
8		18	5.4	1.7	0.57	0.23
9		23	6.7	2.2	0.71	0.28
10		27	7.7	2.5	0.83	0.33
12		35	11	3.5	1.2	0.46
14		40	13	4.2	1.4	0.54
16			17	5.7	1.8	0.62
18			21	6.8	2.3	0.88
20			28	8.0	3.0	1.2
22			32	9.9	3.4	1.3
24			34	12	3.7	1.5
26			38	13	3.8	1.7
28				16	5.1	2.0
30				17	5.8	2.3
35				23	7.8	3.1
40				28	9.2	3.6
45					12	4.2
50					13	5.1
55					17	6.0
60					19	7.6
65					22	8.7
70						9.7
75						11
80						12
85						13
90						15

TABLE 11.4 FRICTION LOSS THROUGH uPVC PIPES. PRESSURE DROP IN METRES PER 100 METRES. Shaded print indicate water velocities below 1.5 m/sec (5 ft/sec). Flow values limited to flows below 3 m/sec (10 ft/sec)

	Nominal pipe sizes 9 mm ⅜	12 mm ½ in	18 mm ¾ in	25 mm 1 in	32 mm 1¼ in	38 mm 1½ in	50 mm 2 in	75 mm 3 in	100 mm 4 in
Flow (l/sec)	**Internal pipe diameter 14 mm**	**18 mm**	**22 mm**	**28 mm**	**37 mm**	**42 mm**	**53 mm**	**78 mm**	**100 mm**
0.1	0.33	0.05	0.02						
0.02	0.90	0.12	0.04						
0.03	1.8	0.26	0.08	0.03					
0.04	3.0	0.40	0.12	0.04					
0.05	4.0	0.55	0.18	0.06	0.02				
0.06	5.8	0.75	0.25	0.08	0.03				
0.07	7.3	0.98	0.30	0.10	0.04				
0.08	8.8	1.2	0.36	0.12	0.04	0.02			
0.09	11	1.5	0.46	0.15	0.05	0.03			
0.1	13	1.7	0.54	0.18	0.06	0.03			
0.2	40	5.3	1.8	0.56	0.19	0.09	0.03		
0.3	83	11	3.6	1.2	0.40	0.19	0.07		
0.4		17	5.6	1.8	0.62	0.30	0.11		
0.5		25	8.0	2.6	0.88	0.44	0.15	0.03	
0.6		36	12	3.7	1.3	0.63	0.22	0.04	
0.7		45	14	4.7	1.6	0.78	0.27	0.05	
0.8			18	6.0	2.0	0.98	0.34	0.06	
0.9			22	7.1	2.5	1.2	0.42	0.07	0.02
1.0			26	8.5	2.9	1.4	0.48	0.09	0.03
1.2			34	12	3.8	1.8	0.63	0.12	0.04
1.4				16	5.4	2.6	0.88	0.16	0.05
1.6				18	6.3	3.2	1.1	0.19	0.06
1.8				24	7.0	3.8	1.4	0.24	0.07
2.0				28	9.4	4.6	1.6	0.28	0.08
2.2					12	5.2	1.8	0.33	0.09
2.4					13	6.0	2.2	0.38	0.11
2.6					14	6.7	2.4	0.43	0.13
2.8					16	7.8	2.7	0.48	0.14
3.0					18	8.7	3.0	0.53	0.16
3.5						12	3.9	0.70	0.23
4.0						14	4.9	0.90	0.27
4.5						17	6.0	1.1	0.33
5.0							7.0	1.3	0.38
10.0								4.0	1.3
15.0								8.8	2.6
20.0									4.2
40.0									

Imperial (US)

$$\text{friction factor} = \frac{(29 \times 2.31) \times 0.20}{6.56}$$

$$= 2.04.$$

These factors are then related to the friction loss tables 11.2, 11.3, 11.4 and 11.5, so that a pipe is selected with approximately the friction factor calculated above. The exact friction loss for the pipes which have been selected can be determined in the manner described below:

Metric

Points	**Length**	**Flow**	**Pipe size**	**Friction loss from charts (uPVU)**	**Total friction = length in 100 m × loss**
Start to A	200 m	0.5 l/sec	37 mm	0.88 m/100 m	2.0 × 0.88 = 1.76
A to B	10 m	0.4 l/sec	28 mm	1.80 m/100 m	0.10 × 1.80 = 0.18
B to C	10 m	0.3 l/sec	28 mm	1.20 m/100 m	0.10 × 1.20 = 0.12
C to D	10 m	0.2 l/sec	22 mm	1.80 m/100 m	0.10 × 1.80 = 0.18
D to E	10 m	0.1 l/sec	18 m	1.70 m/100 m	0.10 × 1.70 = 0.17
				Total =	2.41
				Plus 10% (for bends, etc.)	0.24
					2.65

So total pressure loss = 2.65 m head or (÷10.19) = 0.26 bar

Imperial

Points	**Length**	**Flow**	**Pipe size**	**Friction loss loss charts uPVC**	**Total friction = length in 100 m × loss**
Start to A	650 ft	10 gal/m	1.5 in	1.4 ft/100 ft	6.50 × 1.4 = 9.10
A to B	33 ft	8 gal/m	1.14 in	2.7 ft/100 ft	0.33 × 2.7 = 0.89
B to C	33 ft	6 gal/m	1.14 in	1.7 ft/100 ft	0.33 × 1.7 = 0.56
C to D	33 ft	4 gal/m	1.14 in	0.8 ft/100 ft	0.33 × 0.8 = 0.26
D to E	33 ft	2 gal/m	0.90 in	0.8 ft/100 ft	0.33 × 0.8 = 0.26
					Total = 11.07
					Plus 10% (for bends, etc = 1.11
					12.18

So total pressure loss = 12.18 ft head or ÷2.31) = 5.3 psi

The total friction loss in such a system should not exceed 20% of the total pressure which is available. In this example a 20% maximum friction loss for a pressure of 2 bar (29 psi) is 0.4 bar (5.5 psi) so that these pipes are suitable.

Using pumped water

The same friction loss charts are used to design a pumped circuit except that a friction factor is not used. Instead a pipe size is selected so that a velocity between 0.75 and 1.5 m/sec (2.5 and

TABLE 11.5 FRICTION LOSS THROUGH uPVC PIPES. PRESSURE DROP IN FEET PER 100 FEET. Shaded print indicates water velocities below 5 ft/sec (1.5 m/sec). Velocities limited to flows below 10 ft/sec (3m/sec)

	Nominal pipe sizes ⅜	¾ in	¾ in	1 in	1¼ in	1½ in	2 in	3 in	4 in
Flow (US gall/min)	Internal pipe diameters 0.55 in	0.70 in	0.90 in	1.14 in	1.5 in	1.7 in	2.1 in	3.1 in	4.0 in
0.2	0.46	0.06	0.02						
0.4	1.4	0.18	0.06	0.02					
0.6	2.8	0.37	0.12	0.04					
0.8	4.4	0.58	0.18	0.06	0.02				
1.0	6.3	0.85	0.27	0.09	0.03				
2	18	2.4	0.78	0.26	0.09	0.05			
3	38	5.2	1.6	0.52	0.18	0.09	0.03		
4	60	7.8	2.6	0.80	0.28	0.14	0.05		
5	86	12	3.7	1.3	0.43	0.21	0.07		
6		16	5.0	1.7	0.57	0.28	0.10	0.02	
7		20	6.5	2.2	0.72	0.35	0.13	0.02	
8		26	7.1	2.7	0.92	0.46	0.16	0.03	
9		33	11	3.4	1.2	0.58	0.21	0.04	
10		38	13	4.0	1.4	0.68	0.24	0.05	
12		53	17	5.4	1.8	0.90	0.33	0.06	0.02
14			22	6.8	2.4	1.2	0.39	0.07	0.02
16			27	8.6	2.9	1.4	0.49	0.09	0.03
18			33	11	3.6	1.7	0.60	0.11	0.03
20			38	13	4.4	2.1	0.72	0.13	0.04
22				15	4.9	2.4	0.84	0.16	0.05
24				17	5.8	2.8	0.87	0.18	0.05
26				19	6.8	3.3	1.2	0.21	0.06
28				23	7.8	3.7	1.3	0.24	0.07
30				26	8.8	4.2	1.4	0.27	0.08
35					12	5.2	1.8	0.34	0.10
40					14	6.8	2.3	0.43	0.13
45					17	8.3	2.8	0.52	0.16
50					19	9.4	3.3	0.59	0.18
55						11	3.8	0.69	0.21
60						13	4.6	0.84	0.25
65						15	5.2	0.96	0.28
70						17	6.0	1.1	0.33
75							6.7	1.2	0.36
100							10	1.8	0.57
200								6.3	1.9
300									4.0
400									

5 ft/sec) is maintained. The total friction loss is then calculated as above and this is added to the required working pressure of the distribution outlets (expressed in metres head or feet head) to determine the pump head which is required. Using the example above, the total friction loss of 2.65 m head (8.09 ft head) is added to the operating pressure or 2 bar (20.66 m head) or 29 psi (67 ft head) to give a total head requirement of 23.31 m head or 75.09 ft head. This of course assumes that the pump and distribution points are at the same level. This information can then be passed to a pump manufacturer who will supply a pump to fulfil these requirements, ie in this example a pump to deliver 5 l/sec with a pressure of 23.31 m head (10 gal/min with a pressure of 75.09 ft head).

CHOICE OF APPLICATION SYSTEM

Water can be applied to plantings in a range of different ways and the most useful techniques for interior plantings are described below:

Drip emitters

Water is released through a number of distinct exit units which are secured to the supply pipe so that a slow, steady and exact amount of water is applied to a specific area. With these low application rates the water seeps gently into the compost and spreads in the form of a drop as shown in fig 11.16 (see page 85). The greater the surface tension within the substrate the greater the area of spread, eg peat composts experience more lateral movement than sand based composts. With a drip irrigation system it is not necessary for a plant to have its complete root system in moist soil and in some cases it has been found that a plant will survive if only one third of the root system is regularly irrigated.

An irrigation system normally comprises a main supply with laterals arranged at right angles (fig 11.9). The laterals usually

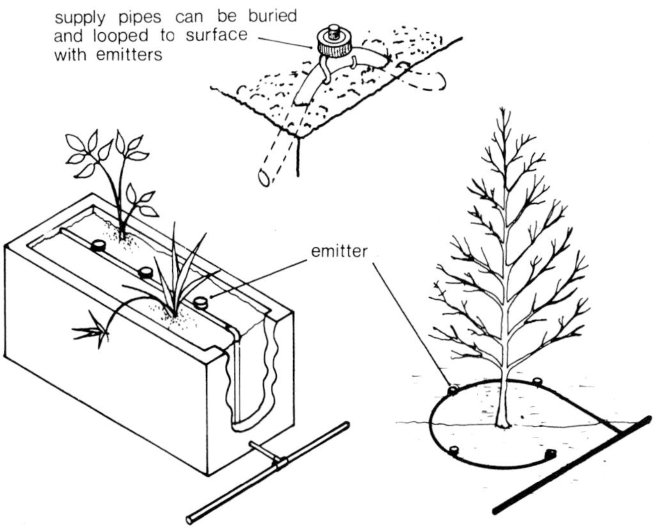

11.9 *Some common pipe layouts*

consist of 12 mm diameter low density black polyethylene tube and can carry in excess of 75 nozzles without a serious loss in pressure. All pipes should be secured with special staples or plastic pipe retainers to prevent movement during operation. There are many types of emitter available which all serve to constrict the point of exit and so cause a positive pressure within the system which ensures an even rate of application. Unfortunately the more simple emitters such as micro bore tubes can suffer from blockages due to solids or calcium deposits, and so the larger more easily cleansed emitters are to be recommended. Emitters usually have a discharge rate of 2 to 9 l/h ($\frac{1}{2}$ to 2 gal/h) depending on the operating pressure, although a new generation of emitters is available which can compensate for changes in water pressure along a supply line. This means that the easiest way of classifying emitters is according to whether or not they are able to compensate for variations in pressure.

Non compensating emitters

These are the more traditional type whose rate of emission is in direct proportion to the water pressure and therefore variable. They are inline or online and usually have a long spiral water path to dissipate the pressure, although some online emitters use a small orifice (fig 11.11). One range of emitters uses a small orifice combined with a vortex chamber which achieves a small degree of pressure compensation (fig 11.12).

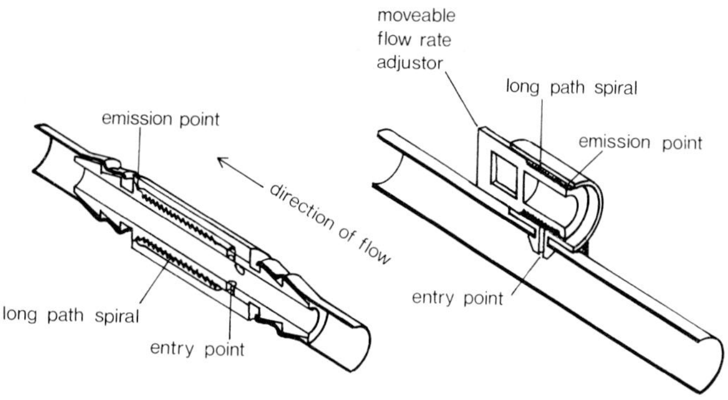

11.10 *Inline emitter (left) and Online emitter (right)*

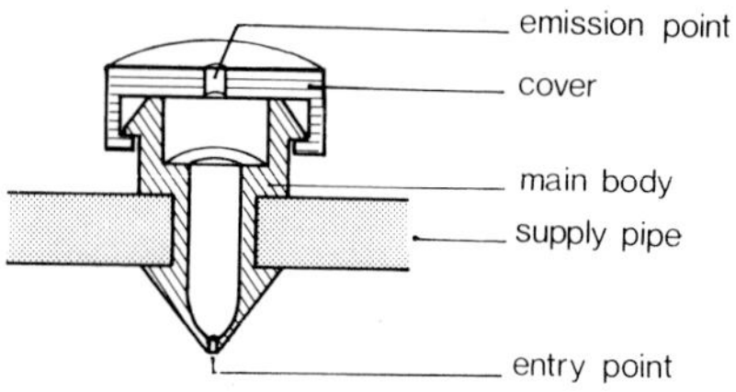

11.11 *Non-pressure-compensating online small orifi*ce emitter

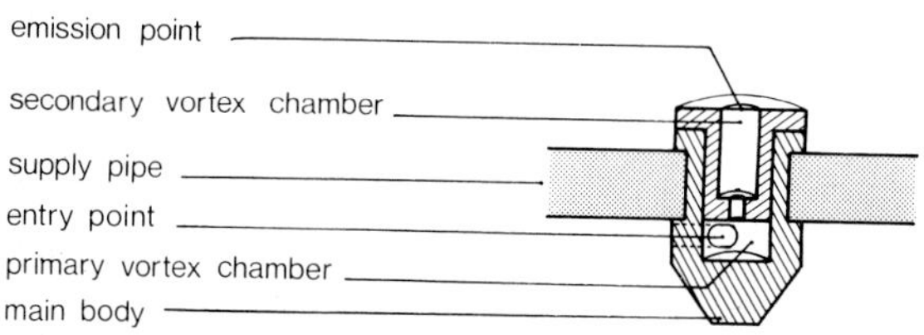

11.12 *Non pressure compensating small orifice emitters: (top) basic form; (bottom) with vortex chamber*

Compensating emitters

The most popular emitters are pressure compensating which have the advantage of discharging water at a constant rate despite variations in water pressure, and so make possible the use of longer runs of smaller bore distribution pipes. The pressure compensating effect is usually achieved by a flexible rubber diaphragm which presses down on the flow path as the water pressure increases and so reduces the cross sectional area of the flow path. Some emitters are also automatically flushed of troublesome particles each time the pressure in the line changes. There are a range of pressure regulating emitters available and some are described below:

1 Rubber tube

This type of nozzle is typified by the ISS "Enternomatic Compensating Emitter" which combines simplicity with excellent pressure compensating qualities. The head of the emitter fits into the pipe wall and the tailpiece projects back into the pipe. There is an 8 mm long groove starting in the tailpiece and ending in the outlet in the head which is covered by a 5 mm long rubber valve tube (fig 11.13). When the pressure is low the entire cross section of the groove is open and small dirt particles are rinsed out. When the pressure rises the valve tube is compressed and so reduces the cross section of the groove, maintaining the flow at 4 l/h (1 gal/h) over a pressure range of 0.7 to 4 bar.

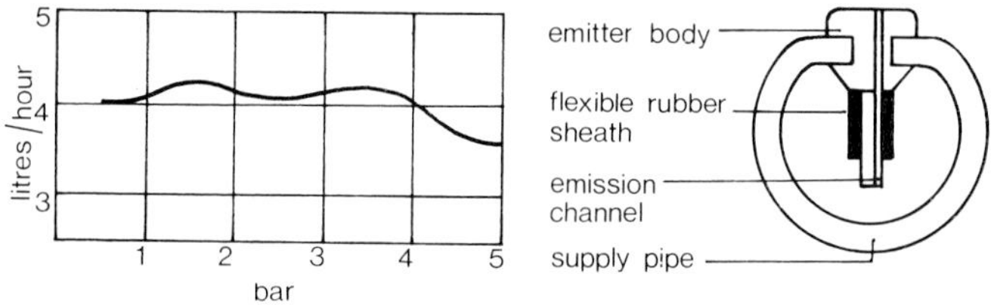

11.13 *An ISS Eternomatic pressure compensating emitter, and a graph of its discharge characteristics*

2 Rubber disc

This type of nozzle is typified by the Reed International "Key Emitter" and the Farrow "Plastif Dripper", and usually have a delivery rate of 4 l/h (1 gal/h) although some models will deliver 8 or 16 l/h (2 or 4 gal/h). These large emitters clip on to the upper surface of the pipe and contain a rubber diaphragm which is forced into a spiral path on a plastic disc when subjected to water pressure (fig 11.14). Such emitters deliver at a uniform rate at pressures between 0.5 and 4 bars, so that runs of 18 mm pipe up to 180 m long can support a nozzle every metre.

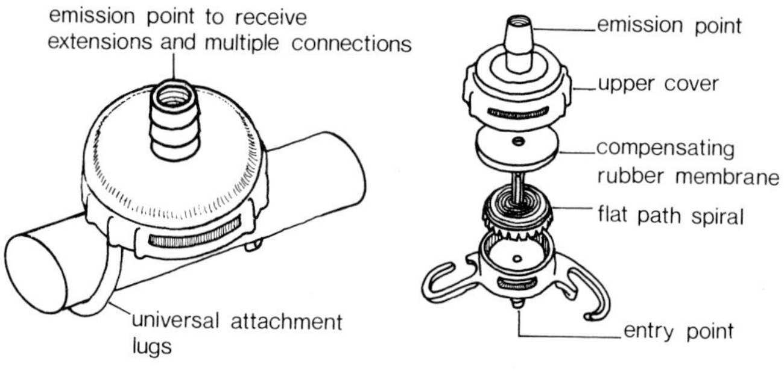

11.14 *A Reed International pressure compensating emitter*

Spray emitters

Recently a range of spray emitters have been developed which produced a variety of fan shapes or even full circle coverage (fig.

11.15). The flow rates vary from 16 l/h (4 gal/h) to 200 l/h (50 gal/h), and the area of coverage from 0.5 m^2 to 30m^2 (5 sq ft to 300 sq ft), depending on the pattern and size of the nozzle. The flow rate characteristics of these nozzles are the same as for non-compensating emitters, so that the same design criteria can be applied – that is to say, the flow is directly proportional to the water pressure. The nozzles are usually fixed directly onto the delivery pipe, but should it be necessary to bury the pipe then they can be raised above the surface on short risers. The ability of these nozzles to produce a low-level spray means that it is possible to secure a pipe, fitted with outward-pointing nozzles, directly onto a wall to produce a particularly unobtrusive system.

The advantage of these emitters is that a low level spray can be directed under the foliage to cover an area either side of the supply line. They provide an economic and convenient compromise between a true drip system and overhead sprinklers by producing a reasonably large wetted area from a spray.

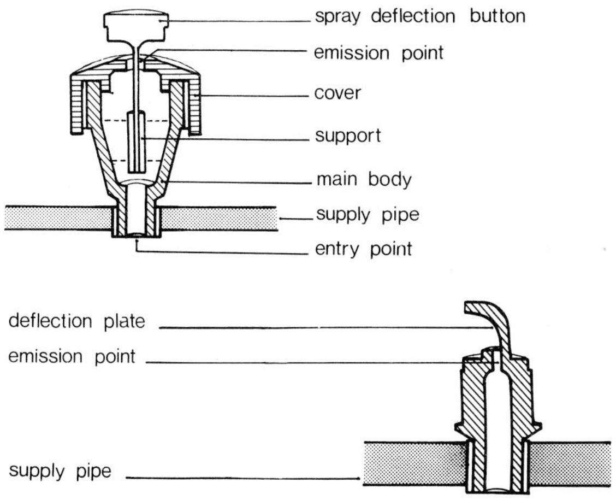

11.15 *Irrigation spray emitters: (top) button spray (360°); (bottom) deflection plate spray (270° max)*

GUIDES TO DRIP OR SPRAY EMITTER DESIGN

An installation should always start with a head unit which contains an isolating valve, a fine mesh filter and a pressure regulator (fig 11.19, see page 87). If liquid fertilisers are to be added then the head unit will also require connections for the dilutor before the filter unit. If the system is operating directly from a mains supply, a non return valve should be fitted to remove the risk of contaminating the water supply. To determine the capacity of the head unit which is required for a drip irrigation system the following simplified standards may be applied.

12 mm (½ in) pipe @ 1.5 m^3/h, eg 180 m drip line with emitters at 500 mm spacing
18 mm (¾ in) pipe @ 3.0 m^3/h, eg 360 m drip line with emitters at 50 mm spacing
25 mm (1 in) pipe @ 5.0 m^3/h, eg 590 m drip line with emitters at 500 mm spacing

The distribution network of pipes are connected to the head unit to carry the water to the planted areas (the sizes being calculated as previously described). Pipes of 16 mm outside diameter or 12 mm internal diameter are then taken off the distribution pipe to the individual areas to be irrigated (fig 11.9). The supply pipes are normally led across the area to be irrigated at regular intervals and placed in a manner which assumes a maximum lateral water movement of 500 mm from the point of application, ie the delivery pipes should be as little as 1 m apart. The emitters can be more frequent than this at regular 500 mm centres although in the presence of a relatively small number of

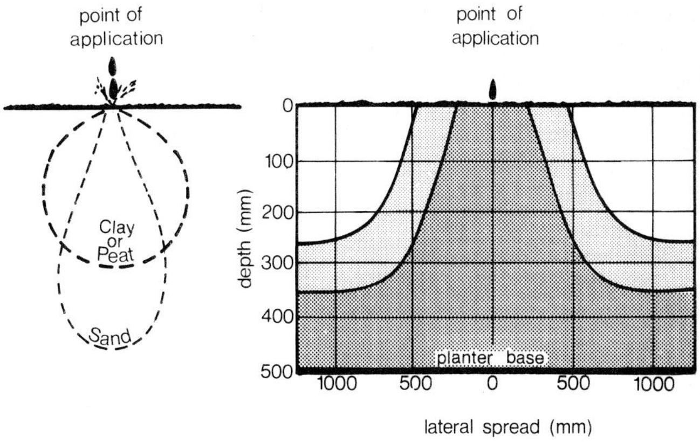

11.16 *The variations in water spread associated with different substrates, and the movement of water in a planter*

choice plants it may be desirable to locate the individual nozzles about 200 mm from the main stem. In the case of large plants two emitters can be installed some 400 mm from and on opposite sides to the main stem. If it is impractical to have several parallel supply lines it is possible to fit flexible remoting leads to nozzles located either side of the supply pipe, or to fit remoting leads to nozzles connected directly to the supply pipe to give an additional coverage of 750 mm either side.

It is necessary to calculate the pressure required at the beginning of a drip line. This will be the operating pressure of the emitter plus the friction loss equivalent in the pipe. This loss should not exceed 20% of the emitter pressure and can be determined from fig 11.16 when the "average flow rate" per metre or per foot has been calculated.

$$\text{Average flow rate} = \frac{\text{No. emitters} \times \text{flow rate}}{\text{length of line}}$$

The pressure loss for the length of drip line can then be read off from fig 11.17.

Example

A 150 m (550 ft) drip line with 4 l/h* (1 gal/h) emitters at 500 mm (20 in) centres.

	Metric	Imperial (US)
average flow rate	$\frac{300 \times 4}{150} = 8.0$	$\frac{300 \times 1}{500} \simeq 0.6$

From fig 11.17 the average flow rate of 8.0 l/h/m (0.6 gal/h/ft) over a pipe length of 150 m (500 ft) shows a pressure loss of 40 m head (120 ft head). This is excessive so another design must be considered, eg three 50 m (150 ft) lengths of pipe:

	Metric	Imperial (US)
average flow rate	$\frac{100 \times 4}{50} = 8.0$	$\frac{100 \times 1}{150} \simeq 0.6$

From fig 11.17 an average flow rate of 8.0 l/h/m (0.6 g/h/ft) over a pipe length of 50 m (150 ft) shows a pressure loss of 2.5 m head (7.5 ft head). If the emitter pressure is 20 m head (60 ft head) a pressure loss of 2.5 m/head (7.5 ft head) is acceptable, ie it is only 8% of the operating pressure. The pressure loss can then be added to the emitters pressure to give the pressure which is required at the start of the line and expressed as a loss of head.

Metric	Imperial (US)
2.5 m head + 20 m head	7.5 ft head + 60 ft head
= 22.5 m head	≃ 67.5 ft head

The volume of water required by each line can then be calculated:

* 4 litres per hour is the rounded-up equivalent of 1 US gallon per hour.

Total flow volume required = (50 × 2) × 4 = 400 l/h or 6.6 l/min (100 gal/h or 1.66 gal/ min).

The three lines in total require a flow of 20 l/min (5gal/min). If a pump is to be used to deliver this flow then a pressure variation factor of 25% should be assumed. With a lateral start pressure of 22.5 m head (67.5 ft head) and a supply main which is say 40 m (120 ft) long, a friction factor can be determined, but it can be seen from tables 11.2 and 11.3 that an 18 mm ($\frac{3}{4}$ in) supply pipe will probably be required. The exact pressure loss due to friction will then be 4.8 head (12 m/100 m) or 9.6 ft head (8 ft/100 ft), therefore a pump is required which can effect the following:

1 Produce the volume of water at the given line pressure 20 l/min (5.0 gal/min) at 22.5 m head (67.5 ft head)
2 Overcome the friction loss with a 10% addition for bends, etc. of 4.8 + 0.48 = 5.28 m head (10.56 ft head)
3 Overcome the static head, ie difference between height of the pump and the discharge point.

With a mains water supply of known pressure the figures calculated above can be used to determine the settings of the pressure regulator at the start of the system.

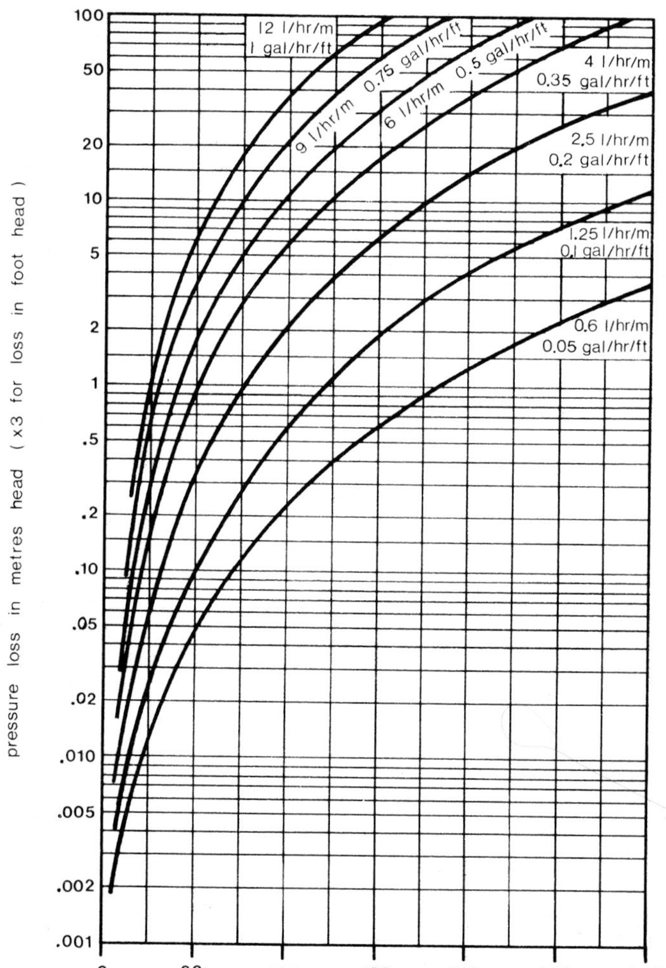

11.17 *The relationship between pressure loss and pipe length, for seven different rates of flow through 12 mm inside diameter ($\frac{1}{2}$ in) drip irrigation lateral pipe. No allowance is made for emitters which can reduce the friction loss to one third in the distal portion of the pipe*

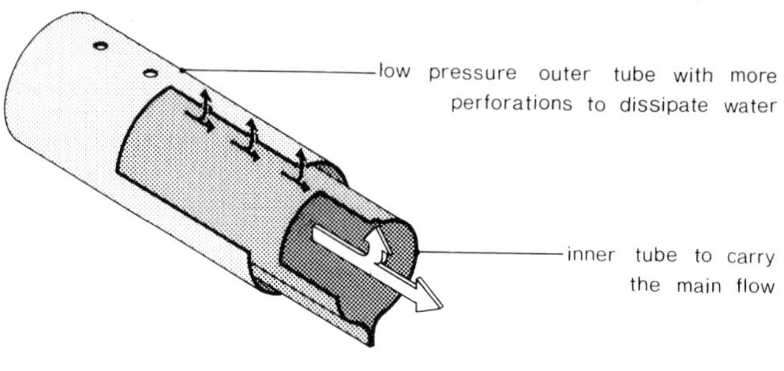

11.18 *Typical section through a Chapin Watermatic "Twin-wall" hose*

PERFORATED TUBES

With emitters the water is discharged at given points, but in certain cases it may be preferable to produce bands of irrigated compost. This can be achieved by a perforated tube system which permits a greater area to be wetted than with emitters and so is very useful with ground cover schemes. There are many types of perforated tube systems available, but most are made of high quality black UV resistant polyethylene between 0.25 mm and 0.50 mm thick. The simplest consists of a folded strip of polyethylene which is stitched along its length. More precise systems use an accurately perforated tube but the most advanced systems consist of two fused tubes, the larger carrying the main flow which is bled into the smaller tube from which it is discharged (fig 11.18). This more complex structure reduces the effect of pressure loss along the length of tubing, which can be significant at the normal low operating pressures of 0.3 to 1.0 kg/cm^2 (5–15 psi). A wide range of perforation frequencies are available to give a discharge rate which is suitable for a given crop, but for most interior planting situations the perforations should be 0.5 mm in diameter at 100 mm intervals. Due to the small apertures the water supply should be passed through a filter with a mesh size no greater than 100 microns. Despite their flexible construction perforated tubes can be installed below ground to depths of between 50 and 200 mm to hide their presence.

WATER SPREAD WITH DRIP IRRIGATION

The typical water spread associated with cultivated soils is shown in fig 11.16. The onion shaped spread indicated in the diagram is characteristic of all substrates. In most loam soils the maximum usable width is from 1.20 m to 1.50 m, whilst in heavy soil the water spreads in a circle approx 2.20 m in diameter but with a reduced depth of penetration. In a sandy soil, the maximum lateral spread of water is reduced to 0.90–1.20 m, while the penetration depth is considerably increased. In a planter where the substrate depth is not great it is estimated that the water spread will be as indicated in fig 11.16. The lowest portion of the water penetration spreads to form a moist layer on the base of the planter and from this water is lifted by surface tension to a height of only 100–200 mm.

The water spreads in the substrate as concentric circles around the drip point so that with shallow rooted plants, which occupy the upper 200 mm of compost, the distance between supply pipes should not be greater than 1.0 m. With deeper rooted plants the pipe interval can be increased to 1.50–2.0 m. Pipes laid underground should be close to the surface because surface tension lift is limited and hence lateral water spread is reduced.

IRRIGATION CONTROL

All irrigation systems require a control input to operate them and this can be supplied in a number of ways:

1 Manual – A human element must initiate the operation as a result of personal observation or the observation of an instrument such as a tensiometer.
2 Time Clock – If the environment is reasonably uniform the human element can be standardised into timed operation, although adequate drainage is important with this technique.
3 Automatic – With existing technology this can be an effective solution to the problem of irrigation control.

The problem of determining the moisture level in a compost can be overcome by regular inspection, but this does represent a considerable ongoing maintenance input. There is still much resistance to fully automatic irrigation controls although their value is proven. If there is any reticence about removing executive control for an irrigation system from the maintenance operatives then sensors can be used to trigger an alert system with a light or buzzer. Possibly the safest compromise is to have an automatic controller connected to the irrigation system and an independent sensor which is connected to an alert system that operates in the event of the primary circuit failing.

Moisture sensing devices

To derive the maximum value from an irrigation system it is advisable to employ a sensor which is capable of monitoring the moisture content of the compost. Of the equipment which is available, two products which have shown themselves to be admirable for this function are described below. The location of such sensors in a comprehensive system is illustrated in fig 11.19. One problem with any automatic system is that, during the first year after installation, the compost and plant root system interact to modify the physical properties of the substrate. As a result it is usually necessary to recalibrate the system every few months until a stable situation develops.

Dielectric constant monitor

There are several instruments available which can monitor electronically the moisture content of a substrate. The "water bug" is one example. The most useful type for planting in buildings is the "Water Bug" HD5 which has a probe which is sited remotely from the electronic controller. The controller is connected to a 24 V solenoid valve on the water supply as indicated in the wiring diagram shown in fig 11.19. The basic control unit measures some 300 × 200 × 75 mm and carries a three pronged probe some 200 mm long and 150 mm across. The probe consists of a U-shaped field transmitter with a central receiving cylinder which is sensitive between 10 mm and 75 mm from the base and is linked to the control unit by a cable which can vary in length from 3 m to 30 m.

The transmitter generates a field which is modified by the substrate and converted by the receiver into a signal current whose strength is inversely proportional to the signal received. This voltage is monitored by two potentiometers which are adjusted to give the maximum and minimum moisture levels. The instrument therefore monitors the dielectric constant of the growing medium, ie it measures the total pore volume of the growing medium and monitors the mass of water which it contains. The advantage of this technique is that it is unaffected by such problems as salt concentrations and being fully electronic should run for at least a decade without replacement.

Tensiometers

Tensiometers make a direct measurement of the matrix potential or suction within the body of the compost. They are largely unaffected by salt concentrations as they absorb salts and are therefore self compensating. A tensiometer consists of a special porous ceramic tip which is filled with distilled water and connected to a vacuum gauge. The ceramic tip is buried in the substrate at a depth where most of the roots are located. As the moisture level in the substrate is reduced by evapotranspiration water flows from the instrument into the substrate and creates a negative pressure which registers on the vacuum gauge, and when the substrate is irrigated the process is reversed. If the substrate is allowed to become very dry (−0.8 bar) air tends to enter the ceramic tip and affects accuracy. The gauge is calibrated in centibars and although the readings have to be taken regularly they are easy to translate into irrigation needs. From 0 to 5 cb is too wet for most plants, but readings for 10 to 25 cb represent ideal water and air conditions. When

11.19 *A proposal for an automatic irrigation system with electronic control unit*

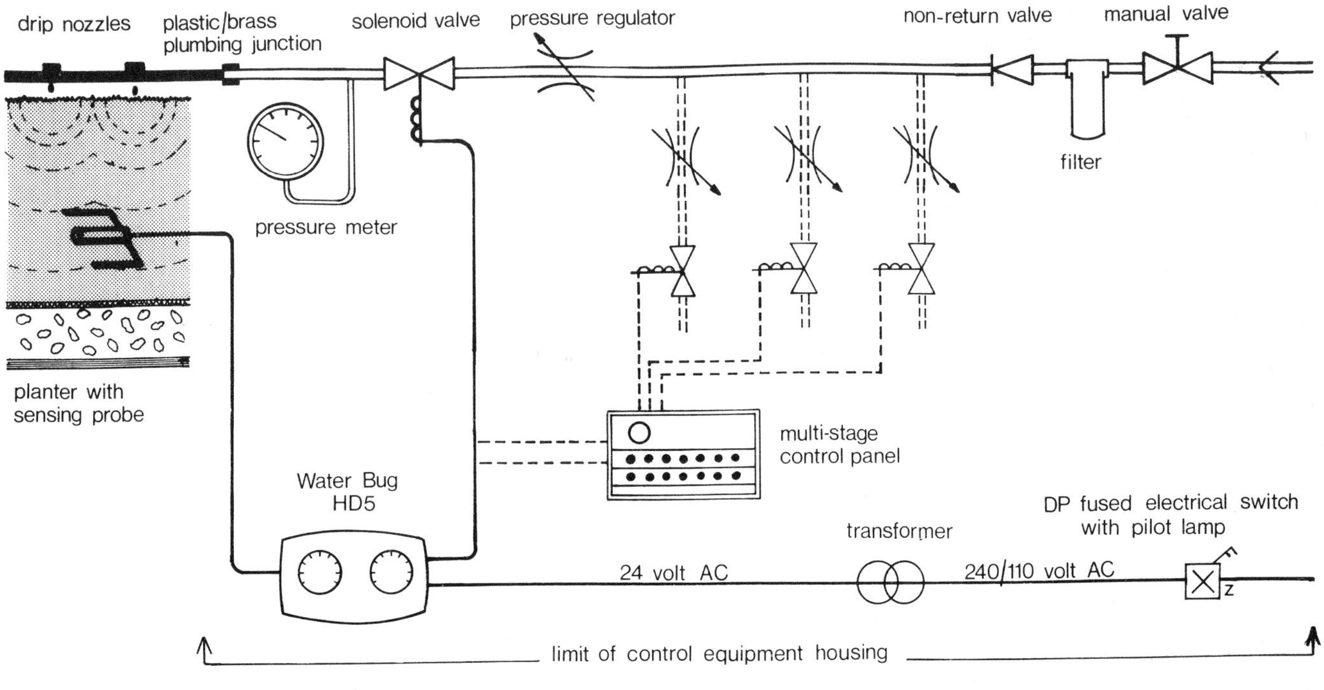

reading exceeds 25 cb water is usually becoming limited to some plants, although most plants with a root system at least 500 mm deep will not suffer from water deficiency until the gauge reading is 40–50 cb. Plants with a root system more than 1.0 m deep will seldom show symptoms of shortage before a reading of 70 cb. Automatic tensiometers are available and these use the theory described above, except that a magnetic switch is attached to the vacuum gauge to be activated when the needle on the gauge passes under it. The signal from this switch can then be used to operate a multi stage control panel and/or electric solenoid valves.

Head unit housing

To prevent interference all irrigation control equipment should be enclosed in a lockable cupboard. Such housing should be securely built, with adequate ventilation to prevent condensation forming on electrical equipment. The floor should be drained as there will always be an amount of free water, if only during maintenance operations. The noise of electric pumps can cause irritation so they are best located in the basement or the service core. Thermal insulation should also be good for, although most components of an irrigation system can be frozen, the temperature of the control gear should not fall below freezing point.

Transformers and solenoid valves

Recently a new range of solenoid valves has been developed specifically for use with irrigation systems which have the advantage of lower flow rate operation, adjustable flow control and manual override. Almost all the solenoid valves operate from a 24 V supply so an AC transformer to reduce the mains supply voltage is necessary.

Multi stage control panels

To avoid the need for a large transformer or the possibility of lowering the water pressure in the building it is possible to operate an irrigation system in sections by the use of a multi stage control panel. Such panels have the advantage of being adjustable so that different portions of the system can operate for different time periods once the sequence has commenced. The panels operate on either 220–240 V AC or 110 V AC and generate a 24 V AC output. The panels usually contain twelve, twenty four, or forty eight channels which can operate in sequence. Each channel can be individually set to any number of one tenth units on a preset base time which can be varied from six seconds to six minutes, although some models are available which work on a base of thirty minutes. The panels are designed for automatic operation but also possess a facility for manual override. These control panels can also be fitted with auxiliary controls to initiate other functions such as water pumps and injection equipment.

INSTALLING A SYSTEM

To eliminate problems with an irrigation system, all proposals should be checked by a specialist. Installation is also best undertaken by a specialist, in which case the responsibility of the main building contract should be limited to supplying a lockable drained housing unit with a fused electrical socket and mains water supply.

Pipe protection

Where possible all pipes should be hidden from view. Some systems can be completely buried (eg Twinwall hose), or at least the delivery mains can be buried (eg drip emitters). If it is desirable that only the emitter should be obvious then the pipe can be looped to the surface where necessary (fig 11.9). If an area fitted with irrigation is to receive pedestrian traffic then the supply lines should be protected by passing through a length of uPVC pipe.

Assembly

It is quite common for emitters and fittings to be connected to the pipe in the factory but often it is necessary to assemble equipment on site. In such situations the pipes should always be cut cleanly without burrs, and to reduce the effort required for assembly the hoses should be softened by warming in hot water. Lubricants like soap, detergent and grease should not be used as they increase the chance of stressing by encouraging the use of excessive force. Naked flames should never be used on plastics as it can cause degradation.

Calibration

The only way to determine if an irrigation system has been adjusted correctly is to excavate holes in the planter to study moisture movement, or to study the drainage system to see if the compost is at "field capacity". Obviously it is necessary to apply water very slowly when calibrating a system, otherwise free water may still be passing through the body of the compost at the time of examination.

It is not possible to generalise on the frequency and extent of irrigation required by a given planting, due to variations in the aerial environment, the behaviour of the plants, and the condition of the root substrate. However, it can be expected that with a fairly low plant density in moderate conditions irrigation will only be required twice a week. At a higher plant density and with good evaporation conditions irrigation may be necessary every two days. When a planting is being installed it is important that no great time period should be permitted to elapse between planting and the commencement of irrigation, particularly if the plants have a tight and well defined root ball.

When a system has stabilised it is possible to check its operation by the use of tensiometers. Two instruments should be placed about 500 mm from an emitter in a typical area of the planting and installed so that the sensing areas lie 300 mm and 600 mm below the surface. If the system is operating satisfactorily the readings should be between 10 and 20 cb.

MAINTENANCE

Only minimal maintenance should be necessary for an irrigation system which operates with mains water. The filter system will require checking and flushing, but this should not be necessary more than once every six months. One problem which can arise in hard water areas is the deposition of calcium salts at the delivery point of small bore emitters. This has traditionally been handled by syringing the nozzles with diluted nitric acid, but is easily avoided by the use of large orifice emitters. A frequent cause of problems are electrical circuits, although these should not occur if the system has been correctly installed.

12 Plant selection

*by Stephen Scrivens, Barry Clare, David Richardson and Christopher Sill**

INTRODUCTION

The plant data and illustrations in table 12.1 have been designed to help with the choice of plant material, and should be read in conjunction one with the other. The major characteristics of the plants are described in the table, but to reduce the size of individual entries certain standard abbreviations have been used and these are explained below:

1 *Name* This is the internationally accepted scientific name of the plant, and should be used when accuracy is necessary. Wherever appropriate each plant also carries a common or vernacular name.

2 *Usual height range* The height ranges indicated are those which can be expected in a building. Many plants will exceed the height limits specified but only in good growing conditions or over a long period of time.

3 *Leaf colour* Where the colour descriptions are split by "&" the colours are in distinct areas, cf variegation.

4 *Leaf texture* Most interior plants have smooth leaves with a shiny surface but some are rough (with a spiky surface) or downy (covered by soft hairs).

5 *Stem colour* Most stems are a basic green but some make a positive visual contribution.

6 *Flowers* Few long term interior plants have visually significant flowers but with adequate light levels some can produce a pleasing display.

7 *Minimum radiation levels* A plant's minimum light energy requirement is critical. The best technique for expressing light requirements is energy in joules. The figures in the table are minima and should be exceeded wherever possible. If continuous healthy growth is desired these levels should be exceeded by a factor of at least 50%.

8 *Minimum light levels* A plant's minimum light energy requirement is critical. The system which expresses light levels in lux is not particularly relevant to a plant but will suffice in the absence of more suitable data. The figures in the plant table are minima and should be exceeded wherever possible. If continuous healthy growth is desired then these levels should be exceeded by a factor of at least 50%.

9 *Tolerance to direct sun* In general interior plants have been selected from shade species and are unable to tolerate direct sun for more than a short time. A plant with a low tolerance should never be exposed to the sun and even those with a high tolerance prefer to receive diffused light.

10 *Minimum temperature regime* It is not possible to make a definitive statement on a plant, as temperature interacts with other environmental factors and so a broad minimum threshold has been indicated. All interior plants have a preferred temperature regime and care is advised in selecting plants with a similar and appropriate preference for a given environment.

11 *Moisture level preference* The safest way to manage compost-grown plants is to allow them to become just dry before watering, but some do prefer more or less water than this norm. Plants with extremes of water preference should not be mixed within the same planting.

12 *Tolerance to leaf cleaner* Many plants are considered more attractive with "polished" leaves. However many are sensitive to heavy applications of "leaf shine" and some can be damaged by even a small application. As a general rule ferns, palms, or leaves with a downy surface should not be so treated.

13 *Tolerance to fluoride* Some plants have a pronounced aversion to fluoride, usually indicated by "die-back" of the foliage.

14 *Availability* This is a variable and often transient factor, but it is possible to make the following generalisations:

Freely available – those plants which can usually be supplied in very large numbers.

Moderately available – those plants which can usually be supplied in moderately large numbers.

Rarely available – those plants which are in production but will require effort to locate in large numbers.

15 *Comments* All statements in this column elaborate an entry in another column (signified by an arrowhead → in the relevant column).

The plants that are shown in the subsequent display illustrations were made available by courtesy of Tropical Plants Display Ltd, London.

* Barry Clare and Christopher Sill are with Tropical Plants Display Ltd, London.
David Richardson is with Rochford Landscape Ltd, Hoddeston, Herts

TABLE 12.1 GUIDE TO PLANT SELECTION

Botanic name (common name)	Usual height range in mm: 0 to 500	500 to 1000	1000 to 5000	5000 plus	Leaf colour	Leaf texture	Stem colour	Flowers	Minimum radiation requirement (400 to 700 nm) in MJ/day	Minimum average illuminance requirement in lux for 12 h/day	Tolerance to direct sun	Minimum temperature regime in °C	Moisture level preference	Tolerance to leaf cleaners	Tolerance to fluoride	Availability: freely	readily	rarely	Comments
1 *Aechmea fasciata* (Urn plant)	●				Green & cream	Rough bloom		Pink →	0.115	1000	Mid	7–10	Mid →	High	High		●		Long pink flower spike – water in leaf funnel
2 *Aglaonema crispum 'Silver Queen'* (Chinese evergreen)	●				Green & grey	Smooth shiny			0.070	600	Mid	13–15	High	Low	High	●			
3 *Aglaonema commutatum* (Chinese evergreen)	●				Green & silver	Smooth shiny			0.070	600	Mid	13–15	High	Low	High	●			
4 *Ananas bracteatus 'Striatus* (Pineapple plant)		●			Green & gold →	Smooth Shiny			0.070	600	Mid	13–15	Mid	Low	High		●		Leaf edge viciously serrated leaves flushed red at centre
5 *Anthurium scherzerianum* (Flamingo plant)	●				Dark green	Smooth shiny	Green	Numerous red →	0.070	600 →	Low	10–13	Mid	High	High		●		Flowers best in Spring – 0.115 MJ/day or 1000 lux for good flowering
6 *Araucaria heterophylla* (Norfolk Island pine)			●		Green →	Smooth shiny	Green to brown		0.095	800	Mid	10–13	Mid	Low	High			●	Needles light or dark green
7 *Asparagus densiflorus 'Sprengeri'* (Asparagus fern)	●				Green	Smooth shiny	Green		0.095	800	Mid	7–10	Mid	Low	High			●	
8 *Aspidistra elatior* (Cast-iron plant)	●				Dark green	Smooth shiny			0.060	500	Low	5–7	Low	High	Mid			●	
9 *Asplenium nidus* (Bird's-nest fern)	●				Pale green	Smooth shiny			0.070	600	Low	10–13	High	Low	High	●			
10 *Begonia rex* (Fan plant)	●				Multi colour →	Rough	Multi colour →		0.105	900	Low	7–10	Mid	Low	High		●		Leaf/stem colours include green/red/purple/white

TABLE 12.1 GUIDE TO PLANT SELECTION (CONTINUED)

Botanic name (common name)	Usual height range in mm: 0 to 500	500 to 1000	1000 to 5000	5000 plus	Leaf colour	Leaf texture	Stem colour	Flowers	Minimum radiation requirement (400 to 700 nm) in MJ/day	Minimum average illuminance requirement in lux for 12 h/day	Tolerance to direct sun	Minimum temperature regime in °C	Moisture level preference	Tolerance to leaf cleaners	Tolerance to fluoride	Availability: freely	readily	rarely	Comments
1 *Chamaerops humilis* (European fan palm)		●			Green	Rough bloom	Brown		0.115	1000	High	5–7	Mid	Low	High			●	
2 *Chamaedorea erumpens* (Bamboo palm)		●	●		Green	Smooth shiny	Green to brown		0.095	800	Mid	10–13	Mid	Low	High		●		
3 *Chlorophytum comosum 'Variegatum'* (Spider plant)	●				Green & white	Smooth shiny		Small white →	0.080	700	Low	7–10	Mid	High	Low	●			On long stalks also bearing plantlets
4 *Cissus antarctica* (Kangaroo vine)		●	●		Green	Smooth shiny			0.080	700	Low	7–10	Mid	High	High	●			Prefers cooler locations
5 *Codiaeum variegatum* (Croton)		●	●		Multi colour →	Smooth shiny	Green to brown		0.115	1000	Mid	15–18	Mid	High	High	●			Leaves green/white/gold/ orange/red
6 *Chamaedorea elegans* → *Bella* (Parlour palm)	●	●			Green	Smooth	Green		0.060	500	Low	10–13	Mid	Low	Mid		●		also called *Neanthe bella*
7 *Cordyline australis* (Cabbage tree)			●		Green	Smooth shiny	Brown	Small white →	0.115	1000	High	3–5	Mid	Low	High			●	Flowers on large spikes
8 *Cordyline terminalis* (Tree of kings)		●			Multi colour	Smooth shiny	Green		0.070	600	High	10–13	Mid	Low	Low		●		Leaves mixed green/red/ bronze stripes
9 *Cryptanthus forsterianus* (Pheasant leaf)	●				Mottled green	smooth			0.095	800	High	13–16	Mid	High	High			●	
10 *Cyperus diffusus* (Umbrella grass)		●			Pale green	Smooth shiny	Green		0.095	800	Mid	10–13	High →	Low	High			●	Prefers very high moisture levels

TABLE 12.1 GUIDE TO PLANT SELECTION (CONTINUED)

Botanic name (common name)	Usual height range in mm: 0 to 500	500 to 1000	1000 to 5000	5000 plus	Leaf colour	Leaf texture	Stem colour	Flowers	Minimum radiation requirement (400 to 700 nm) in MJ/day	Minimum average illuminance requirement in lux for 12 h/day	Tolerance to direct sun	Minimum temperature regime in °C	Moisture level preference	Tolerance to leaf cleaners	Tolerance to fluoride	Availability: freely	readily	rarely	Comments
1 *Dieffenbachia amoena* (Dumb cane)		●	●		Green & cream	Smooth shiny	Green		0.070	600	Low	15–16	Low	Low	High			●	
2 *Dieffenbachia maculata 'Superba'* (Dumb cane)	●				Green & cream	Smooth shiny	Green		0.070	600	Low	15–16	Low	Low	High			●	
3 *Dieffenbachia 'Exotica'* (Dumb cane)	●				Green & white	Smooth shiny	Green		0.070	600	Low	15–16	Low	Low	High		●		
4 *Dieffenbachia amoena 'Tropic Snow'* (Dumb cane)		●			Green & cream	Smooth shiny	Green		0.070	600	Low	15–16	Low	Low	High		●		
5 *Dizygotheca elegantissima* (false aralia)		●			Bronze	Smooth	Brown		0.115	1000	Low	15–18	Mid	High	High			●	
6 *Cordyline stricta* →		●			Green →	Smooth shiny	Green		0.070	600	High	10–13	Mid	High	Low			●	Young leaves have purple tinge. Incorrectly called *Dracaena Congesta*
7 *Dracaena deremensis* (Striped dracaena)		●	●		Green & white	Smooth shiny	Green to brown		0.070	600	High	10–13	Mid	High	Low		●		
8 *Dracaena deremensis 'Rhoers Gold'*		●	●		Green & yellow	Smooth shiny	Green to brown		0.070	600	High	10–13	Mid	High	Low			●	
9 *Dracaena godseffiana* (Florida beauty)	●				Green & cream	Smooth shiny	Green		0.070	600	High	10–13	Mid	Low	Low			●	

TABLE 12.1 GUIDE TO PLANT SELECTION (CONTINUED)

Botanic name (common name)	Usual height range in mm: 0 to 500	500 to 1000	1000 to 5000	5000 plus	Leaf colour	Leaf texture	Stem colour	Flowers	Minimum radiation requirement (400 to 700 nm) in MJ/day	Minimum average illuminance requirement in lux for 12 h/day	Tolerance to direct sun	Minimum temperature regime in °C	Moisture level preference	Tolerance to leaf cleaners	Tolerance to fluoride	Availability: freely	readily	rarely	Comments
1 *Dracaena marginata* (Silhouette plant)	●	●	●		Green & red	Smooth shiny	Green to brown		0.070	600	High	10–13	Low	High	Mid	●			
2 *Dracaena marginata tricolour*	●	●			Multi colour →	Smooth shiny	Green to brown		0.070	600	High	10–13	Low	High	Mid		●		Leaves mixed green/red/ cream stripes
3 *Fatsia japonica* (Castor oil plant) →	●	●			Green	Smooth shiny	Brown		0.060	500	Low	4–7 →	Mid	High	High	●			Also called *Aralia sieboldii*, prefers cooler locations
4 *Fatshedera lizei*		●	●		Green	Smooth shiny	Green to brown		0.070	600	Mid	6–8 →	Mid	High	High		●		Prefers cooler locations
5 *Ficus australis* →			●	●	Green	Smooth shiny	Brown		0.080	700	Mid	7–10	Mid	High	High			●	Also called *Ficus rubiginosa*
6 *Ficus benghalensis* (Bengal fig)			●	●	Green	Downy	Brown		0.070	600	Low	7–10	Mid	Low	High			●	
7 *Ficus benjamina* (Weeping fig)			●	●	Green	Smooth shiny	Brown		0.080	700	Mid	10–13 →	Mid	High	High	●			Sudden changes in temperature can stimulate leaf fall

TABLE 12.1 GUIDE TO PLANT SELECTION (CONTINUED)

Botanic name (common name)	Usual height range in mm: 0 to 500	500 to 1000	1000 to 5000	5000 plus	Leaf colour	Leaf texture	Stem colour	Flowers	Minimum radiation requirement (400 to 700 nm) in MJ/day	Minimum average illuminance requirement in lux for 12 h/day	Tolerance to direct sun	Minimum temperature regime in °C	Moisture level preference	Tolerance to leaf cleaners	Tolerance to fluoride	Availability: freely	readily	rarely	Comments
1 *Ficus diversifolia* (Mistletoe fig)		●	●		Dark green	Smooth	Brown	Red berries	0.095	800	Mid	13–16	Mid	High	High		●		
2 *Ficus elastica* (Rubber plant)			●	●	Dark green	Smooth shiny	Green to brown		0.070	600	Low	5–7	Mid	High	High	●			
3 *Ficus elastica 'Black Prince'* (Black rubber plant)			●	●	Black green	Smooth shiny	Green to brown		0.080	700	Low	5–7	Mid	High	High			●	
4 *Ficus elastica 'Schryveriana'* (Variegated rubber plant)			●	●	Green & cream	Smooth shiny	Green to brown		0.095	800	Low	7–10	Mid	High	High		●		
5 *Ficus nitida* (Indian laurel)			●	●	Green	Smooth shiny	Brown		0.080	700	Mid →	7–10	Mid	High	High		●		Similar to *F. benjamina* but more resilient
6 *Ficus lyrata* (Fiddle leafed fig)			●	●	Light green	Smooth	Brown		0.070	600	Mid	13–16	Mid	High	High		●		
7 *Ficus pumila* (Creeping fig)	●	●	●		Green	Smooth	Green		0.070	600	Low	7–10	Mid	Low	High	●			
8 *Ficus retusa* (Chinese banyan)			●	●	Green	Smooth	Brown		0.080	700	Low	10–13	Mid	High	High			●	

TABLE 12.1 GUIDE TO PLANT SELECTION (CONTINUED)

Botanic name (common name)	Usual height range in mm: 0 to 500	500 to 1000	1000 to 5000	5000 plus	Leaf colour	Leaf texture	Stem colour	Flowers	Minimum radiation requirement (400 to 700 nm) in MJ/day	Minimum average illuminance requirement in lux for 12 h/day	Tolerance to direct sun	Minimum temperature regime in °C	Moisture level preference	Tolerance to leaf cleaners	Tolerance to fluoride	Availability: freely	readily	rarely	Comments
1 *Hedera canariensis 'Variegata'* (Canary ivy)		●	●		Green & cream	Smooth shiny	Green to brown		0.080	700	Mid	5–7 →	Mid	High	High		●		Prefers cooler locations
2 *Hedera helix* (English ivy)		●	●		Green	Smooth shiny	Green to brown		0.060	500	Mid	3–5 →	Mid	High	High	●			Prefers cooler locations
3 *Heptapleurum arboricola* → (Green rays)			●		Green	Smooth shiny	Green		0.080	700	Mid	7–10	Mid	High	High	●			Also called *Schefflera arboricola*
4 *Howeia forsteriana* → (Kentia palm)			●		Green	Smooth	Brown		0.070	600	Mid	7–10	Mid	Low	High	●			Also called *Kentia forsteriana*
5 *Laurus nobilis* (Bay tree)			●		Dark green	Smooth shiny	Brown		0.095	800	Mid	3–5 →	Low	High	High			●	Prefers cooler locations
6 *Monstera deliciosa* (Swiss cheese plant) →		●	●		Dark green	Smooth shiny	Green to brown		0.060	500	Mid	10–13	High	High	High		●		Also called *Philodendron pertusum* when small
7 *Neoregelia carolinae* (Blushing bromeliad)	●				Green →	Smooth shiny		Purple →	0.105	900	Mid	13–15	Mid	Low	High	●			Plant centre red – flowers insignificant
8 *Neoregelia carolinae tricolour* (Blushing bromeliad)	●				Green & cream →	Smooth shiny		Purple →	0.115	1000	Mid	13–15	Mid	Low	High		●		Plant centre red – flowers insignificant

TABLE 12.1 GUIDE TO PLANT SELECTION (CONTINUED)

Botanic name (common name)	Usual height range in mm: 0 to 500	500 to 1000	1000 to 5000	5000 plus	Leaf colour	Leaf texture	Stem colour	Flowers	Minimum radiation requirement (400 to 700 nm) in MJ/day	Minimum average illuminance requirement in lux for 12 h/day	Tolerance to direct sun	Minimum temperature regime in °C	Moisture level preference	Tolerance to leaf cleaners	Tolerance to fluoride	Availability: freely	readily	rarely	Comments
1 *Nephrolepsis exaltata* (Sword fern)	●				Pale green	Smooth			0.070	600	Low	7–10	High	Low	High		●		
2 *Pandanus veitchii* (Screw pine)		●	●		Green & gold	Smooth shiny →	Green & brown		0.070	600	Mid	10–13	Mid	High	High		●		Leaves with vicious serrations
3 *Peperomia caperata* (Little fantasy)	●				Dark green	Shiny & crinkled	Red brown	White spikes	0.070	600	Low	10–13	Mid	Low	High	●			
4 *Peperomia obtusifolia 'Variegata'* (Variegated Peperomia)	●				Green & gold	Smooth shiny	Red & yellow	White spikes	0.070	600	Low	10–13	Mid	High	High		●		
5 *Philodendron* X *'Burgundy'*		●	●		Dark green →	Smooth shiny	Green		0.070	600	Low	10–13	High	High	High		●		Underside of leaves with deep red veins
6 *Philodendron erubescens 'Red Emerald'*		●	●		Green	Smooth shiny	Red		0.060	500	Low	10–13	High	High	High	●			
7 *Philodendron longilaminatun*		●	●		Dark green	Smooth shiny	Green		0.060	500	Low	10–13	High	High	High		●		

TABLE 12.1 GUIDE TO PLANT SELECTION (CONTINUED)

Botanic name (common name)	Usual height range in mm: 0 to 500	500 to 1000	1000 to 5000	5000 plus	Leaf colour	Leaf texture	Stem colour	Flowers	Minimum radiation requirement (400 to 700 nm) in MJ/day	Minimum average illuminance requirement in lux for 12 h/day	Tolerance to direct sun	Minimum temperature regime in °C	Moisture level preference	Tolerance to leaf cleaners	Tolerance to fluoride	Availability: freely	readily	rarely	Comments
1 *Philodendron panduraeforme* →		●	●		Green	Smooth shiny	Green		0.060	500	Low	13–15	High	High	High			●	
2 *Philodendron pertusum* →		●	●		Green	Smooth shiny	Green		0.060	500	Low	10–13	High	High	High	●			More correctly a juvenile form of *Monstera deliciosa* with smaller leaves and more upright habit
3 *Philodendron pertusum variegatum* →		●	●		Green & white	Smooth shiny			0.095	800	Low	10–13	High	High	High			●	Slower growing than *Philodendron pertusum*
4 *Philodendron scandens* (Sweetheart plant)		●	●		Dark green	Smooth shiny	Green		0.060	500	Low	7–10	High	High	High	●			
5 *Phoenix dactylifera* (date palm)			●	●	Green	Smooth	Brown		0.115	1000	High	5–7	Mid	Low	High		●		
6 *Platycerium bifurcatum* (Stag's horn fern)	●	●			Grey	Downy bloom →			0.115	1000	Mod	10–13	Mid	Low	High		●		Bloom on leaf will not regenerate once removed by rubbing
7 *Rhoicissus rhomboidea* (Grape ivy)	●	●			Dark green	Smooth shiny	Brown		0.060	500	Low	7–10	Mid	High	High	●			
8 *Rhoicissus rhombidea 'Ellen Danica'*	●	●			Dark green	Smooth shiny →	Brown		0.060	500	Low	7–10	Mid	High	High	●			

TABLE 12.1 GUIDE TO PLANT SELECTION (CONTINUED)

Botanic name (common name)	Usual height range in mm: 0 to 500	500 to 1000	1000 to 5000	5000 plus	Leaf colour	Leaf texture	Stem colour	Flowers	Minimum radiation requirement (400 to 700 nm) in MJ/day	Minimum average illuminance requirement in lux for 12 h/day	Tolerance to direct sun	Minimum temperature regime in °C	Moisture level preference	Tolerance to leaf cleaners	Tolerance to fluoride	Availability: freely	readily	rarely	Comments
1 *Sansevieria trifasciata laurentii* (Mother-in-law's tongue)		●			Green & gold	Smooth shiny			0.070	600	High	7–10	Low	High	High	●			
2 *Schefflera actinophylla* (Umbrella tree) →			●		Green	Smooth shiny	Green to brown		0.080	700	Mid	10–13	Low	High	High	●			Also called *Brassaia actinophylla*
3 *Scidapsus aureus* (Devil's ivy) →		●	●		Green & gold	Smooth shiny	Green		0.070	600	Mid	10–13	Low	Low	High	●			More correctly called *Epipremnum aureus*
4 *Spathiphyllum wallisii* (Peace lily)	●				Dark green	Smooth shiny		White	0.080	700 →	Mid	10–13	High	High	Mid	●			0.172 MJ/day or 1500 lux for good flowers
5 *Spathiphyllum 'Mauna Loa'* (Peace lily)		●			Dark green	Smooth shiny		White	0.080	700 →	Mid	10–13	High	High	Mid		●		0.172 MJ/day or 1500 lux for good flowers
6 *Syngonium xanthophilum 'Green Gold'* → (Goose foot plant)		●			Green & gold	Smooth shiny			0.060	500	Low	10–13	Mid	Low	High	●			Also called *Nephthytis 'Green Gold'*
7 *Tradescantia fluminensis variegata* (Wandering jew)		●			Green & cream →	Smooth shiny	Green		0.080	700	Mid	5–7	Mid	High	High		●		Other forms can contain green/white/cream/purple/red
8 *Vriesea splendens* (Flaming sword)	●				Green & brown	Smooth		Red →	0.115	1000	Mid	13–16	Mid	High	High		●		Flowers on long spike
9 *Yucca elephantipes* (Spineless yucca)		●	●		Dark green	Smooth shiny	Brown	White →	0.095	800	High	10–13	Low	High	Mid		●		Flowers on spike

13 Plant specification and tendering procedures

INTRODUCTION

Most of the plants which are used for interior in buildings are produced many miles from their display location; eg much of the material used in Britain is produced in the Ghent area of Belgium and the Amsterdam area of Holland (fig 13.1). In a similar manner a large portion of the plant material used in North America is produced in Florida, Texas and California. One advantage of interior plant production in the USA is that the climate in the extreme south of the country is sufficiently mild for most species to be grown outside. It is therefore common for large plants to be grown in the open ground for several years before being lifted and containerised. In western Europe most of the plants have to be produced in glasshouses although an increasing number are now being grown outside in Southern Spain. This situation means that there will almost certainly be a permanent shortage of large plants for interior use in Western Europe. Proposals are being considered for large scale importation from the USA. If it were possible to predict the need for a given number of large plants it may be possible to purchase ahead and then grow on in a glasshouse. However the commercial intricacies of such an operation are considerable, eg inflation and rising fuel costs could make the formulation of a contract almost impossible.

With the increasing demand for interior plants there has been a considerable strain placed upon many of the established channels of supply. This is not particularly serious where small plants are concerned but is particularly noticeable with larger specimens which are grown for five to ten years or more before being sold. One of the results of this diminution in supply is that the variability of plant material is even more pronounced than was formerly the case. This variability in standards between companies is particularly pronounced over the extremes of the quality spectrum. Frequently it is difficult to be certain as to the quality and dimensions of plants that are being specified in a given tender price. Unfortunately at present there is no standard specification format for plant material in Europe although one has been produced in the USA by the Florida Foliage Assocation. Until standards are universally accepted it

13.1 *A production glasshouse in the Ghent area of Belgium*

is necessary to specify clearly and accurately those characteristics which are required. The information contained in this section is intended to achieve this aim:

FACTORS FOR THE PREAMBLES

The following should be included in the preamble to all specifications:

1 The plants including their root system shall appear healthy and free from pests and diseases
2 The foliage shall be of good colour which is characteristic of the type, and free from blemishes
3 The plants shall have a form which is typical of their type
4 There shall be no damaged, dying or dead material attached to the plant
5 The plants shall be stable and well rooted in a container of reasonable size
6 The plants shall be rooted in a substrate which contains at least 20% pore space and is free from a high salt concentration
7 During shipment no plant shall be short of moisture, or deprived of light for more than five days unless the journey necessitates such an extended period
8 Compost should only carry a small residue of fertiliser and where necessary the salt levels of the substrate shall be reduced to no more than 1000 ppm before despatch
9 (For large plants which will experience very low light conditions.) The plants shall have been acclimatised under approximately 55% shading for a minimum of three months before delivery

SPECIFICATION

The problem of producing a specification for interior plants is the natural variability which exists with living material. No definitive rules are possible but the following suggestions should be useful, particularly with the larger specimens.

1 *Name* – This should be in botanical nomenclature. Care should always be taken to apply the conventions described below.
2 *Overall height* – The height of a plant can be taken either from the surface of the compost or the base of the container. Usually the height from the compost surface bears more relevance to the ultimate function although in North America the height is usually taken from the base of the container. The top of most woody plants should be taken as the natural dominant apex rather than extraneous side growths.
3 *Stem length* – Where a clear stem is desired the length should be taken from the surface of the compost.
4 *"Cane" length* – With plants that are raised from 'canes" the height should be taken from the compost surface.
5 *Stem number* – The number of stems which support a canopy can be crucial with certain species, eg Yuccas, and may even be significant for plants with a less definite form, eg *Ficus benjamina*, as it indicates the overall foliar density. The number of stems should be taken as those which originate within the first 150 mm of the stem and continue for at least 75% of its overall height.
6 *Stem diameter* – For large specimens the diameter of the main stem may be used to indicate the "weight" of plant which is required and should be measured at 500 mm above the compost surface.
7 *Canopy diameter* – This can be difficult to determine and should exclude extraneous growths.
8 *Container size* – It is seldom necessary to specify the size of production container unless a narrow display planter is to be used when it is necessary to state a maximum size.
9 *Root ball dimensions* – Seldom are interior plants sold without a container except for some large specimen trees. In such situations it is advisable to agree with the supplier as to the size of root ball most likely to succeed.

Plant nomenclature

Plant nomenclature is the subject of internationally accepted codes and is used to ensure that standards of accuracy are maintained. Although the complete system is exceedingly complex there are certain basic conventions which pertain to the writing of names and the more important of these are described below.

Plant nomenclature has arisen from many languages but its grammatical form is based on Latin with a Greek influence. For this reason all names are in Latin or treated as if they are even if derived from other sources. A whole name can be written in upper case but this can lead to errors in reading and so should not be used. More correctly lower case should be used throughout except where mentioned below. To indicate the use of botanical nomenclature the full name should be either underlined or printed in italics, eg

Dracaena marginata or *Dracaena marginata*

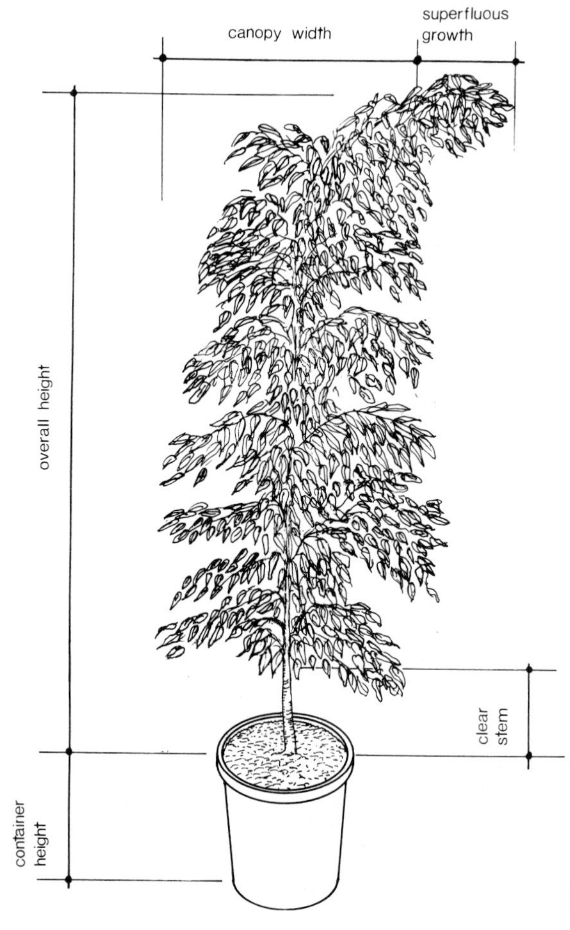

13.2 *Features to consider when producing a specification for plant material*

Family
These indicate broad groups of plants and whilst they can be of practical value they are not part of the plants name. When used they should be written in lower case with a capital initial, eg

Dracaena spp belong to the family *Agavaceae*

Genus
This is the basic naming unit in regular usage and is always a singular noun. It should be written in lower case with a capital initial, eg

Dumb Canes belong to the genus *Dracaena*

If an unspecified species within a given genus is under consideration the generic name should be followed by the letters sp, eg *Dracaena sp*.

If a whole genus is under consideration, or a large group of species within a given genus then the generic name should be followed by the letters spp, eg *Dracaena spp*.

Species
The specific epithet serves to identify the plant within the genus and follows the generic title. It should be remembered that Latin is an inflected language so that the endings of specific epithets, which are normally adjectives, should agree in number, gender and case with the generic name. Sometimes the genus and the specific epithet are both nouns, in which case they should agree, although this is not always the case. Specific epithets should always be written in lower case throughout, eg

Dracaena marginata
(genus) (species)

Subspecies
These are naturally occurring forms of a species which have certain noteworthy characteristics. They should be in Latin and written in lower case throughout after the specific epithet, eg

Dracaena marginata tricolour
(genus) (species) (subspecies)

Cultivars (or, incorrectly, varieties)
These are distinct forms of a species which have been bred or selected for commercial purposes. The majority of interior plants are of these improved forms and most have to be reproduced by vegetative means. As a cultivar is based directly upon an established species the full name should be given, including the specific epithet. The cultivar names are usually vernacular words and should be written in lower case with a capital initial and enclosed in single quotation marks, eg

Philodendron erubescens 'Red Emerald'

If it is desired the single quotation marks may be removed and replaced with the letters cv, eg

Philodendron erubescens cv. Red Emerald

Hybrids
These usually occur in cultivation by inter breeding between two or more species. As a result they no longer belong to an ancestral species and so a specific group of crosses may be given a collective name. This should be written in lower case throughout and separated from the generic name by a multiplication sign, eg

Philodendron × *wend-imbe* (ie P. wendlandii with P. imbe)
However, if the hybrid exists in only one form it is given a single clonal name. This is not usually in Latin and should be written in lower case with a capital initial and enclosed by single quotation marks, eg

Philodendron × *'Burgundy'*

Name reduction
When the name of a plant is to be written both the generic name and specific epithet are necessary. If a list of species within a genus is to be written then the generic name can be reduced to its initial. In such usage all specific epithets are assumed to relate to the last complete generic name even if they are located through a text, eg

Dracaena deremensis
D. godseffiana
D. marginata

A similar approach may also be applied to a list of cultivars and/or subspecies, eg

Hedera helix 'Chicago',
H.h. cristata,
H.h. 'Glacier'

INSTALLATION COSTS

Once a planted container has been installed it will require regular maintenance if it is to remain in good condition. Many organisations prefer to undertake their own maintenance, but unfortunately it has often been found that unless the maintenance operatives are of a high standard there is a steady decline in quality. The trend of local authorities to utilise staff who have no specialist knowledge of this field, for reasons of economy, can be most detrimental, although it is to be hoped that training procedures will develop to overcome this problem. Such difficulties can be avoided by the use of a specialist company to undertake maintenance on a regular basis. With large contracts such companies may well second an employee to a specific scheme, and so reasonable facilities should be provided for their operations.

Wherever possible the initial maintenance contract should be with the plant supplier and should last for at least one year after planting. This contract should include plant replacement when necessary so that the scheme is complete on hand-over. This approach also ensures that any major design problems are overcome before the planting becomes the responsibility of the occupant. With large schemes it may well be beneficial to extend this contract for two to four years to cover the period of establishment.

After installation the control of interior planting often passes to the premises manager and with it the determination of standards for maintenance contracts. Obviously such a situation can be difficult for a person who is not familiar with plants and so it is advisable for the design team to recommend a suitable maintenance organisation. If at a later date it is found that other companies are more competitive the arrangements can be changed but at least standards will have been determined.

MAINTENANCE COSTS

Plants in an office can be bought directly or rented. The cost of renting a planted container (and including its maintenance) is usually found to be three times that of a maintenance service alone and so may be considered excessive. The cost of maintenance is normally based on a rate per planter with reference to the total number of planters in the scheme. Some companies may refuse to service small schemes with, say, less than five planters, although others, who are geared to such operations, are delighted to do so. The more usual size categories for plantings are:

Under 5	–	very small
5–20	–	small
20–50	–	medium
50–200	–	large
over 200	–	very large

The service offered by interior plant companies fall into three main categories:

1 *High class* – This implies a high density of good quality specimen plants which are replaced every few weeks and maintained to the highest possible standard. This is an expensive service, with maintenance on a weekly basis, but it may be acceptable in prestige situations.

2 *Standard* – This implies good quality plants used in such a way that their chances of survival are high, eg some companies may not accept responsibility for plants in very low light conditions. Maintenance is of a high standard with visits at two to three week intervals.

3 *Basic* – This implies moderate quality, small sized plants whose maintenance is dubious. Unfortunately the number of small operators who fall into this category are rising due to the profits which are to be made from such "cut price" operations.

SELECTION OF TENDERS

There are an increasing number of small companies which can offer low price maintenance because they have a limited number of staff and few overheads. However their ability to provide a continuous high quality service with technical support is very dubious. For this reason to accept a low bid for a maintenance tender can mean selecting a company with low standards. Unfortunately there are still situations where regulations require that the lowest bid be accepted, but these can be avoided by accurately specifying the requirements. It is common for many bids to be similar – companies tend to study the pricing policy of their competitors. Often one company will try to be selected by attempting to undercut the competition on the initial planting cost so as to secure the maintenance contract.

For the maintenance of large schemes, tenders should be requested only from large established companies with at least five years' experience. Where possible it is advisable to visit at random several schemes maintained by these companies to inspect the quality of their work and to ascertain the level of existing customer satisfaction. Often there are only four or five well known companies who are in a position to tender for a given project, but this is usually sufficient to provide fair competition.

14 Maintenance

INTRODUCTION

Many views have been expressed concerning the level of maintenance necessary for successful interior planting. As a result a whole spectrum of standards exist. These range from the very highest, where high quality plants are changed every few weeks, to a self-help policy, where individual employees are encouraged to identify with a specific group of plants. In Britain and North America this personal responsibility for a plant would appear to be less satisfactory than in, say, Holland. Therefore in practice it is usual for the appearance of any planting to be closely related to maintenance expenditure. Maintenance requirements vary according to the location, type and size of installation, but the most important factors for consideration are the following.

WATERING

One of the most important factors for reducing the rate of growth is a lack of water. If water stress is removed growth is often stimulated, although overwatering must be avoided as a thin layer of water will halt gaseous exchange. If such a condition continues for more than 24 hours damage can result. The symptoms of a waterlogged plant can be similar to those of a dehydrated one, as both situations can result in the root system failing to deliver sufficient water to the foliage. Therefore an indication of prolonged overwatering is wilting, even when the compost is moist, due to the root system malfunctioning. Probably the most serious effect of overwatering is "root rot", caused by soil borne fungi and bacteria invading tissue damaged by low oxygen levels.

Water is best applied in heavy doses at well spaced intervals so that the compost moisture content fluctuates between "field capacity" and barely moist. If the plants are to experience a period of low temperature the compost moisture content should be reduced to avoid the possibility of cell damage and infection. At lower temperatures plant growth is usually minimal so that the effect of such water stress should be marginal. The extent of this reduction will depend on many factors but a drop of 50% on the available water content should suffice.

The characteristics of manual and semi-automatic irrigation systems have been fully described in chapter 7.

FEEDING

When a planting is assembled the compost will usually contain sufficient fertiliser for at least six months' growth. It should be remembered that in most interior situations the plants can require as little as 10% of the nutrient concentrations which they required during production. For this reason the fertiliser content of any substrate should be low, and excessively high salt levels may require leaching from production containers before use.

Most plants will benefit from small additions of "liquid feed" every four to six weeks during periods of active growth or every two months during the winter.

The nutrient value of organic fertilisers can be very variable and their efficacy hard to predict, which is why they are not recommended for use indoors. Controlled release fertilisers which remain effective for over nine months can be used, although care is necessary when determining the application rates. The fertiliser requirement of certain species can be determined from table 14.1, but in very low light situation even these application rates can be reduced by half. With a hydroculture system an ion exchange resin is usually applied at six monthly intervals, although a little liquid feed may be necessary in soft water areas to allow the resin to function. Foliar feeds are available for spraying onto the leaves, but these should only be considered when a plant is recovering from root damage.

Occasionally plants may exhibit symptoms of nutrient deficiency. It is often difficult to determine the exact cause by visual assessment but each specific deficiency does tend to manifest itself in a slightly different way. The most usual symptoms are a yellowing of the foliage by death. It may prove possible, however, to determine the exact nature of a deficiency by reference to table 14.2. If a more accurate assessment is desired then a sample of foliage should be sent to a commercial laboratory for complete chemical analysis.

CLEANING

A well established plant will generally require some training and pruning to maintain its form. All pieces of dead plant material and rubbish should be removed at regular intervals (fig 14.1). If planters are used as repositories for tea and coffee dregs, replanting will certainly become necessary.

TABLE 14.1 FERTILISER APPLICATION FACTORS FOR INTERIOR PLANTS AT DIFFERENT RADIATION LEVELS (400 TO 700 NM) IN MJ=DAY OR AVERAGE ILLUMINANCE IN LUX FOR 12H=DAY.

Requirement group	Typical species	Low	Medium	High	Very high
		.06 to 0.09 MJ/day	0.09 to 0.18 MJ/day	0.18 to 0.30 MJ/day	0.30 to 0.60 MJ/day
		500 to 750 lux	750 to 1500 lux	1500 to 2500 lux	2500 to 5000 lux
low	Ferns & peperomia spp.	3	7	10	17
medium	Aglaonema, Cordyline, Dieffenbachia, Dracaena, Howea, Philodendron, Scindapsus, & Syngonium spp.	7	13	20	25
high	Ficus, & Schefflera spp.	10	20	25	33

1 For the chosen fertiliser determine the weight of nitrogen in each kilogram. From this determine the weight of fertiliser which will contain one gram of nitrogen ie.

$$\frac{100}{\text{Nitrogen content (\%)}} = \text{fertiliser in grams}$$

2 Multiply this weight of fertiliser by the light/species factor determined from the table above in gms/m^2/year.

3 Determine the actual rate per application by dividing the annual application rate by the proposed number of applications per year.

14.1 *Any debris which has been placed in a planter should be removed as soon as possible (for it may encourage others to add to it)*

TABLE 14.2 NUTRIENT DEFICIENCY SYMPTOMS

Symptoms	Diagnosis
1 Symptoms general throughout plant – most extreme in older tissue	
a foliage light green turning yellow then light brown – growth retarded with small leaves which seldom fall when dead	low nitrogen
b foliage dark green but turning yellow or purple between veins – petioles (leaf stalk) may turn purple – overall growth retarded with premature leaf fall	low phosphorus
2 Symptoms pronounced on older leaves	
a foliage mottled with yellowing starting from extremeties – Margins later die and curl – older leaves fall	low potassium
b foliage yellowing particularly between veins – margins curl – leaves die suddenly between veins	low magnesium
3 Symptoms on new leaves with terminal buds alive	
a foliage pale or yellow but veins still green – leaves can die back from margin	low iron
b foliage pale or yellow but veins still green – dead spots appear on leaf surface	low manganese
c foliage pale but veins lighter than adjoining areas – dead spots may appear on leaf surface	low sulphur
4 Symptoms on new leaves – with terminal buds dead	
a foliage die-back from margins – root system severely damaged	low calcium
b Stems and leaf bases brittle – root tips severely damaged	low boron

In many schemes attempts are made to cover large areas with plants. It is unfortunate that inside many buildings dust accumulates which soon detracts from the value of the display. If there is a small quantity of foliage then it may be practical to remove the dust by hand. Such manual cleaning usually involves wiping with a damp cloth although in North America the use of a feather duster is popular. The effect of wiping with a damp cloth can be increased by the use of a mild detergent or the use of dilute citric acid, although such materials should be used with extreme caution. Over large areas such techniques may be impractical, so spraying the foliage with clean water at regular intervals may be the only solution. For this function a fine fogging or misting nozzle should be used if surrounding surfaces are not to be drenched. If the foliage is to be sprayed at regular intervals soft water must be used otherwise a white calcium deposit will form.

To ensure that the accumulation of dust does not cause difficulties provision should be made to reach all foliage or to at least be able to spray it with water. "White spirit" or "leaf shine" can be used to reduce the tenacity of a dust layer but should be used with care as they are harmful to some plants and will damage all plants if used in excess. No plant should be cleaned with leaf shine more than once a month and if possible much less frequently. The potential hazard with leaf shines is that they may block or even enter the leaf through the stomatal apertures. For this reason they should only be used on the upper surface of dicotyledonous leaves, where there are few stomata, and not on monocotyledonous plants, such as palms, which have an equal number of stomata on either surface.

PLANT DISORDERS

At some time most plants will undergo periods of stress due to irregularities in their environment or attacks by pests and disease pathogens. It is fortunate that of the many potential plant problems there are few which are common. Of the plants which die in buildings it has been estimated that losses can be attributed to:

1	Incorrect lighting	50%
2	Incorrect watering	40%
3	Pests and diseases	5%
4	Others	5%

The diagnosis of plant problems can be difficult as some of the symptoms can be produced by a range of causal agents. Often the symptoms of pathogens are similar to those of a deficiency or excess of nutrients. In a similar manner some plants, for example, ferns, can exhibit disease-like symptoms if planted too deeply. Some like *Philodendron scandens* or *Syngonium podophyllum* exhibit symptoms of fungal attack if sprayed with cold water. Temperatures below 10°C can cause some *Dieffenbachia spp* and *Aglaonema spp* to progressively yellow. However in general the more obvious causes should be considered before the more exotic.

The more common symptoms of a distressed plant with their probable causes are described in table 14.3. If the problem is associated with a specific individual in a group there is a high chance that the symptoms are due to disease. Where a plant is exhibiting stress it is usual to try and assess the cause by observing the aerial components of the plant. If the problem is particularly severe or if many plants are involved, then it may be informative to expose a complete root system for examination.

PESTS AND DISEASE

It is to be hoped that when plants are introduced to interior locations that they will be relatively free from pests, although it is almost inevitable that some will be present. As a result it is good practice to cleanse the plant before installation by the use of a strong commercial insecticide and a soil drench. Once they are in use there are few pests and disease organisms which will attack the plants. However, the low light levels which are common indoors adversely affect the carbohydrate economy of the plant and so reduce disease resistance. Tables 14.4., 14.5 and 14.6 indicate the most common pests and diseases found on interior plants, with a suggestion for chemical control. There are many materials which can be used to control those organisms which adversely affect plants. The term pesticide is a generic title for such compounds as insecticides, fungicides, herbicides and rodenticides. Of these the first two are the most important to interior planting and are considered below.

Insecticides

These are applied to destroy insects and mites in one or more of the following manners:

1 by direct contact
2 by leaving a small deposit which is later eaten
3 by being taken into the sap of the plant and then being consumed, ie a systemic insecticide.

The first two are described as contact insecticides and are widely used against creatures which actively consume the plant, eg caterpillars. The last is used mainly against those creatures which suck sap from the plant, like greenfly and mealy bug. Many of the popular commercial chemicals which are available for the control of insects and mites are effective in more than one role, eg systemics are usually effective as contact insecticides. Unfortunately the less aggressive compounds which are more commonly used indoors are effective for such a limited period that they can only be considered as having a contact effect. The use of chemical pesticides is regulated in North America by the US Environmental Protection Agency and in the UK by the Government Approved Pesticide Safety Precaution Scheme. These organisations require the manufacturers of a chemical to ensure that the formulation is safe for use in the situation for which it is intended. They also require that the chemical be sold in suitable and clearly labelled containers. To date, the regulations applying to the household and amateur market are the only ones appropriate to building interiors. As a result the range of formulations is limited and tends to be somewhat "dated" in view of recent develoments.

The most popular chemicals for controlling pests on interior plantings are those based on pyrethrum and resmethrin. These are a group of compounds, found in certain plants, which have a low mammalian toxicity. Of the many synthetic compounds which are available, malathion and kelthane are popular for this reason, although their smell can be offensive. If odour is a problem it may be practical to spray at the start of a weekend to allow time for the odour to dissipate. If a more aggressive chemical control is desired then it may be necessary to remove the plants to an isolated location for treatment. Most companies who deal with interior planting prefer to use insecticides based on pyrethrum or related compounds as they are inoffensive and yet adequate for aphids and red spider mites. The more tenacious problems such as mealy bug and scale insects are often controlled by dabbing individually with methylated spirits.

It is hard to determine the frequency of spraying which is necessary to control or prevent an attack. If the plants are apparently free from pests it may be possible to dispense entirely with spraying except for a bi-monthly protective spray against eggs or young larvae. If a plant is heavily infested it may be advisable to give two sprays at weekly intervals followed by a three weekly cycle until the attack is controlled. Very regular spraying has been found to be unnecesary with the less tenaci-

TABLE 14.3 PHYSIOLOGICAL DISORDERS (CAUSES IN ORDER OF OCCURENCE)

Plant symptoms	Cause	Comments
Foliage wilting	**a** Prolonged drought	irrigate more frequently
	b Overwatering	irrigate less frequently
	c Root Damage	inspect, determine cause and treat
	d Excess sun and/or heat	relocate in darker situation
Little overall growth	**a** Normal in moderation	may occur in some situations
	b insufficient light	increase illumination
	c insufficient water	increase frequency of irrigation
	d insufficient nutrient	apply feed more frequently
	e root damage	inspect, determine cause and treat
Young leaves pale in colour	**a** insufficient light	increase illumination
	b insufficient nutrients	apply feed more frequently
	c waterlogging	reduce frequency of irrigation
	d toxic gases	increase ventilation or relocate
	e excess nutrients	leach thoroughly and feed less frequently
Mature leaves yellowing	**a** insufficient light	increase illumination
	b insufficient nutrients	apply nutrients more frequently
	c excess salt	leach thoroughly
	d viruses	discard plant
Leaf yellowing followed by fall	**a** normal for occasional leaf	occurs with age after 2–3 years
	b cold draughts	relocate
	c overwatering	reduce frequency of irrigation
	d insufficient nutrients	apply nutrients more frequently
Sudden leaf fall	**a** sudden environmental change	relocate
	b insufficient water	increase frequency of irrigation
	c root damage	inspect, determine cause and treat
	d toxic gases	increase ventilation or relocate
Brown lesions on leaves	**a** bright sunshine	relocate in shade
	b hot dry air	relocate
	c disease	inspect, determine cause and treat
	d gas fumes	increase ventilation and/or relocate
Browning of leaf tips or margins	**a** hot dry air	relocate
	b insufficient nutrients	apply feed more frequently
	c fluoride damage	change compost and aerate irrigation water
	d excess nutrients	leach thoroughly and feed less frequently
	e root damage	inspect, determine cause and treat
Flower Bud fall	**a** insufficient light	increase illumination
	b insufficient water	increase frequency of irrigation
	c overwatering	reduce frequency of irrigation
	d sudden environmental change	relocate

14.4 (**a**) *powdery mildew;* (**b**) *fungal leaf spot;* (**c**) *fungal black blotch;* (**d**) *root rot (Crown copyright, Agricultural Science Service Slide Collection)*

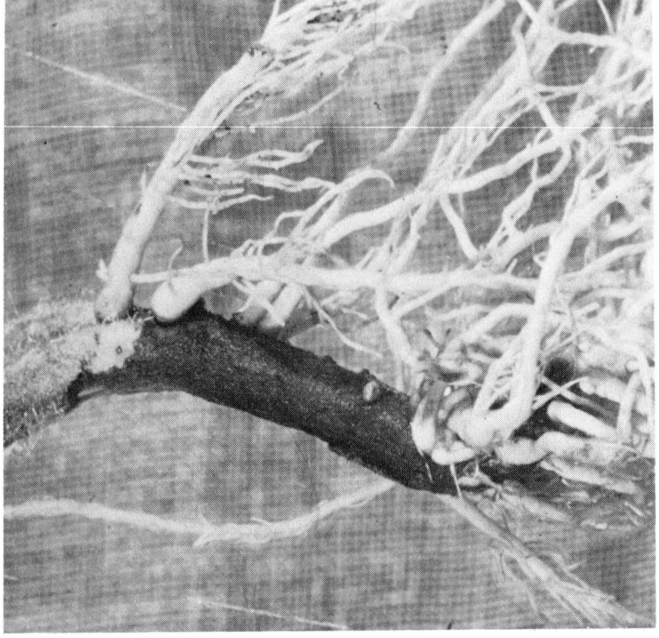

14.2 (**a**) *scale insect;* (**b**) *white fly;* (**c**) *caterpillar;* (**d**) *root galls (nematodes)* (**b**, **c** *&* **d** *Crown Copyright)*

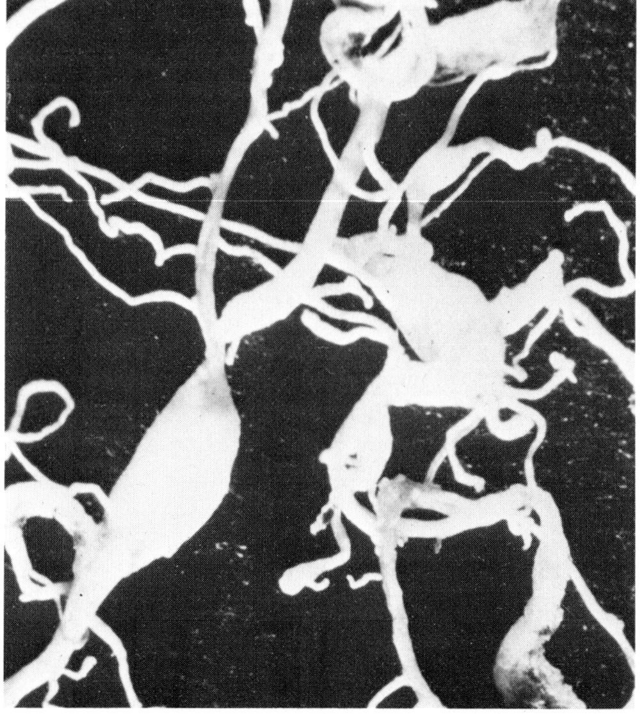

TABLE 14.4 PESTS – AERIAL

Pest description	Plant symptoms	Where to look	Control
Aphids Adult – small green, white or black round bodied fly Juvenile – as above	Young plant growth weak and distorted – lower leaves sticky with honeydew*	On young growing tips and leaves	Resmethrin Liquid Derris Malathion Pyrethrum Pirimiphos – methyl
Leaf miner Adult – small brown fly Juvenile – brown grubs burrowing inside leaf	Dead meandering strip running through the leaves	In the more mature leaves	Dimethoate
Mealy bug Adult – flat ovoid white insect usually remaining in white furry protective covering Juvenile – as above	Mild attack – white cottony deposit and lower leaves sticky with honeydew* Severe attack – stunted weak plant growth. Premature leaf fall. Black fungi on lower leaves.	Base of leaf at centre of plant	Dab with methylated spirits Dimethoate
Foliar nematodes Adult – tiny round colourless worm Juvenile – as above	Severe attack – stunted weak plant growth. Black or or brown patches appear inside the leaves Mild attack – twisted growth. Black or brown patches appear inside the leaf.	On stems and leaves In the more mature leaves	None available
Red Spider Mite Adult – minute red spider just visible to the naked eye Juvenile – as above	Mild attack – surface becomes pitted with yellow patches Moderate attack – white webbing visible Severe attack – leaves become brittle and fall off	On the underside of leaves starting with the youngest	Liquid Derris Malathion Dimethoate Diazinon
Scale Insect Juvenile – small immobile waxy brown shells	Mild attack – brown lumps over whole plant. Lower leaves sticky with honeydew* Severe attack – stunted weak plant growth	On stems and leaves particularly of compact plants	Dab with methylated spirits Dimethoate
White Fly Juvenile – small white moth-like insect	Mild attack – foliage becomes mottled and lower leaves sticky with honeydew* Severe attack – stunted weak plant growth	On the underside of leaves but fly readily if the plant is disturbed	Liquid Derris Malathion Pyrethrum Pirimiphos – methyl Resmethrin Permethrin

* Honeydew: small sticky droplets of plant sap secreted by insects which can act as a food source for black fungi

TABLE 14.5 PESTS–SUBTERRANEAN

Pest description	Plant symptoms	Root characteristics	Control
Fungal gnats Adult – tiny black fly with wings and long legs (max 3 mm long) Juvenile – thin grub-like body with small black head	Plants usually unaffected but can be unaesthetic	Larvae free in compost but adults free flying	Diazinon soil drench or granules Regular aerosol spray
Nematodes Adult – tiny round colourless worm (max 3 mm long) Juvenile – as above	Root system damaged so plant exhibits signs of nutrient deficiency and/or wilting	Roots develop knots, galls, black spots, or become excessively branched	None available
Root Mealy Bug Adult – small flat ovoid white insect (max 2 mm long) Juvenile – as above	Plant shows weak stunted growth	Small white fluffy lumps on roots containing females with eggs	Diazinon soil drench or granules
Springtails Adult – small wingless brown insect which may jump (max 2 mm long) Juvenile – as above	Plants usually unaffected but can be unaesthetic	All stages free living in compost, most will jump when stimulated	Diazinon soil drench or granules Aerosol spray or regular spray

ous pests like aphids or red spider mites as a weekly application gives at best a 10% improvement over a three weekly one. The more tenacious pests like mealy bug require at least four weekly sprays to check an attack before a controlling spray programme is adopted.

The latest developments in systemic compounds have not been related to interior situations because of the apparent unwillingness of the manufacturers to gain approval for such a limited market. One noteworthy systemic insecticide which has not been submitted for approval for use indoors is Temik 10G. It

TABLE 14.6 DISEASES

Name	Plant symptoms	Physical control	Chemical control
Downy Mildew	White mould on stems and leaves	Move plant to improved growing location with good ventilation	Thiram Zineb
Powdery mildew	White powdery mildew on stems and leaves	Ditto	Benomyl Carbendazim Dinocap
Bacterial spot	Dark green watery spots on leaves later turning yellow or brown	Move plant to improved growing location with good ventilation – thin any dense foliage	Copper
Fungal leaf spot	Dark spots covered with minute black dots	Move plant to improved growing location with good ventilation – thin any dense foliage	Benomyl
Root rot	Stem base and roots rot – usually in winter due to overwatering	Mild attack – water sparingly Severe attack – replant in sterilised compost	Captan Benomyl Zineb
Black mould	Dense black mouldy covering over leaves and stems – growing on honeydew secreted by pests	Control pests and wash off the mould	Not necessary
Viruses	Variable – spots or rings may appear on leaves – often leaves yellow in patches	None known – best to destroy plant	Not possible

TABLE 14.7 INSECTICIDES WITH SOME COMMON BRITISH AND AMERICAN TRADE NAMES

Major chemical constituents	Common trade names: British	Common aerosol names: American
Dicofol	Murphy Combined Pest and Disease Spray	Science Clover Mite and Red Spider Spray
Diazinon	Fisons Combat Soil Insecticide Root Guard May and Baker Soil Insecticide Granules	
Dimethoate	Murphy's Systemic Insecticide Bio Systemic Insecticide Boots Systemic Greenfly Killer	
Malathion	Boots Greenfly Killer Malathion Greenfly Killer Murphy Greenhouse Aerosol Murphy Liquid Malathion	
Permethrin	Ambush	
Pirimiphos – methyl and synergised pyrethrins	Sybol 2 Aerosol Kerispray	
Pyrethrum and piperonyle butoxide		Raid House and Garden Bug Killer
Pyrethrum and Resmethrin	Bio Sprayday Plant Pest Killer House/Garden Pest Killer	
Resmethrin and Rotenone		Pratt House Plant Spray
Bio-resmethrin	Cooper's Garden Spray Fison's Combat Whitefly Insecticide Perfect Plant Insect Spray	Ortho Home and Garden Spray Pratt Whitefly Spray Resmethrin Shell House and Garden Spray Whitmore No. 1200 Aerosol Generator
Rotenone	Liquid Derris Murphy Derris Liquid	

should therefore not be used in public buildings, although its use in conservatories, etc. may be considered. Being systemic, Temik will control most pests and is particularly useful for large specimens but is unfortunately highly toxic to mammals. The granules are applied at a rate of 4.5 g/m^2 and watered well in. When used in public areas the granules should be buried under the surface to avoid human contact.

The traditional techniques of trying to control certain pests such as red spider by regular spraying with water are now acknowledged scientifically as being pointless.

Fungicides

There are few fungi which attack interior plants and most of these are controlled by systemic fungicides provided that they are applied at an early stage of infection (table 14.8) (fig 14.2). If there is a danger of attack, preventive spray can be applied which should remain effective for two to three weeks. Infections can be controlled in young tissue by a programme of three or four sprays at seven to ten day intervals.

There is some evidence that certain fungal diseases such as Pythium and Rhizoctonia are less vigorous at temperatures of 25–30°C than say 15–20°C. However it is normal for some fungi to be active in both high and low temperatures and humidities.

Application of pesticides

In most interior situations the problem of pest control is application. Good equipment and well trained personnel are necessary to effect a uniform application of insecticide. Although the concentration of active ingredient in most "domestic" formulations is low, the manufacturers' instructions should be carefully followed at all times. For small scale operations an aerosol is to be recommended, whilst an electrically operated blower is best for spraying large areas.

TABLE 14.8 FUNGICIDES WITH COMMON BRITISH TRADE NAMES

Common chemical name	Trade name
Benomyl	Benlate
Captan	Murphy Orthocide Captan Fungicide
Carbaryl	Sevin
Carbendazim	Bavistin
Dinocap	Murphy Dinocap Mildew Fungicide XLALL Mildew Wash
Thiophanate-methyl	Murphys Systemic Fungicide
Thiram	ICI General Garden Fungicide
Zineb	Dithane

It is often convenient to use pesticides in an aerosol form but the effect of the propellant can be harmful if the discharge takes place within 400 mm of the plant. The symptom of such damage is burn or scorch marks on the foliage. In all situations only sufficient spray should be used to dampen the foliage and not enough for the foliage to "drip". It is possible to treat a plant in situ but care must be taken to avoid the risk of drift onto work surfaces and people. Often it is more efficient to collect the plants into one area for treatment, eg in a central thoroughfare.

Besides posing a potential hazard to people, certain pesticides can damage interior plants. This damage or phytotoxicity usually takes the form of yellowing, with dead leaf tips or margins, and the appearance of scabby black or dead spots with young leaves becoming twisted. The damage is most likely to occur if pesticides are applied during unfavourable environmental conditions or when plants are stressed. To avoid such damage pesticides should only be applied to well watered plants in cool conditions which are conducive to rapid drying. The plants should always be kept out of bright sunlight as the spray droplets can act as magnifiers and damage the leaves. Ferns are particularly sensitive to the effects of chemicals and should receive only minimal applications.

Notes on the use of chemicals

1 Adhere strictly to the manufacturers' recommendations
2 Only use the recommended doses, as higher rates may reduce the effectiveness of the compound and may cause damage
3 Spray in dry, overcast conditions – not in bright sunshine
4 Wash equipment thoroughly before and after use
5 All personnel should wash after applications
6 Never mix chemicals unless the combination is specifically recommended by the manufacturers
7 Never discharge aerosol within 400 mm of the foliage
8 Apply insecticides and fungicides at the first sign of attack and continue at regular intervals for as long as is necessary to effect a control
9 Store chemicals in a cool dry cupboard which does not experience very low or freezing temperatures. Lock such a store cupboard to prevent access by unauthorised personnel
10 Do not store diluted chemicals as they usually degenerate
11 Dispose of surplus chemicals down a foul water sewer as those which are used in buildings are relatively harmless. No chemicals to be tipped into a surface water drain as these may link directly with a natural watercourse.

REPLACEMENT

It is inevitable that some plants will die and need to be replaced, and this should be done as soon as there are obvious signs of stress. If a plant is removed sufficiently early it may benefit from a period of convalescence, provided that it has not been heavily infested by disease. In some situations it may be practical to rotate plants between the good and difficult situations but this is seldom commercially viable.

It is usually advisable to enter into a maintenance contract with the firm who installs the planting. They will ensure that the plantings do not become overcrowded and ensures that someone is available to determine the cause of continual problems. In dark inhospitable locations the effective life of plants can be as little as four months. In marginally better conditions where the light levels are at the compensation point the plant may survive, yet not have the reserves to replace the leaves when they fall naturally after one to two years. As a result of these problems it is usual even in the most successful plantings to expect losses of at least 10% per annum, and 20% may be considered reasonable. It is fortunate that such a loss is usually associated with the smaller plants in the base of the planters rather than the large specimens, which normally recover after the shock of introduction to dominate the rest of the planter.

CONCLUSION

Many of the plants sold for interior work deteriorate or even die after a relatively short time due to either poor environmental conditions or inadequate maintenance. It is probably true that "the best house plants are those which die slowly", but this need not be so, for with careful forethought and maintenance the life of interior plants can be almost limitless. The technical data on interior planting is limited but it is to be hoped that this publication will help the designer, user and maintainer of plants to resolve some of their technical problems.

15 Planting check list

Planning

1 Seek technical advice from the initial planning stage
2 Avoid planting public thoroughfares unless there is continuous supervision
3 Ensure that all plants are easily accessible for maintenance

Environment

4 Avoid extremes in temperatures
5 Avoid temperatures below 13°C unless hardy plants are used
6 Never allow temperatures below 7°C unless outdoor plants are used
7 Avoid the outlets of heating systems
8 Avoid draughty situations

Lighting

9 Never plant in areas receiving under 0.06 MJ/day (500 lux for 12 h/day).
10 Avoid direct sunlight with most commonly grown interior plants
11 Avoid lamps with a high emission outside the 400–700 nm range
12 Select lamps with a well spread spectrum
13 Avoid continuous illumination

Planting systems

14 Avoid waterlogging of the compost
15 Avoid drying out of the compost
16 Avoid relying on hand watering
17 Use self-watering techniques where possible
18 Plumb water to large planters wherever possible
19 Supply drainage to large planters whenever possible
20 Leach high salt levels from substrate before placing in low light conditions

Plant selection

21 Do not expect flowers in low light levels
22 Avoid selecting plants with coloured or variegated leaves for very low light levels
23 Do not overcrowd plants just to achieve an instant effect if they have the potential to grow well
24 Permit a period of acclimatisation before introducing plants to difficult situations

Maintenance

25 Arrange for adequate post-planting maintenance
26 Do not overfeed plants
27 Do not use leaf shine on palms, ferns, or downy-leaved plants, or those plants that are sensitive to its use
28 Inspect plants at regular intervals for pests and disease
29 Control pests and diseases when they appear
30 Replace all dead and dying plants as soon as possible

Glossary

The definitions contained within this section have been kept as non-technical as possible. For more complete definitions the titles of two technical dictionaries are given at the end of this section.

Acclimatisation. The process of preparing a plant for difficult environmental conditions after leaving the production area.

Available soil moisture. That quantity of moisture which is available in a substrate for use by plants: see *field capacity* and *permanent wilting point*.

Calorie (c). A unit of energy replaced by the joule in the SI system: the energy required to raise the temperature of 1 cm^3 of water by 1°C

Cambium. The mass of special plant cells which divide to produce conductive tissue in stems and roots.

Capillarity. The elevation of liquids up fine-bore tubes as a result of surface tension.

Carbohydrate. An organic compound produced during photosynthesis from carbon dioxide and water.

Cation exchange capacity. A quantitative measure of the ability of a soil or compost to retain nutrients.

Centibars. A unit of pressure equal to one hundredth of a bar (1 bar is approximately one atmosphere).

Chlorophyll. A green pigment found in plants, which traps light energy as a part of the process of photosynthesis.

Chloroplasts. Distinct units within a plant cell, each being surrounded by a membrane and containing chlorophyll.

Colour appearance. The colour of a truly white surface when illuminated by a given source, in terms of its apparent "warmth".

Colour rendering. The perceived colour of an object under a given electric lamp, relative to its appearance under a standard light source (which is normally taken to be daylight).

Compensation point. A condition which exists when a plant is able to photosynthesise sufficient carbohydrates to maintain its structure, but not new tissue formation.

Daylight factor. A method of expressing the level of illumination in a room, as a proportion of that which would be experienced at the same point from an unobstructed hemisphere of overcast sky.

Dicotyledonous plants. A large group of plants which have two embryo leaves within each seed.

Epidemiology. The study of the spread of disease.

Erg. A unit of energy: the work done by a force of 1 dyne moving through 1 cm.

Electromagnetic spectrum. The range of frequencies over which waves of energy are generated. The lowest frequencies are radio waves, and the highest are X-rays, with visible light falling midway between these extremes.

Ethylene. $H_2C = CH_2$; a gas which occurs naturally in plants and which can stimulate a number of changes in a plants' structure and behaviour.

Epidermis. The outermost layer of cells of a plant.

Field capacity. A condition which is found in a soil when the maximum volume of water is retained in conditions of free drainage.

Grp. Glass reinforced plastic (known formerly as glass fibre).

Hydroponics. The technique of growing plants without compost by immersing the roots in a nutrient solution.

Hydroculture. The form of hydroponics used with interior planting and usually employing an inert supporting medium in which the root system develops.

Halogens. A group of elements which include fluorine, chlorine and bromine.

Ion exchange fertiliser. A fertiliser which consists of special resin impregnated with chemicals in such a way that they can be exchanged in a controlled manner with others in a surrounding solution.

Joule. A unit of work, energy and heat: the work done by a force of 1 newton when a point advances 1 m (1 joule = 10^7 ergs = 0.24 calories).

Lightweight expanded clay aggregate (LECA). A low density aggregate which is produced by firing pellets of clay in such a way that they expand to give a foamed structure.

Luminous flux density. The quantity of luminous flux emitted through an angle of one steridian by a point source of one candela and weighted according to a scale of differential visual sensitivity; lumens/m^2

Lux. The unit of illumination based on the sensitivity of the human eye; 1 lumen/m^2.

Monocotyledonous plants. A large grouping of plants which have a single embryo leaf in each seed.

Osmosis. The process by which water passes through a semi-permeable membrane from a solution of low concentration to one of higher concentration.

Permanent wilting point. The soil moisture content at which a plant is no longer able to extract water, with the result that the plant wilts and dies.

pH. A system for expressing the acidity of a chemical solution such that pH 7 to 0 indicates increasing acidity whilst pH 7 to 14 indicates increasing alkalinity. Plant growth is usually optimised at pH 6.5.

Photomorphogenesis. The modification of a plants structure as a direct result of being exposed to light.

Photoperiodism. The response of certain plant activities to changes in day length (eg, flowering).

Photosynthesis. The production of carbohydrates from carbon dioxide and water in the presence of chlorophyll and light.

Phytotoxic. Harmful to plants.

Quantum. The basic unit of light energy whose magnitude is dependent upon its "colour", with red light containing more quanta than blue.

Phototropism. A response of certain growth patterns in plants as a result of being illuminated (eg, shoots grow towards light).

Radiant flux density. A measure of the "brightness" of a light source expressed as radiant power per unit area; mW/m^2

Stoma (stomatal aperture). A microscopic pore in the surface of a leaf through which gases may enter and exit.

Transpiration. The loss of water by plants mainly through the stoma of the leaves, at a rate which can to some extent be regulated by the plant.

Vascular tissue. Distinct areas of tissue within a plant which are able to conduct water, mineral salts and carbohydrates.

Watts. A unit of power which is equal to 1 joule/second.

Xerophyte. A plant which is adapted to survive in areas in which the water supply is limited.

More complete technical definitions may be obtained from the following publications:

Chambers dictionary of science and technology – Volumes 1 and 2. Edited by T. C. Collocott and A. B. Dobson. Publisher: W. & R. Chambers Ltd.

A dictionary of biology. by M. Abercrombie, C. J. Hickman and M. L. Johnson. Publisher: Penguin Books Ltd.

Table of common plant names

Algerian ivy	*Hedera canariensis*
Aluminium plant	*Pilea cadierei*
Aralia ivy	*Fatshedera lizei*
Asparagus fern	*Asparagus plumosus*
Australian palm	*Araucaria heterophylla*
Australian umbrella tree	*Brassaia (Schefflera) actinophylla*
Bamboo palm	*Chamaedorea erumpens*
Banyan tree	*Ficus benghalensis*
Bay tree	*Laurus nobilis*
Bengal fig	*Ficus benghalensis*
Birds nest fern	*Asplenium nidus*
Black rubber plant	*Ficus elastica "Black Prince"*
Blushing bromeliad	*Neoregelia carolinae tricolor*
Boston fern	*Nephrolepis exaltata*
Cabbage tree	*Cordyline australis*
Canary Island ivy	*Hedera canariensis*
Cast iron plant	*Aspidistra elatior*
Castor oil plant	*Fatsia japonica*
Ceriman	*Monstera deliciosa*
Climbing fig	*Ficus pumila*
Corn plant	*Dracaena fragrans "Massangeana"*
Creeping fig	*Ficus pumila*
Croton	*Codiaeum variegatum*
Date palm	*Phoenix dactylifera*
Desert privet	*Peperomia magnoliaefolia*
Devil's ivy	*Scindapsus aureus*
Dumb cane	*Dieffenbachia spp.*
Elephant's ear	*Philodendron "Tuxla"*
Emerald ripple	*Peperomia caperata*
English ivy	*Hedera helix*
European fan palm	*Chamaerops humilis*
False aralia	*Dizygotheca elegantissima*
Fan plant	*Begonia rex*
Fiddle leafed philodendron	*Philodendron panduraeforme*
Finger aralia	*Dizygotheca elegantissima*
Flaming dragon tree	*Cordyline terminalis*
Flaming sword	*Vriesea splendens*
Flamingo flower	*Anthurium scherzerianum*
Florida beauty	*Dracaena godseffiana*
Giant dumb cane	*Dieffenbachia amoena*
Glacier ivy	*Hedera helix*
Good luck plant	*Cordyline terminalis*
Goose foot plant	*Syngonium podophyllum*
Grape ivy	*Rhoicissus rhomboidea*
Green rays	*Schefflera arboricola*
Indian laurel	*Ficus nitida*
Ivy tree	*Fatshera lizei*
Japanese aralia	*Fatsia japonica*
Java fig	*Ficus benjamina*
Kangaroo vine	*Cissus antarctica*
Kentia palm	*Howeia forsteriana*
Leopard lily	*Dieffenbachia exotica*
Little fantasy	*Peperomia caperata*
Lizard plant	*Tetrastigma voinierianum*
Madagascar dragon tree	*Dracaena marginata*
Mexican breadfruit	*Monstera deliciosa*
Mistletoe fig	*Ficus diversifolia*
Mother-in-law's tongue	*Sansevieria trifasciata*
Norfolk Island pine	*Araucaria heterophylla*
Peace lily	*Spathiphyllum spp.*
Pagoda tree	*Fatshedera lizei*
Parlour palm	*Chamaedorea elegans*
Pheasant leaf	*Cryptanthus forsterianus*
Platinum plant	*Peperomia hederaefolia*
Poinsettia	*Euphorbia pulcherrima*
Prayer plant	*Maranta leuconeura*
Rabbit tracks	*Maranta leuconeura*
Rubber plant	*Ficus elastica*
Screw pine	*Pandanus veitchii*
Sentry palm	*Howeia belmoreana*
Silhouette plant	*Dracaena marginata*
Spider plant	*Chlorophytum comosum "Variegatum"*
Spineless yucca	*Yucca elephantipes*
Split leafed philodendron	*Monstera deliciosa*
Stagshorn fern	*Platycerium bifurcatum*
Striped dracaena	*Dracaena deremensis*
Sweetheart plant	*Philodendron scandens*
Sword fern	*Pandanus veitchii*
Swiss cheese plant	*Monstera deliciosa*
Ti plant	*Cordyline terminalis*
Tree philondren	*Philodendron selloum*
Tree of kings	*Cordyline terminalis*
Umbrella plant	*Brassaia (Schefflera) actinophylla*
Umbrella grass	*Cyperus diffusus*
Urn plant	*Aechmea fasciata*
Variegated ivy	*Hedera canariensis "Variegatum"*
Variegated rubber plant	*Ficus elastica "Schryvereana"*
Wandering jew	*Tradescantia fluminensis*
Weeping fig	*Ficus benjamina*
Window leaf	*Monstera deliciosa*

Association of Landscape Contractors of America

(Interior Landscape Division)

FORMAT OF LISTINGS

All listings in this Directory are in the following format, listed in alphabetical order according to State

Name of Company
Name of Principal
Company Street Address
City, State, Zip
Phone Number
(Company Size*) Specialty Code†

*Size of Company
AA Annual volume over $1,000,000
A Annual volume of $500,000–1,000,000
B Annual volume of $100,000–500,000
C Annual volume of under $100,000

†Speciality Code
RS Residential
CM Commercial
ID Industrial
GV Government Contract
MN Maintenance

PLANTABILITY
Gene N. Goerke
3335 E. Hatcher Road
Phoenix, AZ 85028
(602) 996–9728
(C) RS, CM, ID, MN

THE PLANT PEOPLE
Raymond L. Brooks
12601 N. 59th Place
Scottsdale, AZ 85254
(602) 991–5170
(B)

THE HABITAT, INC.
Rebecca J. McKay
4637 Colorado Street
Long Beach, CA 90803
(213) 433–0151
(C)

INTERIOR LANDSCAPE DESIGN
Alrie Middlebrook
401 E. Taylor Street
San Jose, CA 95112
(408) 292–9993
(B)

INTERIOR PLANT DESIGN
Jerome A. Gates
P.O. Box 23003
San Jose, CA 95153
(408) 286–1367
(C)

KARP INTERIOR GARDENS
Art V. Karp
P.O. Box 371
Anaheim, CA 92805
(714) 991–1933
(C)

LIVING INTERIORS
Gabriella Leonhard O'Connell
41 Central Avenue
Sausalito, CA 94965
(415) 332–4207
(C)

PLANTCO
Carole Senter
175 E. Dana
Mountain View, CA 94040
(415) 969–3800
(B)

PLANTSCAPE
Nancy Roca
990 Broadway
San Francisco, CA 94133
(415) 885–6335
(C)

PLANTS UNLIMITED
Nancy Goldstein
16450 Kent Avenue
San Lorenzo, CA 94580
(415) 276–2384
(C) RS, CM, ID, GV, MN
*also Exterior

INTERIOR-SCAPE, INC.
Joann L. Spence
100 Indian Cave Road
Ridgefield, CT 06877
(203) 428–3002
(C)

PLANT CITY CORPORATION
Charles K. Oppenheimer, Jr.
P.O. Box 147
Manchester, CN 06040
(800) 525–6043 Ex. 218
(C) CM, ID, MN

INTERIOR PLANTSCAPE CONSULTANTS
Richard L. Gaines
P.O. Drawer AC-1PC
Apopka, FL 32703
(305) 886–1511

EAST MARSH NURSERY, INC.
Jerry Soowal
1900 N. Federal Highway
Dania, FL 33004
Supplier – Grower

LIVING INTERIORS
Laine Craft
1424 Prosperity Farms Road
Lake Park, FL 33403
(305) 842–1823
(C)

LEND-LEAF, INC.
Martin J. Schwartz
3201 Ravenswood Road
Fort Lauderdale, FL 33312
(305) 584–7199
(B)

NATIONAL NURSERIES, LTD.
George Wolf
4850 S.W. 106th Avenue
Ft. Lauderdale, FL 33328
(305) 434–5803
(C)

TROPICAL ORNAMENTALS
Robert T. DeNeve
Rt. 1, Box 661
Woodland Drive
Delray Beach, FL 33445
(305) 278–6147

TURNBERRY CORPORATION
Richard P. Schreier
199th Street @ Biscayne Blvd.
Miami, FL 33132
(305) 931–3110
(C) RS, CM, MN

VOSTERS NURSERIES, INC.
James B. Vosters, Jr.
17000 Old Cutler Road
Miami, FL
(305) 235–2211
Supplier – Plants

NATURE'S WAY PLANTS INC.
Court Stockton
Tony Driskell
580 Pharr Road
Atlanta, GA 30305
(404) 231–9930
(C) RS, CM, MN

SEDGEFIELD ATLANTA
David Korstad
1269 Techwood Avenue
Atlanta, GA 30318
(404) 872–0701
(B)

ALFRED L. SIMPSON & COMPANY, INC.
Alfred L. Simpson
P.O. Box 41025
Atlanta, GA 30331
(404) 349–1432
(A) RS, CM, ID, MN
*also Exterior

EXOTIC PLANTS
Neil Frederickson
300 Florence Avenue
Evanston, IL 60202
(312) 869–2880
(C)

GOOD EARTH PLANTS
Norma Brown
112 E. First St.
O'Fallon, IL 62269
(618) 632–4308
(C)

INSCAPE, INC.
Ron Aisenbrey
1123 W. Washington Blvd.
Chicago, IL 60607
(312) 829–1622
(C) RS, CM, ID, MN

SCAIFE'S FLOWERS
Thomas W. Scaife
960 Clock Tower Drive
Springfield, IL 62704
(217) 546–2030
(C) MN

TROPICAL PLANT RENTALS, INC.
Gerry Leider
P.O. Box 146
Aptakisic Road, Prairie View, IL 60069
(312) 634–3112
(A) CM

GRANT-LEIGHTON ASSOCIATES
Wanda McDade
P.O. Box 991
Indianapolis, IN 46206
(317) 636–2112

NICE GREENHOUSE FLOWERS
Jack Nice
818 West 53rd North
Wichita, KA 67204
(316) 838–1431
(C)

FOLIAGE SYSTEMS INCORPORATED
Bunny Smith
624 Lowerline Street
New Orleans, LA 70118
(504) 899–3334
(C) RS, CM, ID, GV, MN

PLANT INTERIORS & MAINTENANCE
Lucy Price
319 N. Rendon Street
New Orleans, LA 70119
(504) 822–4848
(C) RS, CM, MN

CREATIVE PLANTINGS, INC.
Darryl Kosisky
12247 Nebel Street
Rockville, MD 20852
(301) 770–2440
(C)

TROPICA, INC.
Peter Korstad
2722 Pittman Drive
Silver Spring, MD 20910
(301) 585–2133
(B)

CITY GARDENS, INC.
George Patterson
64 Pleasant Street
Watertown, MA 02172
(617) 924–6573
(B) CM, MN, DB

THE POTTED PLANTER
Polly Gerard
Box 136
N. Scituate, MA
(617) 545–0735
(C) MN

CREATIVE PLANTERS
Donald W. Kiser
50 Tripp Street
Framingham, MA 01701
(617) 875–0839
(C) DB
*also Exterior

GARDEN MILIEU, INC.
Leonard A. Kersch
Nancy Nasset
719 West Ellsworth Road
Ann Arbor, MI 48104
(313) 994–4010
(A)

JENSEN EXOTIC PLANTS LTD.
John F. Ford
P.O. Box 460AX, Back Bay Annex
Boston, MA 02117
(617) 266–0769
(C)

JOSEPH COOK & ASSOCIATES, INC.
Joseph C. Cook
563 So. Eton
Birmingham, MI 48008
(313) 645–0672
(C)

BOTANICAL DECORATORS
Barry L. Wood
277 Notley Road
Silver Spring, MD 20904
(301) 384–8877
(C)

SINGERLING NURSERIES
John J. Singerling, Jr.
13330 168th Avenue
Grand Haven, MI 49417
(616) 846–3820
(C) RS, CM, ID, MN
*also Exterior

GREEN PLANT DESIGN, INC.
Gayle Sarkisian
29645 Highmeadow
Farmington Hills, MI 48018
(313) 855–1335
(C) MN

GREEN SLEEVES
Nancy S. Yang
5711 Cherry Street
Kansas City, MO 64110
(816) 333–3246
(C) CM, MN, DB

GROWING GREEN, INC.
Theresa L. Pesapane
401 North Euclid Avenue
St. Louis, MO 63108
(314) 361–1831/772–1445
(B) CM, MN

THE EVERETT CONKLIN CO., INTERNATIONAL
Everett Conklin
7 Brook Avenue
Montvale, NJ 07645
(201) 391–7300
(AA) RS, CM, ID, GV, MN

FOLIAGE PLANT SYSTEMS, INC.
Donald F. Mastick
P.O. Box 1022
8 Oak Street
Clifton, NJ 07014
(201) 473–0123
(B) CM, ID, GV, MN

PARKER INTERIOR PLANTSCAPE
Lenard Parker
1325 Terrill Road
Scotch Plains, NJ 07076
(201) 322–5552

DAVIS FLORIST, INC.
Albert H. Davis
300 S. Wilbur Avenue
Syracuse, NY 13204
(315) 478–0173
(C) MN

JOHN MINI, INDOOR LANDSCAPES, LTD.
John Minutaglio
269 City Island Avenue
City Island, NY 10464
(212) 885–2426
(C) CM, MN

SOUTHALL CORPORATION
David E. Southall
3236 Main Street
Buffalo, NY 14214
(716) 833–8111
(B) CM, MN

INDOOR LANDSCAPING, INC.
Peggy W. Lambeth
Three Saint Francis Court
Greensboro, NC 27408
(919) 294–1858
(C) RS, CM, MN

INDOOR PLANTS
Joyce Fisher
1 Stoneridge Circle
Durham, NC 27705
(919) 493–1218
(C) RS, CM, ID, MN

PLANTSCAPES, INC.
Sylvia N. Redwine
528–C Rt. 8
Strickland Road
Raleigh, NC 27612
(919) 787–9700
(C) RS, CM, GV, MN

SEDGEFIELD CHARLOTTE
Joanne Brown
2173 Hawkins Street
Charlotte, NC 28703
(704) 372–8278
(B)

SEDGEFIELD LANDSCAPE NURSERY, INC.
Karl Korstad
5000 High Point Road
Greensboro, NC 27407
(919) 299–5529
(B) CM, ID, GV, MN

DOWN TO EARTH PLANT LEASING, INC.
Sherrie Mathis
8447 Foxcroft Drive
Cincinnati, Ohio 45231
(513) 522–9010
(C)

MIDLAND-ROSS CORP.
MATERIAL HANDLING DIVISION
James P. Robinson
10605 Chester Road
Cincinnati, OH 45215
(513) 772–1313
Supplier – Planters

NANCY WYATT, PLANT DECORATOR
Nancy Wyatt
26714 Bruce Road
Cleveland, Ohio 44140
(216) 871–3111
(C)

THE EVERGREEN LEAF
Brian Gilbert
1414 Euclid Avenue
Cleveland, Ohio 44115
(216) 623–1414
(C)

FOLIAGE INTERIORS
Jean Myers
7757 East 106 Street S.
Tulsa, OK 74133
(918) 299–2049
(C)

P & G PLANT COMPANY
Peter J. Norris
9410 SW Corbett Lane
Portland, OR 97219
(503) 246–0336
(C) RS, CM, ID, GV, MN

GRANT-LEIGHTON ASSOCIATES, INC.
Edmond A. Grant
6008 Butler Pike
Blue Bell, PA 19422
(215) 828–6788
(A) RS, CM, ID, GV, MN

INTERGREEN
Howard Roberts
511 W. Courtland Street
Philadelphia, PA 19140
(215) 455–5439
(C) RS, CM, ID

OXFORD DEVELOPMENT COMPANY
Gary S. Barnhart
300 Monroeville Mall
Pittsburgh, PA 15146
(412) 243–4800
(C) CM, MN

PLANTSCAPES, INC.
Carole Horowitz
3801 Liberty Avenue
Pittsburgh, PA 15201
(412) 681–3472
(B) CM, ID, MN

SMITH FOX ASSOCIATES
Summit Greenhouses, Inc.
Donald B. Smith
668 Countyline Road
Telford, PA 18969
(215) 723–1730
(B) CM, ID, GV, MN

RAY BRACKEN NURSERY, INC.
Ray Bracken
42 Pine Knoll Drive
Greenville, SC 29609
(803) 244–9121
(B) RS, CM, ID, GV, MN

ED HINES LANDSCAPE & NURSERY
Ed Hines
P.O. Box 5491
Spartanburg, SC 29304
(803) 574–2090
(B) RS, CM, ID, GV, MN

YOUR FAVORITE PLANTS LTD.
Bob & Lucy Smoak
737 Wade Hampton Blvd.
Greenville, SC 29609
(803) 242–1737
(C) MN

GREENLAWN OF GREENVILLE, INC.
Marion F. Grove
1419 Poinsett Highway
Greenville, SC 29609
(803) 232–3863
(C) RS, CM, ID, MN, DB
*also Exterior

BOTANY CENTER
Richard Ott
3701 Western Avenue
Knoxville, TN 37921
(615) 637–0110
(C) RS, CM, ID, GV, MN

PROVIDENCE PLANT CORPORATION
Green Stuff Division
Janet B. Rattray
62 Elmgrove Avenue
Providence, RI 02906
(401) 272—0968
(C) CM, MN

JOHN F. BIRTLES, INC.
John Birtles
101 Charles Drive
P.O. Box 1080
Bryn Mawr, PA 19010
(215) 525—4646
(C) CM, MN

DOT'S PLANT DECOR
Dorothy Horsley
408 Lindbergh
El Paso TX 79932
(915) 584—7003
Journalist

EDWARD W. BRADSHAW & ASSOCIATES, INC.
Edward W. Bradshaw, Jr.
56 Greenway Plaza East
Suite 1216
Houston, TX 77046
(713) 331—6151
(B) CM, MN, LC, DB
*also Exterior

CHARLIE COOK ASSOCIATES, INC.
Robert O. Walker
P.O. Box 12214
Dallas, TX 75225
(214) 690—9001
Supplier—Plant Broker

THE GREENERY
Len Gallagher
4303 Texas Avenue
Bryan, TX 77801
(713) 846—2838
(B) CM, MN
*also Exterior

LEAF OF DALLAS
George W. Bauman
1514 Easy Street
Dallas, TX 75247
(214) 638—5306
(B) CM, MN

J. D. MILLER FLORAL CO.
J. D. Miller
P.O. Box 10761
Houston, TX 77018
(713) 697—3273
(B)

NORTH HAVEN GARDENS
David R. Pinkus
9150 Forest Lane
Dallas, TX 75243
(214) 341—5375
(AA) RS, CM, MN, DB
*also Exterior

PLANT CARE COMPANY
Don L. Wilson
2265 Joe Field Drive
Dallas, TX 75229
(214) 241—6657
(B), CM, MN

THE SPENCER COMPANY
Greg Spencer
P.O. Box 16113
Houston, TX 77022
(713) 691—3991
(B) RS, CM, MN
*also Exterior

INDOOR GARDENS
Harry Belin
3917 Wheeler Avenue
Alexandria, VA 22304
(703) 823—2660
(A) RS, CM, ID, GV, MN

TROPICAL PLANTS OF GEORGETOWN
David Goldstein
3211 O Street NW
Washington, DC 20007
(202) 337—4458
(C) MN

GROW IT GREEN
Michael A. Jones
4045 Palisades Place, W.
Tacoma, WA 98466
(206) 564—0613
(C)

INTERIORS IN GREEN
Cheryl Trace
1130 N.W. 85th
Seattle, WA 98109
(206) 784—4312
(C)

FAIRFIELD GREENHOUSE, INC.
William W. Allis
7000 North 76th Street
Milwaukee, WI 53223
(414) 353—4040
(C)

R. V. WOOD & ASSOCIATES TROPICAL PLANTS
R. V. Wood
Box 156
Richmond Hill, Ontario CANADA L4C 4Y2
(705) 889—0985
(B) CM, MN

VAN HERRICK'S ENVIRONMENTAL PLANTING, LTD.
Michael Grogan
9945 152nd Street
Surrey, B.C. V3R 4G5 Canada
(604) 584—8505
(B)

Feet and inches (up to 20ft) to metres (exact values)

Feet	Inches 0	1	2	3	4	5	6	7	8	9	10	11
	Metres											
0	—	0·0254	0·0508	0·0762	0·1016	0·1270	0·1524	0·1778	0·2032	0·2286	0·2540	0·2794
1	0·3048	0·3302	0·3556	0·3810	0·4064	0·4318	0·4572	0·4826	0·5080	0·5334	0·5588	0·5842
2	0·6096	0·6350	0·6604	0·6858	0·7112	0·7366	0·7620	0·7874	0·8128	0·8382	0·8636	0·8890
3	0·9144	0·9398	0·9652	0·9906	1·0160	1·0414	1·0668	1·0922	1·1176	1·1430	1·1684	1·1938
4	1·2192	1·2446	1·2700	1·2954	1·3208	1·3462	1·3716	1·3970	1·4224	1·4478	1·4732	1·4986
5	1·5240	1·5494	1·5748	1·6002	1·6256	1·6510	1·6764	1·7018	1·7272	1·7526	1·7780	1·8034
6	1·8288	1·8542	1·8796	1·9050	1·9304	1·9558	1·9812	2·0066	2·0320	2·0574	2·0828	2·1082
7	2·1336	2·1590	2·1844	2·2098	2·2352	2·2606	2·2860	2·3114	2·3368	2·3622	2·3876	2·4130
8	2·4384	2·4638	2·4892	2·5146	2·5400	2·5654	2·5908	2·6162	2·6416	2·6670	2·6924	2·7178
9	2·7432	2·7686	2·7940	2·8194	2·8448	2·8702	2·8956	2·9210	2·9464	2·9718	2·9972	3·0226
10	3·0480	3·0734	3·0988	3·1242	3·1496	3·1750	3·2004	3·2258	3·2512	3·2766	3·3020	3·3274
11	3·3528	3·3782	3·4036	3·4290	3·4544	3·4798	3·5052	3·5306	3·5560	3·5814	3·6068	3·6322
12	3·6576	3·6830	3·7084	3·7338	3·7592	3·7846	3·8100	3·8354	3·8608	3·8862	3·9116	3·9370
13	3·9624	3·9878	4·0132	4·0386	4·0640	4·0894	4·1148	4·1402	4·1656	4·1910	4·2164	4·2418
14	4·2672	4·2926	4·3180	4·3434	4·3688	4·3942	4·4196	4·4450	4·4704	4·4958	4·5212	4·5466
15	4·5720	4·5974	4·6228	4·6482	4·6736	4·6990	4·7244	4·7498	4·7752	4·8006	4·8260	4·8514
16	4·8768	4·9022	4·9276	4·9530	4·9784	5·0038	5·0292	5·0546	5·0800	5·1054	5·1308	5·1562
17	5·1816	5·2070	5·2324	5·2578	5·2832	5·3086	5·3340	5·3594	5·3848	5·4102	5·4356	5·4610
18	5·4864	5·5118	5·5372	5·5626	5·5880	5·6134	5·6388	5·6642	5·6896	5·7150	5·7404	5·7658
19	5·7912	5·8166	5·8420	5·8674	5·8928	5·9182	5·9436	5·9690	5·9944	6·0198	6·0452	6·0706
20	6·0960	—	—	—	—	—	—	—	—	—	—	—

Square inches to square millimetres (to one place of decimals)

Square inches	0	1	2	3	4	5	6	7	8	9
	Square millimetres (mm²)									
0	—	645·2	1290·3	1935·5	2580·6	3225·8	3871·0	4516·1	5161·3	5806·4
10	6451·6	7096·8	7741·9	8387·1	9032·2	9677·4	10322·6	10967·7	11612·9	12258·0
20	12903·2	13548·4	14193·5	14838·7	15483·8	16129·0	16774·2	17419·3	18064·5	18709·6
30	19354·8	20000·0	20645·1	21290·3	21935·4	22580·6	23225·8	23870·9	24516·1	25161·2
40	25806·4	26451·6	27096·7	27741·9	28387·0	29032·2	29677·4	30322·5	30967·7	31612·8
50	32258·0	32903·2	33548·3	34193·5	34838·6	35483·8	36129·0	36774·1	37419·3	38064·4
60	38709·6	39354·8	39999·9	40645·1	41290·2	41935·4	42580·6	43225·7	43870·9	44516·0
70	45161·2	45806·4	46451·5	47096·7	47741·8	48387·0	49032·2	49677·3	50322·5	50967·6
80	51612·8	52258·0	52903·1	53548·3	54193·4	54838·6	55483·8	56128·9	56774·1	57419·2
90	58064·4	58709·6	59354·7	59999·9	60645·0	61290·2	61935·4	62580·5	63225·7	63870·8
100	64516·0									

Square feet to square metres

Square feet	0	1	2	3	4	5	6	7	8	9
	Square metres (m²)									
0	—	0·09	0·19	0·28	0·37	0·46	0·56	0·65	0·74	0·84
10	0·93	1·02	1·11	1·21	1·30	1·39	1·49	1·58	1·67	1·77
20	1·86	1·95	2·04	2·14	2·23	2·32	2·42	2·51	2·60	2·69
30	2·79	2·88	2·97	3·07	3·16	3·25	3·34	3·44	3·53	3·62
40	3·72	3·81	3·90	3·99	4·09	4·18	4·27	4·37	4·46	4·55
50	4·65	4·74	4·83	4·92	5·02	5·11	5·20	5·30	5·39	5·48
60	5·57	5·67	5·76	5·85	5·95	6·04	6·13	6·22	6·32	6·41
70	6·50	6·60	6·69	6·78	6·87	6·97	7·06	7·15	7·25	7·34
80	7·43	7·53	7·62	7·71	7·80	7·90	7·99	8·08	8·18	8·27
90	8·36	8·45	8·55	8·64	8·73	8·83	8·92	9·01	9·10	9·20

Pounds to kilogrammes (to two places of decimals)

Pounds	0	1	2	3	4	5	6	7	8	9
	Kilogrammes (kg)									
0	—	0·45	0·91	1·36	1·81	2·27	2·72	3·18	3·63	4·08
10	4·54	4·99	5·44	5·90	6·35	6·80	7·26	7·71	8·16	8·62
20	9·07	9·53	9·98	10·43	10·89	11·34	11·79	12·25	12·70	13·15
30	13·61	14·06	14·52	14·97	15·42	15·88	16·33	16·78	17·24	17·69
40	18·14	18·60	19·05	19·50	19·96	20·41	20·87	21·32	21·77	22·23

Pounds per cubic foot to kilogrammes per cubic metre (to one place of decimals)

Pounds per cubic foot	0	1	2	3	4	5	6	7	8	9
	Kilogrammes per cubic metre (kg/m³)									
0	—	16·0	32·0	48·1	64·1	80·1	96·1	112·1	128·1	144·2
10	160·2	176·2	192·2	208·2	224·3	240·3	256·3	272·3	288·3	304·4
20	320·4	336·4	352·4	368·4	384·4	400·5	416·5	432·5	448·5	464·5
30	480·6	496·6	512·6	528·6	544·6	560·6	576·7	592·7	608·7	624·7
40	640·7	656·8	672·8	688·8	704·8	720·8	736·8	752·9	768·9	784·9

Degrees Fahrenheit to degrees Celsius (Centigrade)

Part A: Below freezing point of water (below 32°F or 0°C) Figures are negative values

°F	0°	1°	2°	3°	4°	5°	6°	7°	8°	9°
	°Celsius (below freezing point)									
0°	17·8	17·2	16·7	16·1	15·6	15·0	14·4	13·9	13·3	12·8
10°	12·2	11·7	11·1	10·6	10·0	9·4	8·9	8·3	7·8	7·2
20°	6·7	6·1	5·6	5·0	4·4	3·9	3·3	2·8	2·2	1·7
30°	1·1	0·6	0	—	—	—	—	—	—	—

Part B: Above freezing point of water (above 32°F or 0°C) Figures are positive values

°F	0°	1°	2°	3°	4°	5°	6°	7°	8°	9°
	°Celsius (above freezing point)									
30°	—	—	0	0·6	1·1	1·7	2·2	2·8	3·3	3·9
40°	4·4	5·0	5·6	6·1	6·7	7·2	7·8	8·3	8·9	9·4
50°	10·0	10·6	11·1	11·7	12·2	12·8	13·3	13·9	14·4	15·0
60°	15·6	16·1	16·7	17·2	17·8	18·3	18·9	19·4	20·0	20·6
70°	21·1	21·7	22·2	22·8	23·3	23·9	24·4	25·0	25·6	26·1
80°	26·7	27·2	27·8	28·3	28·9	29·4	30·0	30·6	31·1	31·7
90°	32·2	32·8	33·3	33·9	34·4	35·0	35·6	36·1	36·7	37·2
100°	37·8	38·3	38·9	39·4	40·0	40·6	41·1	41·7	42·2	42·8
110°	43·3	43·9	44·4	45·0	45·6	46·1	46·7	47·2	47·8	48·3
120°	48·9	49·4	50·0	50·6	51·1	51·7	52·2	52·8	53·3	53·9
130°	54·4	55·0	55·6	56·1	56·7	57·2	57·8	58·3	58·9	59·4
140°	60·0	60·6	61·1	61·7	62·2	62·8	63·3	63·9	64·4	65·0
150°	65·6	66·1	66·7	67·2	67·8	68·3	68·9	69·4	70·0	70·6
160°	71·1	71·7	72·2	72·8	73·3	73·9	74·4	75·0	75·6	76·1
170°	76·7	77·2	77·8	78·3	78·9	79·4	80·0	80·6	81·1	81·7
180°	82·2	82·8	83·3	83·9	84·4	85·0	85·6	86·1	86·7	87·2
190°	87·8	88·3	88·9	89·4	90·0	90·6	91·1	91·7	92·2	92·8
200°	93·3	93·9	94·4	95·0	95·6	96·1	96·7	97·2	97·8	98·3

Index

Index of plant names: scientific